The Wish

A Prophecy of Love

JLHayes

Cover Design and Artwork by multiple-award winning artist, Darlene

First edition 2020. Printed in the United States of America

JLHayes

The Wish, A Prophecy of Love

ISBN: 978-0-9911776-6-0

Here's what love is:

"Love is a smoke raised with the fume of sighs;
Being purged, a fire sparkling in lovers' eyes;
Being vexed, a sea nourished with loving tears.
What is it else? A madness most discreet,
A choking gall, and a preserving sweet."

—William Shakespeare, *Romeo and Juliette*

♥ ♥

Prologue

San Diego, California—1981

Jill Simpson, grasping the steering wheel as if she could choke the life out of it, sucked in a breath and forced one out, as the car roared toward the exit of her apartment building parking lot. Swinging a sharp left onto the street, she headed east. For some ungodly reason, Jill had agreed to meet her former lover and likely con-artist, Clay Clarkson, in the bar at the Hilton Hotel, to listen to his excuses and pleas of innocence.

It had taken two unexpected telephone calls, one originating from 3,000 miles away, in New York City, and the second, less than three miles from her apartment to ignite a sequence of events that sent Jill's mind reeling. *"I knew he was lying. It showed in his eyes, voice, and body language. Yet, I continued to trust him, and now he has left me with the worst form of betrayal; over a decade of secrets."*

She continued scolding herself. *"I ignored those warning signs: His spur-of-the-moment suspicious phone calls in private;*

Vivian repeatedly insisting that he's a phony and not the man for me; and my daughter, saying she can't believe her mom is in love with a perfect stranger... a man with a deep dark history."

Jill attempted to fool herself into thinking the sole reason she agreed to this encounter was to take pleasure in hearing him try to explain his way out of this damnable situation. On her way over to the Hilton, she silently pleaded, *"Oh God, please... please help me! Every instinct tells me he is nothing but trouble. But why, oh, why do I still love this deceitful bastard?"*

♥ ♥

Clayton Clarkson, in a cab traveling from the airport, knew he had to come clean and rid himself of his haunting secrets. When he walked in, Jill, as dependable as ever, was seated alone at the bar. Being met with a cold greeting reserved for two conflicting spouses in a divorce court, he attempted to kiss her on the lips, but she turned sideways for a kiss on the cheek.

Now seated at what once was considered their favorite table, a thin, young waitress with brunette hair, approached to take their order. "Jill, what would you like... Chardonnay?"

Looking at the waitress, Jill said, "Just a glass of water, with lemon, please."

Clay responded, "I'll have a glass of Chardonnay." A serene silence swept across the table until the drinks arrived.

He picked up his glass, holding it as if preparing to make a toast. Jill made no effort to acknowledge his attempt, she just stared at him.

"Okay, here I am. What is so important that demanded you

fly in from New York to talk with me?"

Silence reigned again; tears filled his eyes. Clay peered out towards the lobby, trying to avoid eye to eye contact with Jill. Chiding himself, "*Shit, this is all my fault, and I need to man-up.*"

While waiting for Clay to pull himself together, Jill sighed, feeling her shoulders sag as she began thinking, "*I can't believe that I made such a huge mistake with this guy.*"

Clay shifted his focus back to Jill only to find that she was peering sharply at him. He could see it in her eyes, "*She's thinking about leaving in a couple of minutes or so. If I fail to prove how much I love her, I will lose her forever.*"

"Sorry, this is so difficult. But I came here to tell you the truth in hopes that you will understand why I did what I did, and that I never meant to hurt you." He struggled to breathe as he started to spill his guts. Clay talked about two decades of his past. Jill listened intently, seldom speaking, except for whispering only one word, "Strange!"

He responded, "Strange, yes... But my alternatives were terrible."

She looked into his agonized eyes and said, "Oh God! Tell the waitress to bring me a nine-ounce glass of Chardonnay."

♥ ♥

Chapter 1

San Diego—December 1980

Jill Simpson, forty years old, had reached a defining moment in her life; divorced and now struggling to create a stable lifestyle and rid herself of the demons she had encountered during her two decades of marriage. As she jogged along the streets of her low-key but not-so-low-priced neighborhood, Jill had learned that one of the best ways not to get bored while jogging was to keep her mind focused on past events.

Her childhood was near perfect, at least by her standards. She was raised on a small farm just outside of Saint Paul, Minnesota, along with her five brothers.

Suddenly as if out of nowhere, a police car with emergency lights flashing whizzed by causing Jill to jump onto the sidewalk. She watched until the vehicle turned left a couple of blocks down. *"No sirens sounding, I wonder what's up?"*

Back in the street, she went refocusing on the memories of

her past, "*Staunch Catholics, Daddy, and Mom always went to Mass every Sunday morning, and it didn't take me long to recognize they sacrificed a lot to send all of us to Catholic schools. Being the only girl in a group of six siblings had its advantages, or so I thought. Growing up, I loved to hang around with Daddy every chance I got. One of my favorite pastimes was going with him on those early Saturday mornings just before dawn to help sell our tomatoes, carrots, spring onions, radishes, and a few other vegetables at the farmers' market in downtown Saint Paul. My older brother, Charlie, told me that I was the only one dumb enough to get up at 4:30 a.m. to help load the truck.*"

Jill, waving to the refuse truck driver, stepped from the street onto the sidewalk staying out of the way of the vehicle that was busy picking up her neighbors' throwaways and recyclables. She smiled, thinking, "*What the boys didn't know was that on each trip as a special reward, Daddy would give me ten cents to buy candy at the little store near our produce stall, so Charlie, I wasn't as dumb as you boys thought!*"

Her pleasant memories continued. "*Daddy was a good and honest man, had a set of rules for practically everything, and was a real stickler for having us follow his principles of conduct. First were his moral laws: never steal, lie, cheat, and always trust people until they give you a reason to not.*

"*He also had his common sense principles: Don't go out in the cold with a wet head after washing my hair, always cover my head during the bitter winters, and to steer clear of any stranger who tries to lure me into their car.*

"*He always encouraged my brothers and me to do kind things: Always be polite and hold doors for the elderly, women, and children; help our elders whenever we could; and for me to always give our farmers market customers a little extra."*

Grinning from ear to ear, Jill remembered, *"Daddy's rules fit the image of who he was, and he was far from being naïve. I always thought one of Daddy's best set of teachings was what he called his, Rules for Happiness.*

"He would tell my brothers and me, 'All close relationships have their problems. When you marry, it's forever. That is the rule; no exception.' So naturally, as a child, I dreamed of falling in love, being swept away by my very own Prince Charming, marrying, and having four or five kids of my own." Another smile lit up her face, *"After all, I am Catholic."*

Daddy had other happiness rules, and I obeyed them all but two: Never move away from the family enclave. I got married, and my new husband and I moved to San Diego. I convinced myself that I was happy, and I was for a while.

"The second was never to divorce. After twenty years of marriage, Roy and I divorced last year. I couldn't stomach his bizarre and selfish ways any longer. Daddy's rules held meaning for me. For Roy, I am not sure. I'd hate to know what Daddy would think of me now."

Smiling, as she steadily kept her jogging pace, *"Daddy was fun to be around. Sometimes he joshed with me about silly things; like the way, he taught me to pour him a cup of coffee. He had me hold the pot high in the air and pour it into the cup sitting on the table.*

"Why that way, Daddy? I asked. He said it allowed the coffee to get more oxygen on its way down. Silly Daddy! It took me years to learn he was spoofing me, and here I am three decades later, still absorbing the humor we so enjoyed."

To the outside observer, it appeared Jill Simpson didn't have a care in the world. But underneath her charade was a troubled woman determined not to contaminate her business or personal life. Admonishing herself to cast aside negative thoughts and only think of happier times, she murmured, "*I often wonder if the only blessed things to come out of my marriage were my three children; all now nearly adults. I love them so much!*"

Up the street, she went past well-manicured yards, a few with rock pathways intertwined with landscape mulch—others with palms, eucalyptus, and fruit trees spread throughout. An occasional rose bush with its delicate petals glistening with dew would catch her eye as she trotted by Mrs. Sysmore's white stucco home.

"*What a beautiful morning to be living in San Diego,*" she thought as the early morning sun was lazily starting to rise over the rooftops.

At the first cross street, Conroy, she slowed for the stop sign, looking both left and right, before moving through the intersection. Jill increased her pace, continuing down the street.

"*Great morning, isn't it, Mr. Albanesi... you're up early,*" as she took note that he was already out washing his precious 1971 Mercedes, 280 SL convertible.

He answered, "Beautiful morning, happy lady."

"*What he doesn't know,*" as her pace held, "*Love is on my mind, Mr. Albanesi. Furthermore, I'm going to reinvent myself and find a man who will make me happy forever, now that my two decades of marriage has ended. Damn, that makes me sound old.*"

She stopped near the crosswalk as an ambulance, flashing lights and siren, sped through the intersection. She sighed... "*Dream on girl. All the good ones anywhere near my age are already hooked.*"

After a glance at her wristwatch, Jill turned left just before entering the crosswalk and headed home. "*Got to shower, get dressed, and then go meet Phyllis Tyrell at the Sunrise café for a quick cup of coffee before I go to work. What's on her mind?*"

Makeup applied and dressed for work Jill paused before walking out the door for a glimpse in the mirror; distressed at what she saw. "*Crow's feet starting in the corners of my eyes and bags underneath.*"

She rubbed her hands over her face. "*I now realize at my age. I've lost the looks that I so need to be an asset in my job of making women even more attractive. I look like crap. Now I know why Phyllis wants to meet off-site. As senior manager of the Cosmetic Department of San Diego's Marine Corps Recruiting Depot, or MCRD, as most people would say, she's not happy with my looks, and she didn't want to embarrass me in front of the others.*

Everybody knows she's a stickler for her girls to always look their very best... after all, we are promoting and selling beauty products."

Over the past few days, Jill had slept little, and it showed in her reflection. A workaholic, avid jogger, and on top of those two, she felt like an emotional train wreck.

"*Why?*" she asked herself. One by one, she performed a self-diagnosis: "*Betrayed Daddy by the divorce; now in a small claustrophobic apartment after living in a large four-bedroom house for more than twenty years; lonely for the love of a man; the dating scene a bust; and my only roomie, my engaged daughter, is seldom home. It's no wonder I am having difficulty sleeping. Besides, I look like I have aged at least ten years. It's no wonder I look like hell!*"

Leaving her car, Jill didn't know what to expect, so she mentally braced herself for whatever calamity Phyllis would deliver at their coffee klatch.

Pulse pounding in her head, Jill walked into the café. Looking around, she spotted an attention-getting wave coming from the rear. It was Phyllis, seated near the back wall. Moving past six or eight booths and fewer tables, Jill made a beeline to her boss.

From the looks of things, Phyllis had chosen the least popular spot in the place, near the door to the kitchen. Her behavior, and the briefcase she was carrying, indicated this clandestine get-together was strictly business—nothing social.

The young waitress, pad and pencil in hand, approached to take their order. "Two coffees, mine black," Phyllis said. Jill followed, "Mine with cream on the side."

Already nervous, Jill became more so as she watched Phyllis remove an official looking envelope from her briefcase. Her pulse kicked up a couple of notches. *"Oh God, I am about to get canned, but why?"* With the suspense percolating to a boiling point, and nearly losing her voice, Jill said, "Phyllis, are you getting ready to fire me?"

"Heavens no, Jill. Quite the contrary. I had you meet me here to give you a confidential message before Colonel Cooperswaite lets the cat out of the bag during Friday's meeting."

"Message? What message?" Jill asked as her insides started to cool down.

The waitress returned. "Two coffees, cream on the side," she said, as she set two cups down and carefully placed two small containers of cream within easy reach of both women.

Reaching across the table, Phyllis handed Jill the envelope. "Jill, inside this envelope is the announcement that you are one of two finalists nominated for our Western Region's Retail Salesperson of the Year Award. Congratulations, my dear! We are so proud of you, and as I said, the Colonel will make it official this Friday. So look your best and also... pretend to be surprised when he tells our girls."

"Oh Phyllis, I am so honored, thank you... thank you!"

"All the particulars are in the envelope, Jill, and I just know you'll enjoy that weekend at the magnificent Ritz-Carlton in Los Angeles."

Noticing Jill had already finished her cup, Phyllis took one last swallow and called out to the waitress as she passed by, "Check, please."

Turning to face Jill, "Well, we'd better get to the Exchange before we are missed. See you there. Remember, act like the Colonel's announcement is a big surprise."

"Oh, I will. Thank you again, Phyllis."

Back in her car, Jill noticed the heavy rush hour traffic was making for a slower drive than usual back to MCRD. While her heart was pounding with excitement, Jill winced as she tried to fight off her taunting inner voice, "*Jill, this dimension of your life is sinking. So forget ever finding your Prince Charming. Your love life is cursed; mark my word.*"

She muttered, "*How much worse can this get? Damn you ... Damn you! Why do you keep doing this to me? I am not a bad person.*"

♥ ♥

Chapter 2

New York City—December 31, 1977

"I *expected this day to come, but I didn't think it would end in a disrespectful manner,"* Clayton Clarkson mulled while seated in the presidential suite's reception area. "I'd *prefer to be making my rounds, going office to office, and saying my goodbyes."* It was now well past the scheduled two o'clock exit meeting with his boss, Bob Como, the new CEO.

The more Clayton glanced up at the eighteenth-century French mahogany clock on the mantle above the unlit fireplace, the slower time passed... fifteen minutes... thirty minutes.

"Ah, ha, keep him waiting and show him who's boss," Clayton imagined that was what Como was thinking. *"That bastard likes to think he is in total control. But Bob, I also know how to play the game of cutthroat politics in big business... Forester's is no different."*

With Forester's Department Stores for nearly five years, Clayton had been hired away from a large Boston-based retail chain to replace the retiring and former New York City police commissioner who— more likely than not—had been given his prestigious position at Forester's as a face-saving move to help out the Borough's political fathers.

Big business politics was nothing new for Clayton; he had survived one major coup in Washington, D.C., during an abrupt change in leadership, but not this time. The survival of his executive team was not in the cards. A political decision by the bigwigs in the parent corporation that owned Forester's had already executed their plan. Two of Clayton's closest associates, along with his highly regarded boss—the former CEO—were now history.

To help pass the time as he waited for the ax to fall, Clayton's memory drifted back to his roots. The son of a West Virginia coal miner, his childhood was one very few would wish upon themselves. He was intimately familiar with what those words, 'the other side of the tracks,' meant.

During his younger years, he had learned firsthand about the separation of classes. The mining bosses were the privileged. They lived in beautiful mansions within a wealthy enclave on a landscaped knoll on the other side of Norfolk & Western's railroad tracks. Clayton, his family, friends, and other miners of different nationalities and races lived in the poorer and segregated communities in small company-owned row houses, less than a stone's throw from three sets of dangerous N&W train tracks.

Clayton particularly enjoyed sneaking up to the bosses' seldom used, private swimming pool. There he would lay in the grass beneath a huge old oak tree and watch Chuck, the pool's part-time lifeguard, lounge in the sun or perform a few pool cleaning chores in case someone in the restricted neighborhood would show up for a quick dip. Clayton could never understand why the pool was forbidden to ordinary folks.

When asked, "Why?" his Mom would only say, "We aren't allowed, and if you get caught in that pool, besides the trouble you would be in, your Dad could lose his job."

Young Clayton was known to be on the stubborn side, and it took more than a verbal warning from his Mom or Dad to make him stay away. During those hot summer afternoons, Clayton could be seen sneaking across the tracks just to hang out near the pool, while none of the other kids dared join him.

He was determined to break that god-awful rule, but how? After volunteering to help Chuck clean up debris and leaves, plus a lot of begging, Chuck finally relented. He told Clayton he would let him take a dip, but first, he had to swear to secrecy.

"You can never tell anyone. Not your folks, and especially not your brother, Hunter."

"I swear, no fingers crossed, not anyone." Once his secret pledge was confirmed, Clayton, torn jeans, no shirt, and barefoot, jumped in. Upon hitting the water, a non-swimmer, he began desperately flailing his arms, trying to get out. He hadn't given any thought to this pool's water coming from a very cold mountain stream. After that blistering hot Friday, Clayton's parents often wondered why the youngster never spoke of wanting to go into the bosses' private pool again.

Clayton, now sitting alone in the reception area, quietly chuckled, "*That damn water wasn't cold... it was ice!*" He waited a long moment as if to organize his thought, then murmured, "*Those times back then taught me at least one vitally important lesson: If you want something bad enough, you can make it happen; just make sure it's what you truly want."*

Looking up at the clock, he thought, *"Being raised in near poverty didn't hurt me nearly as much as it helped give me the drive to succeed. Besides, I realized that if you had never been exposed to a better lifestyle, you had no idea of what you were missing."*

The longer Clayton waited for his soon-to-be-former boss, the more uncomfortable he became. It was New Year's Eve, and for him, an amazing and life-altering day. Once again, peering at the clock, *"Damn, that clock just keeps ticking away; thirty minutes... forty-five minutes."* Clayton reminded himself, *"In exactly two hours and thirty-three minutes, I will go from being a well-paid senior executive to just another statistic among the ranks of the unemployed."*

While waiting, his attention shifted to listening. *"That's Como's voice coming from behind the wall. What he's saying isn't business-related. It's just casual bullshit mixed with a few spurts of laughter."* This discovery annoyed Clayton even more. *"Bob Como is deliberately keeping me waiting... that son of a bitch!"*

Finally, tired of waiting, reminiscing, and giving that French clock the once-over for the umpteenth time, Clayton told Gloria, the CEO's secretary, he was returning to his office. "Please call me once Como is free enough to see me." She smiled, acknowledging his message. Clayton turned and headed in the direction of his office.

As he walked into his office complex, his staff and several guests shouted, Surprise! A few seconds later, a CD commenced playing Elvis Presley's *My Way*. The message was clear. He smiled. "It's time to party!"

Clayton knew it was time to get the hell out. He and his boss were at odds on several issues. He discreetly smiled as he remembered his exact words when Como asked him to do what he considered an unethical thing, "Bob, no way am I going to do that shit!"

With that single sentence, Clayton knew he just severed any chance of forming a working relationship with his new CEO. The second reason was less ambiguous. Clayton's renewal contract was ready for his signature. "*Sign it, and I'm good for another two years.*"

But he also knew that within a month or two, he would be telling his boss to go to hell! Likely burning a bridge behind him, something he had always discouraged. The third and most pleasant reason: Clayton had always wanted to operate his own business. The timing couldn't be better. He was well-known throughout multiple industries and had built an impeccable reputation over fifteen years in the private sector. "It's *now or never.*"

Shortly after 3:15 p.m., more than an hour past his scheduled meeting, Clayton was summoned to the CEO's office for one final meeting. Clayton raised his glass as if to make a toast and discreetly whispered, "*Sorry, Bob, it's now your turn to wait.*"

Chapter 3

Los Angeles—January 12, 1981

"*P*hyllis was right-on when she said I'd enjoy my weekend at the Ritz-Carlton." Sitting on the sofa in her luxurious suite, sipping the second cup of Kopi Luwak coffee brewed in her coffee maker, Jill Simpson was motivated.

"From this day forth, I am going to forget that my life is in turmoil and stop wallowing in self-pity. It's a new year, and I am going to make it a good one. I recently celebrated my fortieth birthday, quit smoking on New Year's Eve, finalized my divorce last year, and moved into a furnished two-bedroom rental apartment with my twenty-year-old engaged daughter, and now doing a little casual dating.

"Even my other two kids, both boys," chuckling, she thought... *"or should I say, young men had reluctantly agreed to stay in our family home with their Dad until they completed their final years of college. Afterward, the house is to be sold as agreed in our divorce decree. And, just last evening, my dream of winning a prestigious*

business award became a reality. Life is good!"

Feeling upbeat, Jill looked down at the coffee packet and wondered if it was the caffeine in this expensive coffee that was making her so optimistic.

She sighed, thinking, *"Now this is living! An elegant room furnished with a dark mahogany cadenza, or ... could it be rosewood? Those gold and scarlet draperies are something to behold, not to mention the marble and granite bathroom, with its plush Egyptian towels and embroidered cashmere bathrobe. The scent of wealth is everywhere."*

Suddenly, she returned to reality after barely hearing a soft knock on the door. *"The bellman,"* she thought. *"It's 6:15 a.m. and he's right on time. I guess that teensy knock is so other guests will not be disturbed."*

Removing her stylish black Calvin Klein double-breasted trench coat from the closet, she turned and took a final sweep to ensure she had all of her things.

"After you," said the bellman, standing with her single piece of luggage in hand, holding the door. Stepping into the carpeted hallway, the muffled sound of the closing door was in sync with a polite whisper from behind, "I'll meet you downstairs at the checkout desk. The elevator should arrive momentarily. I pushed the button."

"Thank you."

Once inside of the elevator, Jill became aware of the soft, soothing, classical music emanating from the ceiling speaker.

"Hold the door please," a shout coming from halfway up the hall caught her attention. Jill responded by pressing and holding the *Open Door* button.

"Thanks," the laughing woman carrying a jacket over her arm

mused. "The fourteenth floor is definitely too far to walk down." Looking back at her slow moving companion as she came trudging up the hall, their conversation continued as if it had not been interrupted. "She just said 'No?' Oh, what a shame." After the elevator door closed and the downward descent now underway, Jill became content just listening to the gossip.

The second woman, likely in her sixties, and certainly not shy, spoke up, "If a man as wealthy and handsome as Marco proposed to my daughter, I'd say 'Yes' before she could utter a word."

"Excuse me, ladies, this is the street floor."

"Oh, we are getting off here."

Overhearing that conversation brought forth Jill's dream of someday falling in love with a man who would be kind to her and one whom she could trust... while wealth was certainly not a priority, it would be nice. Silently grinning to herself, she thought, "*I need a guy like Marco.*"

Jill Simpson's world was far from perfect. But, on this bright and crisp Monday morning, she had every reason to be in a joyful mood. Her weekend stay at the five-star Ritz-Carlton hotel in the heart of Los Angeles was filled with enjoyable entertainment, good conversation, and exceptional food and drink.

As expected, the bellman was waiting at the desk. Once he found out Jill had left her car with the valet, he turned her weekender bag over to the doorman. A slight cough and eye contact signaled he was anticipating a tip before walking away. The hotel doorman, now in possession of her bag, stood at the curb until the valet delivered her car.

The precision with which these men operated intrigued Jill. "*Like clockwork and in unison*," she thought as she watched the doorman open the trunk, carefully place her bag inside, and close it without a hint of slamming. *"I bet that doorman has learned a silently closed trunk lid generates better tips. Three bucks, another nice tip for just placing one small overnighter in the trunk,"* she thought.

A split-second later, the valet moved into position alongside the driver's door, holding out his hand awaiting surrender of the validated parking ticket; and, of course... his tip.

"It was obvious that once my five-dollar bill was in his hand, this guy cared little about holding the car's door for me. Oh well, what he didn't know was that I was not the one eating the cost of my three-night stay at one of L.A.'s most expensive hotels... or did he?"

Once in the driver's seat, Jill buckled her seat belt, started the engine of her borrowed BMW, and pulled from the curb without hesitation. From the turning lane, she swung a left at the light and headed towards the entrance to the I-5 Freeway. Two lights ahead, right turn, and onto the freeway's south ramp. A quick glance in both the side and rearview mirrors showed no speeding vehicles approaching in her lane. Flooring the gas pedal, the Beemer's engine growled and showed its full power.

"Smooth sailing," she thought. *"Providing traffic conditions are halfway normal, my drive back to San Diego should take less than two hours."*

Cruising down the freeway, Jill reminded herself this weekend was everything Phyllis indicated. *"I believe she said it would be magnificent."*

It was her employer's tenth-annual conference and awards banquet. A conference newbie, Jill was nominated for the Western Region's Retail Salesperson of the Year award. As with most conferences, the days were filled with sessions designed to educate and motivate the employer's personnel; both the Saturday and Sunday calendars were packed full of excellent workshops and demonstrations.

During the afternoon of the awards banquet, and upon returning to her room after lunch, Jill found a single red rose and an engraved invitation neatly placed in the center of her freshly made bed. 'Your presence is requested at Table 3, at 6 p.m.' This invitation came as no surprise. She was tipped-off by Jerry Smythers, her Regional Manager.

As Jill stepped into the breathtaking contemporary banquet room, the first thing to catch her eye was the sweeping wash of an array of light from ceiling pendants and recessed lamps that cast their sparkle onto the clusters of pink tablecloths throughout.

Waiting just inside the door was Jerry Smythers. "Good evening, Jill; you certainly look marvelous. May I escort you to your table? Number three, I believe."

"Yes, Jerry, how nice of you." As the two moved in the direction of Jill's table, Jerry whispered, "Savor the moment, Jill. Win or lose; you will forever remember this night."

"You bet I will!" As they approached the table where seven of the eight nominees, plus the CEO, Mr. Levine and his wife, Claire, were already seated.

Startled that she was the last arrival, Jill took a quick look at her watch and said to Jerry, "I'm not running late, I am four minutes earlier than the time noted on the invitation."

"Your timing is fine," he replied. "Sort of like making a grand entry. You couldn't have pulled it off better, even if planned."

"Oh, don't be silly. The only thing on my mind is that I cannot allow my nerves to spoil my entire evening."

Tables 1 and 2 also had eight nominees, plus a senior executive and spouse. In total, twenty-four nominees were present. However, only twelve would be receiving top honors, one for each division. The runners-up would receive honoree plaques, but nowhere near the prestige of those winners capturing first-place.

Taking her place at the table after introductions were completed, Jill continued to be awestruck, *"The table's décor is something to behold."*

Each table arrangement consisted of Fuchsia napkins, elegant gold-rimmed china, and sterling place-settings, along with a centerpiece of red roses carefully arranged in what appeared to be a medium size fishbowl. Locked in Jill's mind were only two words... *"unique and magnificent."*

The small talk diminished and shifted to business as dinner progressed. Mr. Levine and his wife, Claire, she insisted everyone call her by her first name, were more interested in grilling those nominees seated at their table.

"Each wanted our individual thoughts about the Company's latest products and its marketing strategies. The quality of the night's meal or timeliness in service were secondary," Jill thought, *"A good-natured, but meaningful interrogation of the captured."*

♥ ♥

Chapter 4

New York City—Monday, January 8, 1978

Before leaving Forester's, Clayton spent numerous evenings making phone calls and pounding the pavement searching for a particular office space. He found it two weeks before striking out on his own. *"Today, I am moving into my one-room office on the fifteenth floor of 415 Madison Avenue, New York City. Oh, how I love this address. A mark of success, and I don't even have my first client."* Clayton's lucky stars were aligned. Not only did he find his ideal and affordable office space, but he also pulled off an inconceivable coup. *"I was able to sublet this space, including the use of a part-time secretary, along with sharing my landlord's telephone operator."*

"Mr. Clarkson, you have a call on line three," the pleasant voice of Clayton's shared telephone operator/receptionist sounded over the intercom. "Thanks, Irene." Picking up the phone, he said, "Clayton Clarkson speaking." Listening for several seconds to the caller, he responded, "Where is she now?"

Once that brief conversation concluded, Clayton nervously grabbed his topcoat from the coat rack, "Irene, I have an emergency. Please take messages, but since this is my first day at work, don't be surprised if you are bored to death waiting for someone to call me.

"Oh, I almost forgot. If Taylor Lee was to call, tell her I'll call her later. Please don't tell her I left on an emergency. She's my girlfriend, and that would likely make her very nervous."

Clayton immediately left the office building, removed his car from the parking garage, and drove to his second wife's house on Long Island.

"Here I am setting in the hospital's waiting room hoping that Lorre can make it through this, her latest life-threatening episode. As I explained to the RN, that phone call I received less than three hours ago from Mrs. Bartlett, our slightly nosey, but caring neighbor likely saved Lorre's life.

"She said that Lorre, in a drunken stupor, had fallen on the sidewalk and she helped her inside the house, but was fearful of her condition. After driving twenty-two miles to the house that Lorre and I still owned in Rockville Centre. I went to the front door. She didn't answer when I rang the doorbell, which was not unusual. I used my key to go inside. There I found Lorre at the bottom of the stairs in our split-level house, unconscious. Had she fallen down all three flights? Thank God, she was still breathing.

"Lorre was transported to the hospital by the town's rescue squad ambulance. Shortly after that, the emergency room doctor diagnosed her as having had a stroke."

While continuing to wait for Lorre to be assigned a hospital room, Clayton's interrogation by the R.N. continued. He was well aware that she was checking for the possibility of domestic violence.

So, he proceeded without objection to tell his story: "*Three years ago, I separated from Lorre, who is a hopeless alcoholic—in and out of multiple treatment centers—and never would admit to having a problem. Even though we had parted ways, she still lives in the house we jointly own, and I continue to support her. Checking on Lorre was nothing unusual. I generally go to the house a couple of times a week or so. My visits have nothing to do with love or romance, I feel sorry for her, and for some reason, I cannot bring myself to file for divorce.*"

Seated alongside Lorre's hospital bed as she slept, Clayton had chosen not to wake her. With tears in his eyes, his mind filled with several memories revolving around the early years of their marriage.

"*Lorre was a real trooper throughout most of our ten years of marriage. During those times, I held executive positions in Washington, D.C., Boston, Massachusetts, and New York City. She was always opposed to being uprooted. When I was planning to leave D.C., she made it clear to me that if we moved, she would never work again.*

"*I had no concern about her not working. If I was to achieve success, relocation was a necessary part of the game. We moved three times, and she held to her word. Looking back, I was likely stupid, dumb, or even greedy, because I never gave any thought to the damage that my quest could be inflicting upon Lorre's mind.*"

Now going through self-analysis of why he was so against putting up with anyone who drank alcohol excessively, Clayton recognized that Lorre's excessive drinking brought back memories of himself as an adolescent.

"*I still remember, as if it was last week, how Mom and I*

would beg Dad year after year, and to no avail, to just stay sober on Christmas Eve... Please, Dad, please. This was all we wanted; to enjoy celebrating the holiday. Now here I am again caught up in the destruction that alcoholism can wreak on families."

Clayton remembered the pledge he made to himself more than two decades ago. *"I swear to God I will never again tolerate living with anyone who has a drinking problem."* His Dad, a working alcoholic, passed at the age of sixty-three.

Clayton also had a troubling track record with women during his early adult years. He divorced his high school sweetheart after a short marriage, had several brief romances or one-night stands, and at the age of twenty-three, he and Lorre met; she became his first true love.

During Lorre's three weeks in the hospital, Clayton visited her bedside nightly while Taylor Lee waited in the visitors' lounge. Once Lorre's health had improved, with only minor damage from her stroke, her doctor said she would be scheduled for release within five days.

As for Lorre's post-hospital care, Clayton scoffed, thinking, *"She has no one else to look after her. Her only living relative is a religious—and I do mean religious—sister and her family. The sister knew of Lorre's drinking problems but stayed away. It was as if she refused to accept reality. The sister offered all kinds of excuses as to why she was not available to help."*

Now scheduled for release, Clayton told Taylor, "I again spoke with her sister, Bernice, to no avail. I am the one having to assume responsibility. It didn't matter that Lorre and I had been separated for three years, and there was no turning back. I even told Bernice I knew that if Lorre was able to return home alone, she would be hitting the bottle in nothing flat. She just ignored what I said... Can you God damn believe that shit? Bernice professes to be so righteous and God-loving! Bullshit! Bullshit!"

Clayton's facial expression changed. Now looking calm, he muttered to himself, "*I will find the best solution for Lorre... Let's see, what are my alternatives? I move back to Rockville Centre to live with her? No way, not an option. I live with Taylor in Manhattan as I have done so for the past two years. Drop Lorre at her sister's home and insist she is her responsibility? Another 'No way!' Take her back to the house and let her fend for herself, or die from an alcoholic overdose? No, No, No!*

"*So, damn it... What am I to do?*"

♥ ♥

Chapter 5

Los Angeles—January 1981

Jill realized she was getting more nervous as the evening moved forward. *"Oh God, I pray I don't get sick... and vomit."*

With dinner over, tables cleared, and coffee and other drinks poured, Mr. Levine excused himself and went to the podium. *"From his mannerisms, it was obvious... this was not Mr. Levine's first rodeo,"*

The awards presentations moved along, and finally, Table 3 was next. When the names of those other regional nominees at her table were announced, Jill watched closely and saw either emotions of happiness or sure signs of sadness in their eyes.

"Which category will I be cast," she thought. *"Finally... my region's turn."* Her stomach churned and knotted as Mr. Levine adjusted the microphone and announced, 'The next award is for the 1980 Western Region's Retail Salesperson of the Year.'

Jill, without uttering a word, but thinking, "*I could swear he was looking at me when he said, 'and the two nominees are, Alexis Lewis and Jill Simpson.'*" Jill looked over to Table 1, where Alexis was seated. "*Damn, I wanted to see if she looked as nervous as I am feeling. But Jerry is blocking my view.*"

Mr. Levine opened the envelope, read its contents, looked up, and paused. "*Just like those awards I watch on television,*" Jill thought.

"This year's award for the Western Region's Retail Salesperson of the Year is..." The audience broke into thunderous clapping, cheering, and gave a standing ovation once the name... "Jill Simpson" flooded the room.

Jill burst into tears, spouting the words, "Next to the birth of my three kids, this is the happiest moment of my life!" Claire Levine, seated next to Jill, rose from her chair and at once began hugging and offering her congratulations.

The audience continued with their applause. Jill, tears flowing down her cheeks, returned Claire's hug while saying, "Pinch me, please pinch me."

"Why?" Claire asked laughing as she looked at the sobbing Jill. "Why?"

Jill answered, "I just want to make sure this is real and not a dream!"

"Okay, where do you want me to pinch you?"

"Oh, I don't care. On the arm will do."

After Claire's pinch, Jill gave a big smile and responded, "It's real..."

Upon being called to the stage, Jill reached into her jeweled evening purse, removed a folded piece of stationery, carrying it with her. Smiling as she casually walked up the aisle, she looked stunning for a forty-year-old. Standing five-foot-five, slender build, bright blue eyes and, a real surprise for a California woman... moderately long, naturally blond hair. Jill Simpson fit the image of a professional cosmetician perfectly.

As customary after the presentation of the award, each winner is expected to give a speech. It was now Jill's turn. She stepped up to the microphone, carefully unfolded the piece of paper, looked at it, then at the audience, and said, "I didn't want to be unprepared in the remote possibility I would have to come up here, so I jotted down my short speech. She looked at the piece of paper, looked up at the audience, paused, and said, "Thank you!"

It was apparent the audience wasn't going to let her leave the stage with a simple 'Thank you.'

Someone shouted, "More... tell us more."

For a split-second, Jill looked nervous, and then in a friendly, relaxed manner, she placed her notepaper aside. Looking up and smiling, she said, "I may have enough time to extend my thank you. As Jerry Smythers was escorting me to my table this evening, he said, 'Jill, savor the moment for just being here. Win or lose you will forever remember this night.'"

Looking towards where Jerry was setting, she held up her plaque, gestured toward him, and said, "Jerry to you and everyone who helped me achieve this award, I say, 'Thank you so very much.' To you, Mr. and Mrs. Levine, I believe I can speak for everyone here and say, 'We greatly appreciate your kindness and thoughtfulness in all you do for your employees.'" Finished, Jill stepped back from the microphone and waved to the audience.

A standing ovation lasting two or three minutes erupted. The applause continued as Jill, still smiling and waving, headed back to her table. Not a single person in the room suspected that underneath Jill's happy façade was a woman filled with a bundle of heartaches.

Less than forty-five minutes into her drive south, Jill's joyful memories of the weekend surrendered to her wretched inner voice: *"How could my life have spun so far out of control? I was always a good and caring wife and mother to our three children during our twenty years of marriage."*

While searching for something or someone to blame, a gasp escaped from deep in her gut as she focused on her ex-husband, Roy. A year or so before their divorce, the relationship between the two had reached a point well beyond repair. Unfaithfulness was not the problem. Jill never cheated, and she had no reason to suspect Roy had a lover on the side.

"My Dad would have scoffed at the very thought of divorce, let alone me actually following through with what he would have considered such a shallow thing."

Reminding herself of why she was really pissed at her ex-husband, one by one, Jill started to go through a number of items she referred to as part of Roy's shit list: *"Even though I had been a loyal wife, held a full-time job, nursed him during his prescription drug addiction, he never once showed any appreciation.*

"But my biggest peeve revolved around our three kids. I always made it a point to place them first... they were my priority. Roy was so absorbed in his own world that he rarely devoted any special time to them by doing much needed fatherly things, or expressing his love. I sincerely believe that he deeply loves all three, but he had an inferior

way of expressing it."

Jill's most vivid memories focused on Roy going behind her back and doing some peculiar things. *"On one occasion, he came home and proudly announced he had purchased several large containers of purified water and a twenty-year supply of dehydrated foods for stockpiling. His reasoning: This would help the family survive in the event of a deadly earthquake.*

"He reminded me that our house was located close enough to the San Andreas fault line to suffer a devastating impact. While having Roy's stockpile returned, I discovered he was in negotiations with a contractor to dig an underground shelter in our backyard. I canceled that deal before he was able to sign on the dotted line... whew!"

Jill believed Roy was living in his own little world, and no one else mattered. As if asking another person, she mumbled, *"Can you just imagine, coming home and discovering a significant amount of money was missing from your family's savings account? With the bank statement in hand, I called the bank; they verified that my husband made the withdrawal.*

"Once home, Roy admitted that he secretly removed $10,000 from our savings account and invested that money in a bag of silver coins. His reasoning: To protect the family in the event of a catastrophe such as an earthquake, the U.S. dollar would likely collapse. If so, silver would be in demand.

"The only positive thing, if anyone chooses to call it positive, coming out of Roy's heist took place during our divorce settlement... I now have a bag full of silver coins, nowhere near the value of the $10,000. My damn faultfinding list just kept growing. Roy was never one to make any effort to help around the house, even though he knew I had to put in more hours at work than he with his cushy

city government job as an administrator within the City's mental health division."

The more those negative thoughts churned in Jill's mind, the higher the speed of her BMW. Both her mind and the movement of her Beemer had reached intense levels. Finally, back to reality, Jill looked down at the speedometer; she was driving thirty-eight miles per hour over the posted limit. Shocked, she quickly slowed the car back to sixty-five.

"Damn, speeding can mean jail time, a $1,000 fine, or both. I wonder if they would accept silver coins for payment of a fine?"

Back driving at a reasonable speed, Roy was still in Jill's crosshairs as she continued to mentally recite Roy's shit list.

"There was also a slew of petty things that burned my butt. Like the time I asked him to cut the small lawn in front of our house, and he refused, saying he was too tired. The next thing I knew, he had left the house and had gone to play basketball at the playground up the street.

"All of Roy's crap was really building up and making me ready to explode. But the straw that broke the camel's back took place on one Sunday afternoon. Our car had gotten filthy after being driven several days back and forth through a muddy construction area. I asked Roy to wash it. He snapped at me, saying, 'Today is Sunday, and God doesn't want us to do any labor on this holy day.'

"Well, less than two hours later, we both saw our Catholic priest, Father Timothy, who lived on the next block, out in front of his home, and guess what? He was busy washing his car. I looked directly at Roy. He paused, and after a couple of seconds or so, all he said to me was, 'I am going over to the golf range to hit balls.' I then got out a bucket, connected the hose to the house's faucet, and washed

that damn car."

Roy was diagnosed as having a manic-depressive illness. This mental disorder was causing periods of depression along with abnormally elevated mood swings. He always refused treatment in a hospital, even though all of the behavioral signs were there: agitation, depression, and his dependency on prescription drugs for self-medication. Other symptoms included absenteeism, refusing to get out of bed, irritable mood swings, and periods of excessive spending.

Moments later, as Jill turned off the I-5 Freeway onto Washington Street, she relaxed her grip on the steering wheel. Only a couple lights more, and she would be at her destination, MCRD.

Within a block of the base, she smiled, thinking, *"Upon arriving at the base's Gate 5, after literally following the same boring procedure two hundred or more times, I knew the routine well. First, stop and produce my civilian I.D., vehicle registration, and wait for the gate guard to record all pertinent information, including my borrowed BMW's blue color, and ensure the registration matched the vehicle's license plate number. The final step for my okay to enter was a salute accompanied by the guard's firmly spoken words, 'Permission to enter granted.' Yes, I had it all down to a T."*

♥ ♥

♥ ♥

Chapter 6

277 Park Avenue, New York City— January 5, 1981

Clayton, seated in his brown leather high-back office chair, with a mug of black coffee in hand, said to a smiling Guy Devine, "It's almost three years to the day since I left Forester's and moved into my first office over on Fifth Avenue. And, look at us now. Time flies when you're having fun, right?"

"You bet it is fun, and I must add... exciting," Guy said as he moved from his chair to the window and looked down upon the flood of Yellow Cabs making their way north up Park Avenue.

With three on the payroll, including himself, and a pool of top-notch subcontractors, Clayton had come a long way since he went out on his own. "Damn, Guy, I'll never forget my first day at work as an independent contractor. I didn't have a care in the world." Rethinking that statement, Clayton said, "Well, that's not totally true. There was pressure on me knowing that come next week, I wouldn't have one penny coming in. Not one penny!"

Guy responded, "That has to be tormenting. So, how did you cope?"

"I didn't. I never got the chance. In less than one hour in the office, my peaceful day turned into a horrific nightmare."

"Are you serious... what happened?"

"It started with a devastating phone call about my ex, Lorre, having a stroke. That traumatic experience, along with knowing that I no longer had any money coming in... changed my world forever. But I survived, and it wasn't easy."

Guy quietly asked, "How?"

"The support of close friends, business associates, and a couple of competitors," Clayton said with a warm smile. "Even Taylor was encouraging me to go see a shrink. Can you see me lying on a couch in some psychiatrist's office?"

"Not really, but I could add, only if your shrink is a woman."

"Funny, real funny, but this was no joke," Clayton scornfully responded. "Between Lorre's problem and my not focusing on coming up with clients, a couple of times it looked awful for me. Then, honest to God, Guy, I was sitting in my chair, and I remember saying to myself, 'Come next week you will not have one penny coming in.'"

"So, what did you do?"

"I jumped out of that damn chair, saying to myself, 'Then what the hell are you doing sitting here?'"

"What happened with your ex?"

"Well, she's another story. Too long for now. I'll tell you about her someday when we are on a long flight."

"Clayton, do you know what today is?"

"Come on, Guy. I'm not so old that I would forget this date. Besides, it corresponds with the day I moved into our Madison Avenue office."

It was the third anniversary of Clayton's practice, and what a three years it had been. His business was rapidly growing, and within that short time-span, he was able to add a number of high profile organizations to his U.S. client list that included Forester's parent company, a prestigious NYC real estate firm, the top stock exchange corporation in the world, one of the nation's top accounting firms, and the United States Marine Corps.

With the addition of international clients in Italy, France, England, Canada, Argentina, Brazil, Paraguay, and New Zealand, Clayton recognized potential advantages in changing his firm's name from Clayton L. Clarkson & Associates to Clayton L. Clarkson International, Inc.

The only physical change to take place otherwise was his office move two weeks ago to a larger and more luxurious office building over on Park Avenue.

"Hold on a second, Guy. I don't want to forget this." Clayton reached over and jotted a note on his desk calendar: 'double-check with Myrna to ensure that she has my airlines, hotel and rental car travel plans confirmed for the next two months.' Clayton looked up and said, "Myrna is the best and most dependable travel agent ever. But it always pays to double-check."

First, on his agenda was the trip to San Diego, California. At the request of Colonel Cooperswaite, his Marine Corps contact, Clayton, along with Guy Devine, would be making a three-day visit to the U.S. Marine Corps Base in San Diego. This trip would be Clayton's second in less than three weeks. Knowing Clayton would be in Europe for a month, the Colonel wanted to confirm that his project was on schedule. Once this visit was complete, the plan was for Guy to return to Manhattan, while Clayton continued to Milan, Italy.

Chapter 7

San Diego, Marine Corps Recruiting Depot (MCRD)
—January 19, 1981

"*F*inally! I am so glad to hear that polite gate guard say, '*Permission to enter granted.*'" Pulling forward, Jill found an empty parking spot about fifty or so yards inside the gate.

As she parked, she took a couple of extra minutes to digress. "*The only interruption to this smooth five-day-a-week process was that every once in awhile, I would be driving my daughter's car or a loaner. Then all hell would break loose when I couldn't put my hands on the registration without a frantic search.*

"*From the reaction of those vehicles in line behind me, you would think I had committed some mortal sin, as nonstop horns blaring set in. If their timing was better, I bet several could create some new tune with the synchronization of those horns. Pissed, you bet they were pissed, and as they sped past me if looks could kill, I would have expired several months ago.*

"Every once in a while, I would feel extraordinarily brave and give the finger to one or two as they drove by shouting obscenities. Then, I would remind myself... this is a Marine Base filled with a bunch of macho jocks; what else could I expect?

"I am lucky. I love my job, and my winning that prestigious business award was the greatest; a good omen... I hope?"

"Hey babe, you look great! Let me hold the door for you?" There was no mistaking the fact that this young recruit was flirting. Quickly rejecting his unsolicited offer, Jill gave a dirty look and replied, "Knock it off Marine, I am old enough to be your mother."

She then grabbed her purse off the seat and started walking towards the Exchange, a distance as far as a city block. She entered the building through the employee door. From here it was a short walk to the porch where she would meet her best friend, Vivian.

Entering the area, she thought, *"The piped-in music was dull, and for some odd reason today, it reminded me of the old Lawrence Welk shows I watched as a kid. Those old songs did little to improve the porch's almost sterile ambiance. Another 'you get what you pay for' thing wasting the military's money."*

The two always got together at their favorite table, unless occupied, for lunch. Vivian, mostly spontaneous with her eating habits, was nearly unpredictable. One day it was an apple and a few grapes, the next day a slice of pizza, or a deli sandwich and vanilla shake; impulsive. The opposite, Jill, was predictable. Vivian often lightheartedly criticized her for bringing peanut butter and dill pickle sandwiches.

However, today would be different. Jill had driven straight from L.A. with no stop for a snack in between. After being filled in with all the gossip from the conference, Vivian still refused to share her chicken salad sandwich and pretzels. But she did give Jill the banana she was saving for her afternoon break.

Their table of choice always had a decent view of the goings-on. Today the two decided to turn the thirty-minute lunch break into a people-watching affair. Still, on a high from the glorious weekend at the Ritz-Carlton, Jill was in a silly mood, when a well-dressed man in civilian clothes sitting across the porch caught her eye.

"Look at that guy over there. Doesn't he look just like Gene Wilder in *Charlie and the Chocolate Factory*? That was my kids' favorite movie! Look at his face, eyes, and nose. Let's name him 'Charlie,'" exclaimed Jill.

Something unusual about 'Charlie' caused her to keep staring at him. Vivian, snacking on her pretzels, watched the nonverbal communications between Jill and her new guy, 'Charlie.'

Jill proceeded to take a big bite out of the peeled banana, and sure as heck, there he was staring at her. Vivian, first glancing at the gyrations Jill was going through with each bite of her banana, and then over to 'Charlie,' she began giggling.

"*Obviously because of some obscene thought,*" Jill blushed like a seventh-grader in the back of the bus kissing. "How embarrassing. Did he know what we were laughing about?"

"Probably not," replied Vivian. Jill felt giddy the rest of the day for some unknown reason.

The next day both Vivian and Jill looked for 'Charlie.'
He was nowhere around. He would have been easy to spot as he really stood out among the officers and recruits in his fancy three-piece suit, white French-cuff shirt, and tie. "*Impeccably dressed,*" Jill thought. However, she was not feeling as whimsical at lunchtime today.

"*Sometimes, I wonder if there's something wrong with me. Perhaps I am becoming a literary romantic, but no man ever turned me on like that guy. It was his eyes, his bright greenish eyes.*" No words were necessary; they spoke volumes.

Suddenly, Jill's often recited verse from Philip Glass and Robert Wilson's classic opera, *Einstein on the Beach* drifted into her mind: "*Two lovers sat on a park bench with their bodies touching each other, holding hands in the moonlight. There was silence between them. So profound was their love for each other, they needed no words to express it. And so they sat in silence, on a park bench, with their bodies touching, holding hands in the moonlight.*"

Whenever feelings of sadness swept across Jill, she would replay that verse in her mind. However, for some strange reason, this time, she added a few extra words, "*I just want to be loved and find true happiness... Is that asking too much?*"

Jill's heart was pounding as she felt a ripple of strong feelings for what might have been. "*Stop wallowing in self-pity,*" her inner voice chastised as she embraced the reality that she may never see 'Charlie' again.

Jill was in the kitchen when she heard the apartment front door open and close. Looking at the wall clock, it's five-thirty. She knew it was Wendy. No surprise, she snickered, "*Only Wendy and I live here.*"

"Mom," Wendy called. "I was surprised to see your car out front. I thought you and Vivian were having dinner out. Why are you home? Is something wrong?"

Jill smiled and set the salad bowl on the kitchen counter. Sunlight was penetrating one of the slightly opened slats on the Venetian blind just enough to remind Jill of her daughter's beauty.

Her blond hair and blue eyes, an inch taller than her Mom, Wendy walked with perfect posture, at least in Jill's mind, and she was perhaps a little too thin. *"Those eyes... It was the brightness of her eyes! Just like those bright hazel-green* eyes *of that guy, I named, 'Charlie.'"*

"No," she said. "Nothing is wrong. Vivian's car was acting up, and she thought she had better get it taken care of while it is still drivable. God, I'd hate to have to go out to Del Mar to pick her up tomorrow morning. With you now engaged and out almost every night, I thought it would be nice for the two of us to spend a quiet dinner and evening together, that is until your fiancé, James shows up once he gets off his second job at the airport."

"Mom, come on. I can tell something is bothering you. What's the matter?"

Jill, in what Wendy interpreted as a dodge to her question, responded, "Nothing. I'm fine."

"Ah, Mom, please. Is it something James or I did?"

Jill, with a shake of her head, "No, this is about me." Nervously, she pulled two chairs away from the table. "Okay, let's have a seat, and I will tell you."

Jill had never talked to Wendy about her love life, and her stomach felt unsettled at the very thought of revealing her inner self, especially to her very own daughter. Lowering her eyes, she swallowed hard and managed a weak smile.

"Mom, you haven't said anything, and you are scaring the bejeebers out of me."

"Oh, Wendy, I don't mean to." She reached across the table and squeezed Wendy's hand. "I'm just afraid you are going to laugh at me."

"Oh, Mom, I would never make fun of anything you thought

to be serious."

"You know that occasionally I have gone out on casual dates, and once I even went on a blind date. So, you can see I am going out since the divorce became final."

"I assumed so, but since you never brought anyone home, I just figured they were all bummers."

"Wendy, do you believe in coincidences?"

Wendy paused, thinking, "I guess I do."

Sensing that she now had Wendy's attention, Jill said, "This guy showed up on the porch at work when Vivian and I were having lunch. Wendy, I had to force myself to take my eyes off of him; he was also staring at me. I am not talking about some flirting episode. Even though we never exchanged a single word, the chemistry between the two of us was unbelievably strong."

"Well, what happened?"

"Nothing! Vivian and I had to get back to work. The next day, he wasn't around. I never saw him again, but I still feel unbelievably connected and convinced our paths will cross again. I just know we are meant to be together."

"Mom, I pray it will work out for you."

For some reason, those bright eyes of Charlie' floated into her mind. Jill looked up and said, "Wendy, I'm sorry; I don't mean to cry."

♥ ♥

Chapter 8

San Diego—January 19, 1981

The plane from New Jersey's Newark airport with Clayton and Guy touched down at Lindbergh Field shortly after midnight on Monday. After only four hours of rest at the Hilton, Guy settled into the driver's seat of their Ford Fairmont rental. Exiting the parking lot, he pulled into the left traffic lane for the short drive to MCRD.

With Guy at the wheel, Clayton thought, *"I can't help but think about how nice it is to once again be in sunny California."* The day before, his part-time driver, Arthur, had done everything he could to maneuver the 1979 Cadillac Seville along the New Jersey Turnpike in stop-and-go traffic as it crawled its way out to Newark Airport.

Clayton couldn't resist comparing San Diego's weather to the conditions he just left back East. *"The weather was crappy; filthy remnants of a sloppy mixture of slush and road salt were wavering against the alternating icy and thawing temperatures. And, it would be sinful to fail to mention a road full of potholes and those foul-smelling gas refineries stacked along the turnpike sucking practically every speck of breathable air away from our lungs.*

"I felt like lowering my backseat window and shouting, 'Welcome to the land of the Big Apple.' But I dared not. If I did, my first hire and most loyal associate, Guy, would likely bail thinking I had finally flipped my lid, and never work with me again. Both he and Arthur, another convert, would believe that I had gone completely bonkers."

Fifteen or so minutes later, the rental car was in line at Gate 5 for entry into the base. After a short delay, Guy pulled alongside the guard with all the required documents and IDs' in hand. A quick review of papers, the guard stated, 'Permission to enter granted,' saluted, and added, "Colonel Cooperswaite is expecting you."

Next stop, not anything either man would ever have dreamed of in New York City, a reserved parking space in front of the Commanding Officer's complex was waiting. Clayton said, "Ten minutes early for our scheduled 0900 hours meeting."

Guy smiled and said, "Oh yes, once on the base, we must convert our schedules to good old military time."

At 1100 hours, the Colonel told Clayton and Guy that he had to deal with an emergency and would rejoin them for lunch at 1200 hours in the officers' mess. "Until then, you are welcome to use the vacant office. You know the one; next door to Gunny. Feel free to make phone calls, or tour the retail area of the Exchange." With that, the Colonel departed.

"Come on, Guy, follow me."

"Where are we going?"

"You remember me telling you about that gorgeous blond I

saw having lunch on the porch during my last trip?"

"How could I not. She was all you talked about while boarding the plane that evening."

"Well, I want to find her. Hopefully, she is not on day-off."

"Are you sure you want to do this," Guy said, "Remember, what you always preach, 'Even a dog has more sense than to shit where he eats.' Clayton, I am sure that I don't have to remind you that this is our eating place and a well paying one at that. Besides, what about Taylor, your live-in back in the City?"

"Guy, you don't have to remind me of my screwed up personal life. As you know, I have erased most of my past from my mind. It's now my deeply buried secret, one that I hope I will never have to unearth."

"Clayton, you know better. Things like that you cannot simply pretend they never took place. They did happen, and someday your secrets are going to come back and bite you square in the ass... mark my word!"

"I know Guy is right. But I can't get that blond beauty out of my mind. Really weird, and although we never spoke a word between us, there was an unbelievable attraction. One like I had never encountered before. I don't even know if she is married, although she was not wearing a wedding ring when I saw her last. A looker like her has to have a husband, boyfriend, or perhaps she's in a situation like mine, living with someone?"

As Guy and Clayton left the office complex and turned left into the sales area, Clayton's eyes lit up, "Look, there at the Estee counter, with her back to us stands my dream girl. Come on, Guy."

Chapter 9

Clayton walked up to the counter and couldn't resist saying what had to be one of the dumbest pick-up lines ever, "You have the most beautiful blue eyes I have ever seen."

Startled, she turned to face him. "Charlie!" she excitedly said. "Oh, sorry, please forgive me. I know your name is not Charlie."

"Tell you what; I'll forgive you on one condition. Have a drink with me after work."

She responded, "I don't even know your name."

"Nor do I know yours."

"My name is Jill Simpson."

"Mine is Clayton Clarkson, and my associate, Guy Devine. If I can get Colonel Cooperswaite to vouch for me, will you go?"

"I know the Colonel well, and if he says you are safe, I'll consider it. I get off at six, so come back before then, and I'll give you my answer."

Clayton had barely returned to the office area before Jill, after speaking with the Colonel, began to have second thoughts.

"What an impulsive move by me. Cooperswaite told me this guy is okay. But can I believe and trust the Colonel?"

Jill dialed Vivian's extension and excitedly asked her if they could meet in the ladies' room in five minutes. "Let's do it now; I'm not busy."

"Now is good."

"Vivian, guess what? Remember that guy we saw on the porch a couple of weeks ago, the one we named Charlie? He's back, and I need a big favor. I told him that if the Colonel gave him an okay, I would meet him for a drink after work. Colonel Cooperswaite likes him, and said that he's a civilian from New York and is here doing consulting work for MCRD."

Excitedly, she continued, "He's to come by my counter before six for my answer. I'd like to meet him at the Hilton, that's where he and his partner are staying. Vivian, I don't want to go alone... pleeease go with me?"

"Hmmm, that's the *Charlie and the Chocolate Factory* guy that you went bonkers over."

"If you say so. I really want to get to know this guy."

"Well, okay, I guess I could. Besides, I'll get a free drink or two. Look, Jill, only drinks, no dinner, or going anywhere else. I am to meet Marti for dinner at 7:30 at El Torito's in Old Town."

The two ladies walked into the dimly-lit bar in the Hilton at 6:25 p.m. The bar in the lounge was nearly full, mostly men and women dressed in Marine khakis, with only two empty stools remaining. The cocktail tables were just the opposite; only two gentlemen, both in suits and ties, were seated at a cozy table for four, in a slightly secluded corner; the other four tables unoccupied.

Jill and Clayton stared at each other for a second or two, as the ladies approached. Somewhat in unison, the informal greetings between the three again took place. Vivian spoke up, "I'm Vivian, by the way."

The waitress approached with a pad and pen in hand. It was evident from her mannerisms that she knew who would be picking up the tab. Jill ordered a Chardonnay, Vivian, with a slight hesitation said, "Make mine a Silver Patron Margarita on the rocks, no salt." With that, Jill sent an 'if looks could kill' stare Vivian's way. Vivian, without a word, smiled in return.

If the two men picked up on this non-verbal exchange, nary a sign was offered. Clayton also ordered a Chardonnay, and Guy, a Merlot. Once the drinks arrived, Clayton proposed a toast. With glasses raised, he said, "To a long-lasting and wonderful friendship."

Without saying so, Clayton made it apparent his toast was personal and meant only for the beautiful woman seated alongside him. He couldn't take his eyes off her. As expected, the talk around the table was mostly casual chit-chat, that is until Vivian, proposed a second toast to Jill. She briefly told about the award Jill had won in Los Angeles over the weekend. With that, Clayton called the waitress and ordered another round.

Unnoticed by Jill, Clayton had slid his chair three or four inches closer, as the waitress set down her tray and began placing the drinks. Clayton, looking at Jill, said, "Just call me Clay." Almost spontaneously, his hand reached for hers. She didn't pull away. Feeling the heat of his body, Jill thought, "*The temperature in this room is getting warmer.*"

When the next round arrived, Jill wasted no time in taking a sip with the hand Clay had been holding and was glad the glass was chilled. More small talk, and suddenly Vivian in a whisper-shout said, "Oh my God! I have to get out of here! I'm to meet a friend in Old Town. Jill, I need you to drive me back to MCRD."

Pleasantries abruptly ended, but not before Clay asked, "Will you have dinner with me tomorrow night?"

Without hesitation, Jill said, "Yes. I'll pick you up out front at 6:15 sharp."

As she pulled away, Jill thought, *"Is it possible that this meeting between two new acquaintances could take an exciting romantic turn, or perhaps with my luck, turn into nothing more than one of those escapades Wendy refers to as a... bummer? Guess I'll get a better reading tomorrow night, or will I?"*

♥ ♥

Chapter 10

As Jill's car pulled away from the Hilton, Vivian said, "So you didn't like me ordering a Silver Patron Margarita?"

"Well."

"Come on, Jill. Those guys are on expense accounts. They are accustomed to buying top-shelf drinks."

"Okay, okay, I get it. Well, what do you think?"

"I surely noticed that he couldn't keep his eyes off you. I agree, maybe there's some chemistry between the two of you."

"See, I told you that as weird as it appears, no man has ever affected me this way."

"Jill, don't forget he lives in New York, and you here in San Diego. Besides, you don't know a single thing about this guy's personal life."

"I know, but I felt good interactions between the two of us."

"Jill, I don't ever want you to get hurt, so heed this warning… San Diego is a Navy port. Sailors have a girl in every port, and I would suspect the same applies to consultants. Here's my car. I've got to run. See you tomorrow."

First Date

"*If I had known Clay was inconsiderate of other's time,* Jill mused, "*I wouldn't have agreed to go to dinner. Here I bust my butt to be on time.*" Sitting in her car at the main entrance to the Hilton, Jill had been waiting for fifteen minutes past the agreed time to pick up Clay.

"*Not a good start for a first date. Finally, here he comes rushing through the automatic door, suit coat in hand, tie untied, half of his shirt sticking out of his pants; his appearance disheveled. Certainly not the spit and polish looks of the man I spent an hour or so with last evening. What the hell's up with this guy?*"

"Sorry... I am so sorry for being late! But I had no sooner got into my room when the desk clerk called and told me he had an emergency message for me. The news was not good."

"Is there anything I can do?"

"No. But thanks for offering. My former wife's sister died, and I had to deal with a couple of issues. I just hung up the phone, and that's why I am late. Sorry about my appearance. I didn't have time to change or freshen up. Hey, tonight is our night! No more sad talk. Where are we going?"

"Well, I thought it would be nice for us to go to the Rubin E. Lee restaurant, down on Harbor Island. It is a large barge with a replica of a Mississippi paddle wheeler built on top—beautiful place with a great view of the City skyline. Naturally, the place serves all types of seafood, but since I am not what you would call a fish lover, it also has a variety of beef plates. My favorite is the

Delmonico steak."

Upon arrival at the restaurant, several people were standing in the reception area, waiting for a table. Clay saw Jill bypass those waiting and approach the reception desk. She whispered something to the *maître d'* and within less than three minutes, the announcement, "Ms. Simpson, party of two" amplified within the lobby area. The *maître d'* seated them at a premium table for four. The view was spectacular, the best in the house for observing both the sunset and skyline.

Clay thought, "*This table selection wasn't a spur-of-the-moment thing. That's why the whispering between Jill and the* maître d'. *I'll bet she had made reservations and arranged for this exceptional table, and here I came close to screwing up her well-planned evening by being late.*" A quick glance around. "*Not Manhattan, but if my initial impression is any indication of the quality of food, it will be a winner.*"

"I'll have a glass of Chardonnay."

"Wait," Clay interjected, "I'll have the same, Chardonnay, but make it a bottle with two glasses... one of your better brands; a glass of ice on the side."

As the waiter left the table, Jill looking surprised, said, "How did you know I like ice in my wine?"

"I noticed you put a couple of cubes in your glass last night. Mind if I switch chairs?" Before Jill had a chance to respond, Clay was seated alongside her. "The view is better from this angle. Besides, I want to sit close to you."

The waiter gave a low, attention-getting cough and poured Clay the tasting quantity. Given an affirmative nod, the waiter said, "Okay, I shall pour."

The small talk continued throughout the meal, and Jill laughed as Clay told her of the weather and driving conditions they had encountered on their way out of Manhattan to Newark airport.

Now on their second bottle of wine, the two watched as the sky glowed orange and pink as the brightness of the sun moved behind the horizon. Jill muttered, *"An absolutely perfect first date. Good wine and good food,"* as her body language telegraphed her feelings, *"I really like this guy, and best of all, he is acting like a real gentleman."*

With that thought barely processed, Clay leaned over and kissed her, his lips gently touching hers—no time to hesitate or react—Jill tenderly moved her hand behind his head, pulling him closer.

As they were finishing their last glass of wine, Clay became noticeably uncomfortable, and for the second time since their passionate kiss, he glanced at his watch. *"Something is eating at him. But what?"* Jill thought.

"Excuse me," Clay said as he stood up. "I just remembered I need to make a phone call. I'll be back in a couple of minutes." As a waiter passed, "Where's the telephone?" In a split-second, he left the table headed in the direction the waiter had given.

"I may be somewhat naïve, but I'm not stupid," she thought. Believing she could detect risk by spotting the slightest change in a person's behavior, speech, or subtle expression, she mentally visualized, *"Something weird is going on with this guy. Ah crap, too good to be true."*

Chapter 11

Clay, to his word, was gone only four or five minutes. "Clay, I don't mean to sound one-dimensional, but what the hell is going on with you? First, you tell me about an emergency phone call that your former wife's sister just died. Next, throughout the evening, you are not only rude but also antsy over something. Please explain your reasons for constantly looking at your watch and your sudden need to make a phone call? Are you married?"

"No... No, I promise!" Jill looked directly into his eyes, and all she saw was a cloud of confusion. His noticeable nervousness made her uneasy. She reached for her glass and downed the remaining small amount.

Clay called the waiter over. Jill sensed, "*He is going to ask for the check.*"

Instead, he said, "Bring us two glasses of Chardonnay. No, not a bottle, just two glasses of the same brand." With teary eyes and a pleading tone in his voice, Clay said, "Jill, oh Jill, please."

Surprising even herself, she reached down and removed his

hand from the table and squeezed it tenderly, "I don't know what to believe." With a slight quiver of her chin, she said, "Maybe we should just go."

"Please, let's stay and finish our drinks. I have some real fence-mending to do. Just hear me out."

"Okay, but since you used that western jargon, 'fence-mending,' I am coming back to you by saying, 'You pissed on my porch, and now you gotta clean it up.' And, don't try to sell me one of your New York bridges... Brooklyn Bridge, isn't it?" This lightly spoken comment caused Clay to crack a smile, and with his eyes glistening, a tear slowly made its way down his right cheek.

Clayton's first words, as he maneuvered to change the subject to something pleasant, formed a question, "Do you believe in fate? I do, and it brought me here. I knew from the very moment I set my eyes on you, that you were the woman I am destined to love."

That sincere statement got Jill's attention. *"Hold on; he still hasn't told me what's going on,"* she thought, *"Something is seriously wrong here. Clay's actions make no sense unless he's lying about not being married or trying to hide some deep dark secret. Otherwise, why would he be so upset and on edge about that telephone call? It just doesn't make sense."*

Just as sudden as was his first kiss, Jill's inner voice sent a warning, *"Remember Vivian's words of wisdom... 'Sailors have a girl in every port, and I suspect the same applies to worldly consultants.'"*

♥ ♥

Chapter 12

"Jill, as you can see, I am upset. It's been a rough late afternoon, and I must apologize for letting my attention focus elsewhere. However, a serious family problem has arisen, and I am in the best position to rectify this matter. Please believe me when I tell you it has nothing to do with me personally. However, it's something that I do not want to discuss, perhaps later... but not now. For my family's sake, I need to find a solution before I leave for Italy. Please trust me."

The waiter returned with two glasses of wine. Jill picked up her glass, holding it carefully by its stem. Deep in thought, swirling the wine in the glass ever so slowly, *"I must choose my response carefully,"* she thought. In a slow and deliberate move, her focus shifted from the wine glass as she looked Clay in the eye. Her right eyebrow arched, she said, "Why should I?"

He opened his mouth as if to say something, and then paused... thinking. "Look, I know you think I am a jerk."

A slight smile came across her lips, "You're right."

"Honestly, I can't believe that such a perfect date had turned into a petulant encounter, all because I would not divulge a family matter that has nothing to do with me and you. Jill, I'm just stressed, and you are unfair." With that, Clay called to the waiter, "Bring our check, please."

Jill, at a loss for words, leaned forward in her chair, picked up her glass, took one last swallow, and set it on the table. Her inner voice cautioned, "*Here you go again. You can now add Clay to your 'what might have been' list. You are such an idiot. Stupid, stupid move.*"

During the drive back to the Hilton, neither spoke a word. As Clay stepped from Jill's car, holding the door, he turned to face her. With a sad look, he said, "Thanks for spending the evening with me. I am so sorry for what happened... I guess some things, no matter how perfect they appear, are just not meant to be. Jill, I guess this is the last time I will see you. Over the next two days, Guy and I will be in meetings at Camp Pendleton, and then I will be leaving for Italy."

Clay, as he reluctantly closed the car's door, felt a heart-wrenching ache sweep over his entire body as he thought, "*She was the one with whom I could have spent the rest of my life. But now she is gone forever. Guy had warned me that someday my dirty little secrets were going to destroy any hope I ever had for happiness. His prediction may well have come true tonight.*"

On her way to the apartment, a single thought reverberated in Jill's mind, "*I just want to find love and be loved.*" Tossing and turning as she lay in bed, a single question kept playing over and over again, "*Why, oh why... what's wrong with me?*"

Two o'clock... three... four... five. Crying, she murmured, "*No *sleep for the crushed and heartbroken.*"

For the first time in months, Jill rolled over and turned off the alarm clock before it sounded. It was Thursday, and oh, how she dreaded to face the harsh reality that the hours ahead would likely be even more regretful than last night. To make the torment even worse, she awoke with a monstrous headache... one that reminded her of a bad hangover. The past six hours have turned into her worst ever... hellish nightmare.

Preparing for work, Jill showered, reluctantly applied her makeup, and inadvertently put on the same outfit she had worn the day before... a mistake she had never made during her entire business career. As always, she checked herself in the mirror just before walking out the door. Dark circles under her eyes and her hair a full-blown disaster.

Never noticing her wardrobe, she hissed at the image in the mirror, "*Looks like something the cat drug in*"... she closed the door and headed downstairs to her car.

Jill saw Vivian standing in the parking lot as she pulled into an open space. "Well, how did it go?" Vivian shouted so loud that a couple of passersby turned in her direction.

"Terrible!" Jill screamed back, and with that startling response, the nosey passerby stopped momentarily, then moved on.

"God, you look dreadful. What happened? Wait, before I get the rundown, let's go to the ladies' lounge, and I'll make you all beautiful again. You can tell me there."

"Well, our first date got off to a poor start. I had to wait for Clay to come downstairs. This created a slight disruption since I had made reservations with Manny, the maître d' at the Rubin E. Lee. Manny said he would hold a lovely table with a view for us...

and he did. Overall, the dinner and our initial conversations went great. Then I stuck my damn nose into his private affairs."

Vivian questioned, "Married?"

"No, he's not married, or so he says. He was distraught most of the evening, his mind hundreds of miles away. I finally got him to tell me what was bothering him. He said he was trying to deal with a family matter, assuring me that it did not involve him. He kept saying that he was the only person who could fix whatever it was, and this had to be done before he left for Europe."

"Honey," Vivian said, "that's no big deal."

"Oh, Viv, wish it was that simple. I made a big mistake by not dropping the subject ... which I knew was none of my business in the first place. Looking back, my three glasses of wine sure as heck didn't help. Worst of all, we never spoke as I drove him back to the hotel. Oh, Vivian, I am so sick. As Clay was getting out of the car, his last words stabbed me in the heart. He said, 'I guess this is the last time I will ever see you.' From there, everything went to shit. My gut tells me..."

"What? You didn't finish," Vivian fired back.

"I was going to say I know he is the right man for me. Now he thinks that I want to dump him."

Vivian, pausing from fixing Jill's hair, subconsciously commenced stroking her own. Deep in thought, she said, "I hate to say this, but honey, you made a big mistake!"

♥ ♥

Chapter 13

"Gee, Vivian, thanks for telling me what I already know!"

Vivian hugged Jill and continued, "I hate to admit it, Jill, but now, after all the goings-on between you and Clay, I do think you two of you may be a good match. So, you must make a quick recovery. You said he would be up at Pendleton for the next couple days, right?"

"Yes, that's what he told me."

"You know he will most likely remain at the Hilton. He is familiar with its surroundings, and it's an easy commute back and forth. Also, I think he will touch base with Colonel Cooperswaite before he departs. So there's a good chance you can easily connect with him. That is if you want to?"

"Vivian, you know I want to."

"Okay, now you look presentable enough to make those Marine wives and their guests beautiful. Here is one thing you need to take care of at lunchtime."

"What?"

"Go home and change clothes. You have on the same outfit you wore yesterday."

"Shit, shit!"

"By nine or so, the guys should be at Pendleton. So call the Hilton sometime after ten or ten-thirty and leave a message for him. I am sure you know his room number."

"What should I say? I feel like such an ass."

"Be brief; say something like, 'It's urgent that I speak to you. I'll be in the Hilton bar no later than six-thirty.' Jill that is, if you don't have other plans?"

"No plans, and even if I did, I would break them."

As the two women left the lounge, each heading in the direction of their counters, Jill said, "What if he doesn't show?"

"I'll bet money he'll show!"

"I sure hope you are right." Touching Vivian's hand as the two separated, Jill turned to the right, looked back, said, "Thanks."

With a wink and smile, Vivian responded, "That's what friends are for."

Jill followed Vivian's 'orders.' She made her phone call at precisely ten-seventeen, went home at lunchtime, changed into fresh clothes, was promptly out of the Exchange door by six, and was seated at the Hilton bar at six-fifteen.

"A glass of house Chardonnay and a glass of ice on the side, please." The same bartender on duty the first night set the two filled glasses in front of her. "Where's your friend?"

"He'll be here shortly." Jill answered, thinking, "*Oh God, I hope so.*"

Chapter 14

At noontime, as a matter of practice, Clayton called the hotel front desk to check for messages; four were waiting. The first was marked 'Urgent' from Jill; second, from Lorre pleading for him to call her back; a third, 'Taylor called.' The fourth was from a potential client. Clayton immediately returned that call. Afterward, he crossed Lorre and Taylor off his To-Do note pad.

All afternoon Clay thought about Jill's urgent message, sometimes to the extent that it was infringing on his planning session with Camp Pendleton's officers. But Clayton, being Clayton, recovered nicely. The onset of his near mental lapse and lack of sleep went unnoticed by all except Guy.

During their drive back to the Hilton, Guy asked, "Clay, what the hell is going on?"

"I am nearly wiped out from a lack of sleep. Last night, I suffered through a miserable night of tossing, turning, and contemplating how I should handle a couple of personal issues."

"Okay, which one?... Is it Lorre or Taylor, or don't tell me...

it's both?"

Reluctant to give Guy the real story about what had happened last evening, Clayton answered, "Neither."

"Come on, Clayton, I sure as hell know you well enough to recognize something serious is screwing with your mind. If it's not the girls, I know it's not our work, so what's going on?"

He replied, "Jill."

For an instant, Guy took his eyes off the road as he glanced over at Clay. In a slightly raised voice, he said, "Jill... Jill!"

Clay, appearing to be embarrassed, said, "Guy, I know you are trying to look out for me, but believe me, Jill is exceptional. In fact, she is the most special woman I have ever met. I would lay odds on it. Guy, I'm not looking at her as a quick lay."

"What about Taylor?"

"Look, I know Taylor views me as a 'Sugar Daddy' type of guy. She is an attractive socialite with a fetish to be one of the beautiful people. Taylor has shown me what it's like to travel in elite circles, go to snobbish parties, and hobnob in upper-class art galleries with a bunch of wealthy phonies who don't have any inkling about fine art.

"She also taught me about the social value of being seen eating in the finest restaurants and becoming one of the privileged few who always is seated at the best available table. But Guy, I am not going to lie; I loved it!"

Clay continued, "I was reminded of my Dad's coal mining days and how we were not privileged enough to associate with those mining bosses who lived in the mansions on the hill. I wanted to have my very own mansion on the hill. To get there, I had to become successful or at least create the image of being rich. I learned the ways and techniques I needed to show that I belonged.

"Yes, Taylor taught me a great deal about the lifestyles of those fortunate enough to live on the upper Eastside and Westside of Manhattan. Even Arthur, my driver, was part of those trappings. For all she taught me, I am most appreciative... another important step in helping me work towards achieving a few of life's better things. I guess you could say we both used each other without any regret."

Guy listened intently and without speaking a word, but thinking, "He's *unloading on me, and hopefully it will help.*"

"I know it's only a matter of time until Taylor tosses me for some guy with more money, or I drop her first because of her bullshit and screwing around with other guys while I am on the road. Over the two years we have been together, our relationship could be described as pleasant and smooth sailing. But there were also many days filled with turmoil. Many nights, whether at home or away, I lay in bed, asking myself, 'Why don't you get the hell out? Well, I knew the answer. I was just waiting for the right time."

Looking over at Guy, Clayton continued, "I swear as sure as we are in this car, I knew from the moment I first set eyes on Jill, I was intrigued with and attracted to this woman. This thing between the two of us, this bond... it wasn't just sparks of passion, or lust. I knew it was love."

"What the hell's wrong with you?" Guy's question brought Clayton back to reality... San Diego and Jill Simpson. Few knew Clayton better than Guy. The two traveled and worked side-by-side for close to three years. Guy also knew Clayton wasn't the type to agonize over any woman. He was well aware that Clayton enjoyed women, especially those he would meet in their travels. He also knew that Clayton liked to do one-nighters and quickly move on without any regrets. This was always his end plan, and San Diego should be no different, but it was... Guy muttered under his breath, *"Jill Simpson is screwing with Clayton's head."* In Guy's eyes, Clayton was violating his own rules: *'no dating a client's employees.'*

Clayton liked to recite often the saying his old boss had taught him decades ago, *'Even a dog has sense enough not to shit where he eats.'* Next, there was his lecture, *'No matter how difficult never let your personal problems infringe on the work we are doing for a client. Remember, they are paying big bucks for our expertise, and that demands our total time and attention.'*

As the two men talked, Guy reminded Clayton as if he didn't know, what was going on had nothing to do with work or his guarded family issue. It had everything to do with Jill Simpson. "She has tossed you into unknown waters... and now this is tormenting you."

"Agreed, but I am not going to let her bother me."

"Come on, Clayton, you are talking to me, your friend. Remember... how on our very first morning back at MCRD, you wanted to go seek her out?... just like a dog in heat. So, don't try to bullshit me."

"Okay, okay... Look, I'm not going to give her another thought. New York is three thousand miles away from Jill Simpson. Besides, I will be on my way to Italy tomorrow evening. Even as tired and pissed as I am, this evening, I am going to find out what's so urgent in her mind. After all, I don't want her to go running to Cooperswaite and cry on his shoulder." With that comment, a slight smile came across Guy's face as he thought, *"Even a dog has enough sense..."*

Chapter 15

At 6:30 p.m., Clay walked into the bar, and upon spotting Jill, he walked over and said, "Let's move to our favorite table." He ordered the same drink for himself, as he picked up her glass and escorted her to the corner table. A waitress followed, carrying his Chardonnay.

"Can I get you anything else?"

"No, thanks. Not now."

Acting somewhat on the cool side, Clay looked at Jill and somewhat sarcastically said, "Well... what's so urgent?"

"*Just like Roy and all the others,*"

Jill thought. "*He thinks I am here to apologize, and he's going to make me eat crow. If he tries that shit on me, I am going to give him the finger, get up and walk out.*" Wiping tears from her eyes while stammering, Jill, as if attempting to swallow a bitter pill, released the words, "I am so sorry. I had no business prying. Please forgive me."

Once Jill had finally delivered her 'urgent' remarks in person,

Clay... obviously shocked, sat still for two or three seconds trying to process her unanticipated apology.

"You don't need to apologize." He smiled as tears welled in his eyes. Knowing what was at stake, Clay was determined not to lose her. She meant everything to him. He replied, "I thought you were dumping me... not the other way around. Jill, I am crazy about you... make no mistake."

He paused, took a big gulp of wine from his glass and said, "According to Guy, I am about to drown, and only you can save me. So, please rescue me. Let's go to dinner? Your choice, that is, if you are driving?"

"I know just the place you'd like... the Butcher Shop; it's down on Kearny Mesa Road."

"Great choice, Guy and I ate there a couple of times during our last visit. The steaks and chops were good. But the thing leaving the greatest impression on the two of us were those good looking and scantily-clad waitresses... just kidding. Let's go!"

On the way back to the Hilton after dinner, Jill drove slowly, contemplating her next move. She was hell-bent on not letting this fantastic night end. Clayton's last day in San Diego was fast approaching... tomorrow evening. *"Not a minute to waste,"* she thought.

Clayton, abruptly pointing, said, "Pull into that mini-mart, and I'll go in and get us a bottle of Chardonnay and a snack for later."

"Well, with such a high-class offer, I'll tell you what, I'll go up to your room. That is if you'll invite me." Sitting alone in the car while Clay was in the market, Jill was glad Clay was warming up.

She thought, *"Simply being with him, feeling his touch while he looked into my eyes ignited my most sensual feeling ... Oh, God!"*

She didn't try to analyze what was happening; she didn't want to. It wasn't meant to be studied.

Laughing as they got into the elevator, Clayton punched the fourth-floor button; the door closed. "I never thought about mixing the contents from a gift box of Hickory Farms with a bottle of Napa Valley's finest Chardonnay."

Jill, with a big smile on her face, said, "It doesn't matter." Once inside the room, Clayton turned and hung out the *Do Not Disturb* sign. He sat the bottle of the Chardonnay on the desk and placed the Hickory Farms box in the small refrigerator. Looking around, he found and removed the wine bottle opener from the rear of the top writing desk drawer. With the expertise of a wine opening novice, he fought with the cork seal a couple of times before achieving success.

"Oh crap, it looks like we will have to drink our toast in water glasses. Wait... I'll call downstairs and have them bring up a couple of wine glasses."

"No problem with what we have. It would be a waste of time just waiting for someone to arrive. So pour, and let me hear your toast."

"Okay," as Clay moved closer, almost lips to lips, and looking deeply into Jill's beautiful blue eyes. She responded with a smile as she felt the movement of butterflies in her stomach.

"Here goes, 'Hold my hand, and we are halfway there, let me hold you in my arms, and I'll take you there. Here's to us!'"

"Very good, I hope you meant it. I came up here tonight because I love how you make me feel." Laughing, she said, "Think, we can ignite a great love affair with a bottle of Chardonnay and a few bites of sausage? Pull out the sausage... oops, Hickory Farms, that is."

Both laughed as they sipped their wine. His looks were making her heart begin to pound as she had thoughts of holding each other tightly, kissing, and their naked bodies screaming...

"I'm going to the bathroom." She placed her glass on the corner of the desk.

He said, "I'll open the Hickory Farms." Closing the bathroom door, Jill stopped and stared briefly into the full-length mirror. Her lips pinched as she studied her reflection. Jill always tried to look her very best. She told herself... "*The best I have looked in a long time.*"

Jill, a full-fledged romantic, allowed her favorite and often repeated verse from *Einstein on the Beach* to drift into her mind: '*Two lovers sat on a park bench with their bodies touching each other, holding hands in the moonlight. There was silence between them. So profound was their love for each other, they needed no words to express it. And so they sat in silence, on a park bench, with their bodies touching, holding hands in the moonlight.*'

"*Tonight I am going to enjoy myself; no rules, just fun,*" she mused, "*Unfortunately, no sex.*"

She returned from the bathroom and noticed that Clay, with a smile on his face, had placed six or seven slices of the sausages on a paper plate alongside two freshly poured glasses of Chardonnay on the coffee table. Setting down on the small sofa next to Clay, as their warm bodies touched, she sensed his rising expectations. After taking a deep breath, Jill paused for a moment, and then said, "Clay, please don't be mad, but I need to get to know you better before we have sex."

With that startling comment, Clay almost dropped the paper plate he was in the process of handing to Jill. Calmly, he returned the plate to the coffee table, and after a brief pause, said, "Can't let our wine get too warm."

Clay picked up the two glasses as if readying himself for a toast, but he didn't deliver. Looking at her with lust in his eyes, she teasingly said, "I bet I know what you are thinking."

Jill reached out, took the glasses from his hands, and placed them on the table. "Look, we are just getting over a heartbreaking episode. I really... really have strong feelings for you, but it is against my every instinct to jump into the bed with just any guy, especially one that I have known less than a week. Maybe we shall see tomorrow evening, but not now. Oops, since it is now past midnight, let me change that to maybe to this evening. Besides, I remember you telling me that you and Guy have an important eight o'clock meeting at Pendleton. I also have to be at work by eight-thirty."

Clay opened the door, reached down, and removed his wishful privacy sign, gave it a slight wave in Jill's face. They both laughed as he closed the door. Once on the elevator, a couple of kisses, and hugs, while walking hand in hand through the lobby, and out to Jill's car. Clay said, "I really hate this part."

Arrangements were made to meet back at the hotel the next evening after Jill got off work. She also promised to drive Clay and Guy to the airport so they could catch the ten o'clock flight back East. After kissing good night, Jill pulled away from the hotel. Feeling sad, she thought, "*This evening may be our last time together. After that, I wonder if I will ever see him again.*"

Neither Jill nor Clay had any idea that their evening get-together plans would be shattered by noontime.

Chapter 16

It was precisely 0745 when Clayton and Guy walked into Camp Pendleton's meeting facility. "Mr. Clarkson," the duty officer called out as the two civilians walked toward their assigned meeting room. "Colonel Cooperswaite left a message for you to call him at MCRD sometime between 1200 and 1300 hours. *"Lunchtime,"* Clayton thought. *"Mustn't be important enough to disrupt our meeting."*

Following his lunchtime routine, Clayton placed two calls; one to his New York office, the other to his hotel. Today, he chose to call his office first. Marsha informed him, "Lorre had called several times after being told by the Hilton desk clerk that you had checked out unexpectedly and left no forwarding address. What's up? Have you left the Hilton?"

"No, I left word not to accept calls or take any messages from Lorre."

"Also, Taylor called complaining that you were not returning her calls. Clayton, she wanted to 'cry on my shoulder' about the way you are ignoring her. But I didn't want to get tangled in your personal affairs, so I apologized and told her I was too busy and had to go. Oh yes, all business-related messages were given to Guy. You are clear."

Next in his calling order, Clayton checked for messages at the hotel, knowing full well he would have at least one, and he was correct. The clerk said, "Mr. Clarkson, a woman named Taylor, said to give you this exact message, 'I'm sorry for what I said. Please call me.' That was your only message, sir."

Clayton disregarded the messages from both Lorre and Taylor. Next on his call list was Colonel Cooperswaite. Once his conversation ended, and he hung up the phone, he looked at Guy and, in a low, troubling voice, said, "God damn it!"

Guy, who was busy writing, looked up, "Bad news?"

"Well, I guess it all depends on how we look at it. For you, Guy, I would think it is good, but for me, it's the worst shit imaginable. The Colonel and his wife, Martha, want us to join them at their home at 1800 hours *tonight* for dinner.

"To make matters worse, he said a driver would pick us up at the hotel and take us to his home. We are to bring our luggage and plan to stay there until it's time to leave to catch our flight. He said another driver would pick us up at his home and take us to the airport."

"What about the rental?"

"Oh, yes, the rental car. We are to leave the keys at the valet desk, and one of his non-coms will pick it up and return it to Avis. Worse yet, we are to check out of the hotel and be out front and ready for pickup at 1745 hours. I know the Colonel thinks he is doing us a big favor by entertaining us until flight time. He has no idea about

Jill. Damn it, Guy, that's just before Jill gets off from work."

After that disappointing message, Clayton thinking, "*I hate to even think about leaving without seeing her.*" He decided he had one other call to make; Jill's supervisor's office. He remembered that when she gave him the number, she cautioned, "This number is off-limits for personal calls. That is unless it is an emergency."

"*Hell, this is an emergency!*"

He dialed the number. Jill rarely received personal calls at work, and then only when one of her three kids called about something they considered an emergency. When Jill was told she had a personal call, fear ran through her mind, "*One of the kids?*"

Picking up the phone, she heard Clay's voice.

"What's wrong," she almost screamed into the phone. As she listened, tears commenced streaming down both cheeks. Jill's manager, Phyllis Tyrell, overhearing what appeared to be bad news, discretely stepped out of the office, leaving Jill to her privacy.

Once Jill returned to the sales floor, Phyllis asked, "Is there anything I can do?"

Without speaking, she negatively shook her head as she hurried to the ladies' lounge.

Vivian, observing that Jill appeared extremely upset, quickly followed. "Honey, what's wrong?"

The shock in Jill's voice was more unsettling than her words, "Viv, I'm sick." She relayed her conversation with Clay. A streak of desperation surged from her lips, "What in God's name has happened? Am I to treat our encounter as if it was nothing more than a four-day fling and forget about my romantic feelings?"

Not giving Vivian a chance to respond, Jill continued, "Oh God, he's leaving, and we can't even get together long enough to say our good-byes. Oh Viv, how can falling in love, be so wrong? What am I going to do?"

♥ ♥

Chapter 17

After a magnificent dinner and a couple of enjoyable hours of chit-chatting about mostly everything except military matters, which Clayton surmised was done to keep Martha, the Colonel's wife, involved in the conversation. The Cooperswaite's, noticing the excellent rapport between Guy and Clayton, wanted to learn more about their relationship.

Clayton, without hesitation, agreed to give a short version of their relationship. "Guy had proved to be a godsend to me and for my survival in the business world. And it's incredible how it happened.

"About six months into my executive position with a major New York organization, I had one of my senior managers come to my office and tell me he wanted to terminate one of his supervisors who was not doing his job. He said this individual was a five-year employee, and he wanted my okay. Sure, terminate him, I said. We only want to keep productive people. So, get rid of any slackers. After that manager left my office, my senior regional manager walked in and told me he overheard my conversation about firing that supervisor.

"Contrary to what I was just told, he spoke highly of this man's work. I picked up the phone and told the manager to send the man to my office. A short time later, the individual," Clayton gesturing towards Guy, "sat down with me.

To make a long story short, this was the first time Mr. Devine had ever heard that his work was unsatisfactory. I rescinded the termination notice, and based upon my regional manager's recommendation, I promoted and transferred Mr. Devine to our most challenging and newest locations, Rego Park, Queens. He did an outstanding job.

A year later, a competitor 'stole' him away from our organization. Well, after less than a year of operating my own business, guess what... I hired Guy Devine, and the two of us have been working together for nearly three years. So, as Paul Harvey would say, now you know the rest of the story."

After finishing the second glass of wine, one of the Colonel's noncom officers arrived and picked up Clayton and Guy for their ride to the airport. With the ticketing check-in nearly completed, the agent became confused as she attempted to sort out the proper destination of Clayton's luggage. Clayton had told her to send his suitcase only as far as JFK, and not to Milan, Italy.

This unusual request sparked a four-way conversation between the agent, her supervisor, Guy, and Clayton. Once Clayton explained he was going on to Italy and that his California clothes would not meet his needs, and that an associate had already shipped a separate wardrobe by a private parcel service to a hotel in Milan. With that issue resolved, the agent stapled both luggage receipts to Guy Devine's boarding documents... final destination, JFK airport.

Plans were for the two men to separate at JFK. Arthur would meet Guy at the airport and take him to his apartment in Brooklyn. Clayton was to go to the International Terminal and board his Alitalia flight to Malpensa International Airport, Milan.

While waiting in the First-Class Club, Guy watched Clayton fidgety get up from his seat, check his watch, and sit back down. "What's wrong," he asked as if he didn't know.

Clayton, sadly answered, "I am heartsick about not getting to see Jill before we left for the airport."

Guy shrugged his shoulders and said, "Call her."

Before leaving for the gate's boarding area, Clay tried calling her at Wendy's apartment; the recorder picked up. He left a message, "Jill, I will call you again before I get on the plane." Three more attempts, and no success; only that blasted recorder. Just before boarding, Clayton gave it one final try but got the recorder again.

"Jill, I only have your home phone and the emergency number at work. It's almost time to board, and I don't know how else to reach you, but I'll find a way...somehow."

Unknown to Clayton, at the moment his plane was taxiing for takeoff in San Diego, Jill, along with her friend, Vivian Whitney, had driven to Point Loma in some desperate attempt to watch Clayton's airplane take off. Neither of the two women knew which airline or flight number. All Jill knew was that he was going back East on a ten o'clock flight.

Jill was thinking, "*How dumb and stupid I was to have talked Vivian into going with me to Point Loma.*" She rationalized her action by convincing herself she would be climbing the walls if she just sat around, doing nothing. After ninety minutes of waiting for that mysterious ten o'clock flight, Vivian couldn't hold her silence any longer.

"Jill, you mustn't dwell on your fling with this guy. Like I said that first evening when we met him and his associate, some things just didn't fit, especially the way he was evasive when I asked him a few questions about himself. I think he is holding something back... a secret. Besides, he appears to be the type that likely has some piece of tail in every city where he works. Jill, please put Clay behind you."

Vivian's cutting remarks were devastating to Jill as the beat of her heart pounded in her ears. *"He's gone!"*

Vivian reached over and took Jill's right hand in her own. In a clear and authoritative voice, she said, "Honey, I was wrong earlier about the two of you being a good match. He's not the guy for you... Now, let's go home."

♥ ♥

Chapter 18

Well into the flight to New York, and comfortably seated in first-class, the two men attempted to nap. But whenever Guy was ready to snooze, Clayton wanted to talk. "Okay, what's bothering you? Don't tell me it's Jill."

Out of the blue, Clayton responded, "No, it's Taylor."

"Taylor!" Guy shouted, disturbing the lady seated in front of him.

She responded with an equally loud, "Shush!"

"It's bothering me that you are defending Taylor, and you have no idea of the shit she dumps out. Our arguments were bad enough, and I often said to myself, 'I can't believe I am putting up with her selfish ways.' But here's the real kicker. I'm going to tell you something I have kept to myself."

Turning and looking directly at Clayton, Guy said, "What are you saying?"

"Well, I'll tell you just how much she cares about me. At times, when I was traveling, I would call her early in the morning.

She always took my calls and talked. But, I could tell by the sound of her voice, much quieter than usual... almost a whisper. She would tell me to hold on a minute.

"Taylor being Taylor, was not good at deception or covering her tracks. She always failed to cover the phone speaker, and I could hear the bedroom door quietly close. I could tell that she was walking towards either the living room or kitchen of the apartment. Then, within seconds, the tone of her voice returned to normal. I never questioned her about this, but I knew some guy was likely asleep in our bed. How do I know? Well, shortly after we met, I was that guy."

Guy, thinking "*Payback,*" said nothing as Clayton continued with his mind-boggling tale,

"But, my second and best evidence was her diaphragm."

"What?"

"You heard me, her damn diaphragm. A couple of times after arriving home, I would go into our bathroom, and there would be that damn diaphragm on the shelf where she always placed it after washing. Later, I would notice it was in its storage case. It wasn't there because we had just made love, and it sure as hell hadn't been left out during my days away from the apartment. She likes to screw about as much as I do." The two stared at each other and then laughed in commiseration.

With the late dinner meal concluded, the section darkened, and both Guy and the lady upfront of him succumbed to the quietness within the cabin. Clayton remained awake, doing nothing other than staring out the window into the darkness. His thoughts about Jill Simpson made him feel miserable about the way they parted. "*Without even a kiss or a final word of goodbye.*"

The flight touched down at JFK airport in New York at precisely five-fifty-seven local time. The two men parted ways: Guy headed to Baggage Claim to retrieve their luggage. As expected, Arthur was waiting in Claim Four, along with a skycap to handle and transport the luggage.

Arthur jokingly said, "I hope what you are bringing will fit in the Caddy's trunk, or should we rent a truck?"

"No, the Caddy will work fine."

Arthur said, "Guy, something else; Marsha gave me a message from Taylor... you know, the boss's live-in."

"Yeah, I know who she is. What's wrong now?"

"She wanted me to call her when I was ready to leave for the airport. Somehow, she found out that the boss is due to arrive this morning. Most likely, the leak came from that blabber-mouth, Marsha."

"You didn't call her, did you?"

"Of course not!"

"Great, here's the last piece of our luggage. Let's get the hell out of here. Next stop, my Park Slope apartment. "

Clayton, arriving at the International Terminal, noticed the status screen indicating his flight to Malpensa International Airport was already in the process of final boarding.

"*Crap, what luck! I wanted to reach Jill at home; surely, she would be there. After all, it's a little past three in the morning in San Diego. Ah, screw it. I better board the damn plane. With the way my luck has been going the last couple of days, the plane might leave without me,*" he muttered as he handed his boarding pass to the attendant.

Chapter 19

The alarm sounded and Jill, as if on automatic pilot, flung her left arm across her body and turned it off... *"Six o'clock already."* With her body aching, she sat up and looked down. *"Good grief, what the hell? I can't believe I let this happen to me."*

Seeing she had on the same clothes she wore last night,. she mumbled, *"I must have been smashed when Vivian dropped me off. Worse yet, I hope Wendy didn't see me when I came in."*

Looking at the image in her dresser mirror, she gasped, *"I'll be fine. I just need a minute."* Suddenly, reality broke through her foggy brain,

"Oh crap, our section has an eight-thirty meeting with Phyllis and Colonel Cooperswaite, and I am to lead off the meeting with a little pep talk... foggy brain and all. It's already half past six. I can hear the Colonel now, 'What's wrong, couldn't get your ass out of bed? If you were one of our recruits, I would tell you to hit the floor and give me... fifty push-ups.'"

Moving about as fast as an Arizona dust storm, Jill was in

and out of the shower, makeup applied, hair combed, dressed, and out the door. Hitting the steps two at a time, she stumbled as her toe caught the metal edge of the last step. *"Damn, I told the super about that problem. I guess he'll wait until someone falls and really breaks something."*

Muttering, she continued, *"The clock in my car says 7:53. Oh God, I pray the traffic will be okay; I have no time to spare. Think, think... what insightful pitch will Phyllis be expecting me to deliver? I can guess something motivational, especially after winning that award the other day. Oh God, I have about twelve minutes to come up with a plan."*

As Jill pulled into the parking space, up came Vivian, as if she had been waiting for her.

"Do you realize we have been friends for three years?"

"Sure, I do. I even remember the first day I participated in your job interview." Vivian frowned, and then her face brightened. "Oh, I remember, but that's not what we need to talk about."

"Sorry, Viv, got to run. I'll see you at the meeting."

"See you there, but we have to talk... important stuff."

Jill's next stop was Phyllis' office. As she was walking in, she checked the wall clock. *"Still three minutes before Colonel Cooperswaite arrives. He's never a minute early or late. The Marine way, I guess."*

Phyllis wasn't at her desk. For Jill, this is bad... Zero hour is rapidly approaching.

"Morning," Phyllis said as she walked in, placing her purse on top of the file cabinet.

"Hi. Phyllis, help... pleease! What are you and the Colonel expecting me to talk about?"

"Good morning, ladies," the Colonel said as he entered the office. "Little crowded in here. Let's go outside and get this meeting underway. Phyllis, I can't afford to blemish my reputation by keeping all of your fine ladies waiting."

As expected, Colonel Cooperswaite took charge. After a few brief introductory remarks, he announced, "The real purpose of this meeting is to let our exceptional associate know just how proud we are for her winning the Western Region Retail Salesperson of the Year title... Jill Simpson, please step forward."

Jill, in shock and looking stunned, rose from her chair and moved towards the Colonel.

"From the look on Ms. Simpson's face, I would say that you, Mrs. Tyrell, did a great job in keeping this recognition a secret from our honoree. Ms. Simpson was told that she was to address you this morning. However, she was not given any further information. Right, Jill? I hope you don't mind me calling you Jill, or you, Mrs. Tyrell allowing me to call you Phyllis. Sometimes these things get too formal, right Phyllis?"

"Right, Colonel."

With tears streaming down her cheeks, Jill waved and blew kisses to the group as they gave her a standing ovation. Before leaving the room, Colonel Cooperswaite called Jill aside, and in a low voice, said, "Well, Jill, did you and Clayton Clarkson enjoy your dinner at the Butcher Shop?"

Somewhat startled, she responded, "What?"

Smiling, he replied, "Jill, I have spies everywhere."

"Well, Colonel, our dinner went fine. So good that we had plans to go out the next evening... that was until you screwed it up with your dinner plans for Clay and Guy. Colonel, I really like the guy."

"Well, that explains a lot. I also like him. Keep up the great work, Jill." Colonel Cooperswaite then walked away.

No sooner had the Colonel left until Vivian approached. "What was that all about?"

"My talk with Colonel Cooperswaite?"

"You know that's what I meant?"

"We were just talking about the awards dinner in L.A., and he was apologizing for him and his wife not being able to attend." Once Phyllis was out of hearing range, Vivian said, "Jill, as I told you in the parking lot, we need to talk."

"Okay, at lunch. I'll meet you on the porch at twelve-thirty."

Arriving right on time, Jill noticed that Vivian was nearly finished with her lunch and now munching on an oversized chocolate chip cookie. "Got here early, I see?"

"Yes, I didn't want our celebrity of the day to have to wait for me."

"Vivian, don't be silly."

"Oh, you know I am just kidding. Where's your peanut butter and pickle sandwich?"

"Didn't fix it this morning; not enough time. Besides, my brain was in a fog. All I could do was get dressed and fly out the door. In all my rushing, I almost fell down the steps. I tripped on that damn step, I warned you about."

"Here have a piece of my cookie; too many calories to eat alone."

"Thanks."

"Glad to share."

"Okay, Vivian, what's your important message? And, please don't lecture me about Clay. My head hurts, and I am not in the mood."

Vivian's expression stiffened for a moment as she forced a weak smile. Vivian and Jill had grown close and supported one another during their three years of friendship.

Vivian, reaching over and taking Jill's hand, said, "Look, honey, I know you don't want to hear this, but I think you must. Last night was the worst I have ever seen you. Think about what you had us do. Jill, we sat on that God damn hill for over two hours just so you could hopefully get a look at some mysterious plane that might be carrying your short time lover, whom you may never see again.

"Finally, when we left our perch, you practically demanded we stop and buy a pint of Seagram's Seven and a six-pack of Seven-Up. You then begged me to drive back up to our perch, which, like a dummy, I did. Then you drank almost the whole bottle yourself, cried a little, and threw up outside the car before I took you home. And, now you wonder why you awoke this morning with a blasted hangover. Girl, you've got to be kidding."

"Viv, I am so sorry I put you through all of that."

"And to make it weirder, you swore to me that you haven't even had sex with this guy... so how come you are acting the way you are? Are you going crazy?"

Those comments struck Jill hard. She immediately jerked her hand away from Vivian's. In a raised voice, Jill said, "How dare you!" This outburst caused two visitors to look their way.

"Now, calm down," Vivian said. "You misunderstood me."

"Vivian, now I want you to think about this: How could falling in love with Clay be so wrong? That's the bitch about my feelings. I can't control what my heart is telling me.

"As you know, neither of us has ever seen one iota of anything to prove I should ditch him. Perhaps he does have a girl in every city. But even if he does, this is strictly between him and me. So please, no more lectures."

Chapter 20

Milan, Italy

As promised, once landed, Clayton was met in a restricted area by his client's representative, an interpreter, and an airport security escort. The trip through Customs was efficient; no luggage to inspect, and a perusal of his United States Passport was also without delay.

Clayton thought, *"Boy having a police escort certainly helps. I wonder if I get similar courtesies when I travel to those other cities we will be visiting?"* The interpreter, an attractive middle-aged woman named Sofia, told him one large piece of luggage had arrived two days earlier and was now in his hotel room.

The car, a black Mercedes four-door diesel pulled up to the hotel's front entry. Clayton looked around as Sofia filled him in on the surroundings. This boutique hotel was situated directly across the street from the magnificent *Duomo di Milano* cathedral and adjacent to a beautiful shopping galleria.

"Oh, where can I get my suits pressed? I want to be presentable tomorrow morning when I report for work."

She laughingly said, "No, Mr. Clarkson, you do not have to be concerned about your laundry and dry cleaning. The hotel will take care of everything. Just tell your maid what you need."

"Thank you very much! I am certain I will come to rely on you to advise me on many things."

"No problem, that is why I am here. Please, Mr. Clarkson, call me Sofia."

"Good, my first name is Clayton, or if you prefer, Clay."

"If you are not offended, I prefer to call you Clayton and will introduce you as Mr. Clarkson... Clayton Clarkson, to your client's head people. Also, you should know that I am not an employee of your client. They hired me to escort and interpret for you. I will be available every weekday from seven in the morning until I deliver you back to the hotel at the end of each business day. I shall also travel with you and the others to Rome, Florence, and other locations both you and your client wishes. However, I will not be with you on weekends or holidays, such as Easter. Those days you are, as what Americans say, 'on your own.'"

Once checked into the hotel, his passport processed, and both Sofia and Clayton were escorted to the room that would become Clayton's living quarters for the next month. Sofia walked over to the French glass doors and stepped onto a small, but well designed, terrace. The view of the *Duomo* cathedral and the plaza directly in front was in a single word... breathtaking.

"I'm going to like this place!" Clayton thought without saying a word to Sofia or the hotel attendant who was checking to ensure everything within the room was satisfactory.

"Let us go, Clayton. I will take you on a brief tour of the hotel. After that, I will leave you alone, so you may unpack and have the remainder of the day to yourself.

"*Great!*" Clayton thought. "*I need to call Jill.*"

Once alone in the room, Clayton picked up the hotel phone to speak with the hotel operator. "I want to make a person-to-person call to San Diego, California, in the United States." In broken English, the operator said she would assist and asked Clayton for the telephone number and name of the party he wanted to talk.

"Oh sir, you do know there is a nine-hour time difference between here and California. It is three o'clock in the morning there."

"*Oh, crap, I forgot about the differences in time,*" he thought. "Oh, sorry, I forgot. I will place my call later." Clayton hung up the telephone.

"*Nine hours behind us. Well, I know one thing. I can't make that call during work hours or try using a public phone with my credit card without involving Sofia. Think, Clayton,*" he thought, "*No choice. If I call after I return to the hotel, she will be at work and only have access to that 'off-limits' work phone. Hmmm. I may be able to reach her at home. I need to figure this out. If I call around six in the morning here, that will give me an hour before Sofia picks me up.*"

With his clock alarm going off at five, he showered, dressed, and was ready for work just a few minutes before six. Clayton picked up the phone to connect with the hotel operator and received a recorded announcement in Italian and English, "The switchboard and front desk are both closed and will not open until seven if you need in-house assistance, dial two-two. For outside telephone assistance, dial, 0-0. Thank you." Clayton followed the instructions.

Once connected with the telephone operator, he gave his room number and name to the outside operator, hoping she understood English. She didn't; the call never took place. With the clock rapidly approaching the time for Sofia to pick him up, he gave up and headed down to the lobby to meet his ride.

"Damn! I need to focus on the work I was brought over here to perform. Today is my meeting with top La Rinascente's executives, including the Chairman of their retail and supermarket groups, and it must be perfect."

As hard as he tried throughout the day, Clayton could not dispel his thoughts about Jill and what she must think of him; *"Not even a phone call... I'm glad I wasn't just another of his one-nighters!"*

♥ ♥

Chapter 21

Phyllis approached Jill at her cosmetics counter and discretely whispered, "Jill, you have a person-to-person international phone call waiting in my office."

Jill's stomach started churning as she stopped replenishing her supplies and quickly headed towards the office.

"Hello!"

"Damn, I was finally able to reach you."

"Is something wrong?"

"However, I must apologize for calling on your work phone, but I have no choice. The time difference between California and Italy is a nightmare. Trying to reach you at home is nearly impossible without having to wake you and your daughter in the middle of the night."

"Oh, I am so happy you called. I have been praying that you hadn't ditched me for one of those sexy Italian women."

"Never, Jill, you are the only one for me. There'll never be anyone else."

"I have some great news. One of Colonel Cooperswaite's men saw us having dinner at the Butcher Shop, and the Colonel mentioned it to me. He seemed pleased and said he told my supervisor not to say anything about you possibly calling me from Italy. It was as if he understood that you might have a problem because of time differences. He also warned me not to abuse those calls."

"See Jill; the stars have aligned for us."

"I haven't even asked how your work is going, and if you are enjoying Italy."

"That's good you haven't asked—no time for small talk. But really, everything is fine. I have an excellent interpreter, and she is nice to work with."

"Good, just don't get too friendly... as you would say, 'Just kidding.'"

"I must get off this phone or I will be spending all my earnings on telephone calls. One other thing, if the opportunity presents itself, please let the Colonel know I truly appreciate what he did for us. I don't know when I will be able to call next, just be assured I will call. Love you! Bye."

Jill was now the most comfortable she had been since Clay and Guy had left San Diego. After she left the office, she located her supervisor, and with a big smile, said, "Thanks, Phyllis."

"With a smile that big," Vivian said, "people are going to think you just hit the lottery, or... let me guess. You heard from Clay, didn't you?"

"Yes." Vivian's eyes were wide. "He had enough nerve to call you here on that business-only phone?"

"That's right, and our conversation was wonderful."

"So, how did Mrs. Disciplinarian react?"

"Better than I expected." Vivian sensed Jill's coolness, likely still perturbed about their earlier conversation.

As Jill walked away, she turned, looked at Vivian, and then thought for a split-second of giving her the middle finger, but quickly switched to signaling a thumbs-up triumphantly into the air.

After returning to her restocking duties, Jill's favorite verse drifted into her mind: *two lovers sat on a park bench with their bodies touching each other, holding hands in the moonlight...*

Chapter 22

By day three, Clayton had become somewhat familiar with a few Italian customs. For example, sitting down and having a leisurely cup of morning coffee was not something his companions wasted time doing. They would stop on their way to work or elsewhere and quickly consume a small, and strongly flavored, espresso. It was also surprising to learn that having a milky cappuccino after any meal was unthinkable.

Clayton took particular interest in the ways the Italians have lunch, their biggest meal of the day. Many workers go home to eat lunch and enjoy a *pausa pranzo,* similar to the Spanish siesta, as many shops close between one and four in the afternoon.

Since La Rinascente was a large organization, they provided their office personnel and employees working in stores near the corporate office, access to the large cafeteria, if anyone preferred not to go home. Clayton and his 'Italian entourage,' including Sofia, always had lunch here on the days they were in Milan.

"A nice place and excellent benefit," Clayton said to Enrico, his direct contact, through his interpreter, Sofia. He also didn't mention being surprised when he noticed wine was also a mainstay of the lunchtime meal.

After spending three long days with Sofia, Clayton, now more comfortable with her, began to enjoy her company and conversations. "Sofia, let's have dinner. How about tonight?"

"I can't tonight, but tomorrow would be good."

"Great, you pick the place."

Thursday evening, the two stayed a little late at the La Rinascente corporate office and arrived at the place of Sofia's choosing in time for their eight-fifteen dinner reservation.

The restaurant Sofia picked was nowhere near those catering to Milan's tourist trade. It was strictly a place for local clientele; it opened its doors at precisely 8:00 p.m. *"Italians prefer to eat dinner late, and most even consider that time too early."*

Clayton thought, *"No wonder I haven't been able to find a decent Italian restaurant near the hotel. Those nearby only cater to tourists."* Another valuable eating lesson for him to add to those he already had picked up about breakfast, coffee breaks, and lunch hours.

Looking around, Clayton could tell he was the only American in the restaurant. His attire and language were dead giveaways. Sofia did all the ordering after Clayton gave her an overview of his likes and dislikes. With a smile, she said, "Don't be uncomfortable, I promise not to order anything exotic for you. I promise everything I select; you shall enjoy. I even guarantee the wine will be magnifico."

Clayton got to see a little inside of Sofia's personal life. She and her husband lived in a small town just outside of Milan and had no children. She mentioned that her husband did not work because of a disability; no explanation offered. Sofia was mostly closed mouth when it came to talking about her personal life. Prying into another person's life was not part of Clayton's character. He had secrets of his own and understood the need for privacy.

When asked about his family and personal life, like Sofia, he was equally evasive, but did leave her with the impression he was divorced and now living the lifestyle of a bachelor in New York City. However, he couldn't resist bringing up Jill and their California whirlwind encounter, and the way it ended without saying a proper goodbye.

"*Clayton is in love with this woman he had known for only a few days,*" she thought... "*I guess that's possible.*" Looking at him, she smiled and said, "She must be someone extraordinary. Clayton, you are miserable, and I can't help you."

Back to business, Sofia took out her note pad and looking at it, said, "Tomorrow, Enrico is going to tell you that we will be leaving early Monday morning to drive to Rome. He is planning for all four of us to spend a week there visiting their stores and offices. The following Monday, we will drive from Rome to Florence. Since that Sunday is Easter, our team will return to Milan late Thursday, and we shall spend Good Friday with family... good Catholics, you know."

Clayton listened intensely, but made no notes, Sofia continued, "Enrico is also going to suggest that, if you wish, you can stay in Florence over the Easter weekend, and take the train back to Milan. I encourage you to do this. Florence is such a beautiful city, and its *Duomo* and Easter parade are stunning. Michelangelo's original statue of David is currently in the *Accademia Gallery* of Florence. Don't be misled by its copy, which is on display in *Piazza della Signoria.*"

Sofia paused, apparently thinking whether to offer another piece of advice, but decided to continue, "Clayton, are you a superstitious person?"

"Not really... although come to think about it, when I was playing ball, I never liked to see baseball bats crossed, and I would prefer not to walk under a ladder if I could go an alternate way. Black cats running across my path, ah, somewhat. So, am I superstitious? Possibly a little, why are you asking?"

"Well, I am! I would walk ten meters out of the way to avoid a black cat. As for me asking if you are superstitious, my point is that I can see in your eyes and hear in your voice, the love you have for your newly found, Jill."

"Okay, I'll buy that."

"On Monday we will arrive in Rome. Have you heard of the *Fountain of Trevi?*"

"The fountain in the movie... *Three Coins in the Fountain?*"

"Yes."

"Sure, excellent movie and a very popular song in America."

"So here is my suggestion, go to *Trevi* fountain one evening after we stop work. The legend says that if you throw a coin with your right hand over your left shoulder, and with your back to the fountain, your wish will be granted, and you and your love will return to Rome. However, I must also offer a word of caution. Because the *Trevi* is such a popular tourist destination, it's also a well-liked place for pickpockets. Be cautious if you go."

"Tell you what; I'll go if you will accompany me."

"No problem, I shall go also. We shall decide which day once we are in Rome."

"What a great evening I had with Sofia." Clayton thought as he lay in bed. *"So nice to relax and enjoy evenings with someone who speaks near perfect English."* He then let out a low chuckle and added... *"American style English, that is."*

Clayton's telephone commenced ringing. *"Who would be calling at this hour,"* he wondered. Unable to reach the phone, he jumped out of bed, bumping his little toe on the nightstand. As he picked up the phone, Clayton gave out a slightly muffled shriek ..." Shit!"

The voice on the other end responded, "Clayton, is that you?"

"Taylor?"

"Yes, honey, it's me."

"How, why?"

"Guy gave me your number after I begged and pleaded with him. Clayton, I lied to him. I knew the only way he would give up your number was to tell him that it was urgent that I speak with you about Lorre."

"What about Lorre?"

"Oh, nothing, I just said that to get your number."

"Do you know what time it is? I was asleep."

"Well, honey, it's only four in the afternoon here."

"Don't honey me! I told you I was moving once I got back to Manhattan. I have nothing else to say to you, so please don't call again. Goodnight, Goodbye, or whatever."

Clayton slammed the phone back into its cradle. In bed, he turned off the light; his toe still throbbing. *"Shit, if Jill had any inkling of how screwed up my life was..."*

Chapter 23

His review of the operations in Rome was more demanding and much busier than Clayton had anticipated. *"These people are workaholics,"* he thought as he stood waiting for Sofia, Enrico, and Giovanni in the hotel lobby. *"No leisurely morning coffee for this crew. However, occasionally, after a little smile and polite begging, Enrico would give in, and stop for a quick espresso at the stand-up coffee bar.*

This morning was no different. As always, Enrico raised his small cup and said, *'Salude.'* Clayton also raised his, smiling and following Enrico's lead... *'down the hatch.'* Clayton, thinking, *"My Italian associates, while smiling, looked at me as if I was acting a little crazy.*

But Sofia understood and said, "I am well aware of how Americans like to have their coffee." She then explained to Clayton's Italian speaking companions.

That evening, while waiting for Sofia to return, Clayton was thinking, *"Finally, next to our last night in Rome, after work, we split-up for various reasons. I think Enrico and Giovanni want to do some shopping or perhaps break away from the hardship of having to communicate with me, the American."*

As the two men were making their plans, Sofia relayed their plans, of course, in Italian. "I am going to take Clayton on a quick tour this evening so he can see the Vatican, Coliseum, and Trevi Fountain."

"Sofia didn't exaggerate when she said a quick tour. We got a good look at a few interesting places, but I knew her target was the Fountain of Trevi. Once there, Sofia guided me through each step of the tossing of the coin ritual."

"When ready, silently make your wish."

"I will and not even divulge it to you." *"I wish to return to Rome and the Trevi Fountain in love and with Jill at my side."*

"Has your wish been made?"

"Yes, it has."

"Okay, time to go to the hotel. Busy day tomorrow; after work, we drive to Florence."

The next day, after Clayton completed his research and had given a verbal summary of his concerns and recommendations to local management, the team left Rome. Sofia, interpreting for Enrico, estimated the drive to Florence would take three and one-half hours.

The next two days would follow the same scenario as in Rome. After wrapping up Wednesday's work, Clayton, now back in his room and with a glass of wine cradled between his hands swirled the contents while thinking, *"After analyzing Milan's and Rome's functions, and as expected, what I found today indicates issues and risks in Florence will likely be similar.*

As expected, once the briefing session ended Thursday evening, Sofia, Enrico, and Giovanni left Florence to return to their homes to celebrate Good Friday and Easter. Before leaving, a double-check took place to ensure that Clayton's weekend would be without inconveniences. Enrico also took care of the hotel bill and purchased Clayton's train ticket to Milan in advance.

After spending Good Friday and Easter weekend watching the parade and sightseeing in Florence, Clayton, somewhat tired, was glad to board the train back to Milan. He was pleased with his work and was now only a couple of days away from his trip back home. Starting to doze off in his seat, Clayton thought, *"Enrico and the other executives should be very pleased with what I have to report. La Rinascente's cost savings should be substantial."*

Clayton's thoughts were correct. His phaseout meeting with the Executive Committee was all-inclusive. His work in the field had gone so well that the group presented Clayton with a fashionable, premium-grade, leather jacket, in the appropriate size... *"Enrico's and Sofia's doings,"* he thought.

On his last day in Italy, Clayton took Sofia for lunch at a first-class restaurant, one block from his hotel. He thanked her profusely for her help and guidance and handed her an envelope; he suggested she open it later, preferably at home.

Upon their return to the hotel, Enrico was waiting in the lobby. He had Sofia relay to Clayton that the hotel bill was paid in full. Surprised, Clayton responded through Sofia, "I need to reimburse your company for several telephone calls to America." Clayton knew these calls, mostly to Jill, had to be more than $1,000 U.S. dollars. He and the hotel's bookkeeper had kept a running tally.

"No, it is our gift to you!" Sofia cautioned, "Clayton, do not challenge Enrico's offer. It is not polite."

Enrico reached into his briefcase and pulled out an envelope and handed it to Clayton. Unexpectedly, Clayton found it contained twenty $1,000 bills, the final payment of $20,000 in U.S. cash. Clayton accepted the money at the exact moment his luggage was loaded into the trunk of the private car, which was to take him to Malpensa International Airport for his flight home.

The closer his ride came to the airport, the more nervous Clayton became. *"Here I am in a foreign country carrying well over $10,000 that I have not listed on my customs form. Do I get another form, revise it, claim the money, and then probably have to show some proof that the taxes were paid? Or do I not declare the amount and risk having it seized? Shit, this is not an easy solution. If I go the legit way, I will likely miss my plane. Besides, I doubt if the police will pick on an American."*

In the queue to pass through customs, Clayton had misjudged the efficiency of the police. They were on the lookout for anyone fitting the profile of a German terrorist. Clayton was a good fit: Tall, early-forties, dirty blond hair, well built, wearing a black turtleneck sweater, black pants, brown leather topcoat, and carrying an oversized briefcase.

The moment he reached the checkpoint, two officers intervened and escorted him to an adjoining room. One officer checked his passport and other credentials. The second officer opened his briefcase and began rummaging throughout.

The stuffed envelope containing the money sat in plain view in the interior front pocket of the lid. Clayton discretely kept his eye on it while praying the officer would not check inside. The random search moved from the briefcase to his person. Finally, in what seemed like a lifetime, in broken English, the police officer said, "Okay, you can pass."

"Well, I made it past here, but what about U.S. Customs?"

Chapter 24

Wendy asked Jill as they met in the kitchen, "Mom, do you have plans for this evening?" "No, why?"

"James and I would like for you to join us for dinner."

"Sure, what time?"

"Let's plan to leave here at 7 p.m. or slightly after. He doesn't leave work until 6:30."

"Sounds good. Where are we going?"

"It's a surprise; you'll like."

"A surprise! What's the occasion?"

"Mom, just trust me."

"Okay, okay... I'm game. No more questions."

Jill gave little thought to having dinner with the kids. James was always insisting she go out to eat breakfast or lunch on the weekends, but dinner with a surprise was different. The girls knew James would arrive at 6:55, providing nothing delayed him at work.

Like clockwork, the knock on the door; it was James. Unbeknownst to Jill, James flashed a 'thumbs up' sign to Wendy as he entered the apartment. "Ladies, we are having dinner at The Marine Room on the beach in La Jolla."

This unique offer came as a shock to Jill. The Marine Room was well-known as the most exquisite dining experience in the San Diego area. She thought, *"Certainly not the place for a guy like James to be wining and dining two women, especially on his valet parking salary. Something smells here. This is no average dinner invite."*

Once inside the restaurant, James gave his name. The *maître d'* promptly picked up three menus and announced, "Your table is ready, and your guest has already arrived."

As they approached the table, Jill noticed a man, likely in his late forties, brown hair, glasses, and wearing a tan sports jacket, slide his chair back from the table. As he stood, he promptly said "Hello" to Wendy and James. James introduced Jill and Doctor Reid Watson to each other.

Annoyed, Jill sent a disapproving frown to her daughter. This unspoken message was clear; the color drained from Wendy's face. James, in a quick and calm maneuver, asked the server to bring four glasses of house Champagne.

Taking his drink in hand, he said, "I want to make a toast to love and happiness. So please raise your glasses and toast Wendy's and my announcement. We have scheduled Saturday, July 18th, for our wedding." That announcement brought a happy smile to Jill. It was good news.

She would be pleased to have him as her son-in-law. With Jill's responsive, "Cheers," that word had caused the coolness at the table to dissipate.

After listening to Wendy and James talk about their plans, the remainder of Jill's 'blind-date' dinner continued mostly with small talk. Still, Wendy detected an undercurrent of disapproval as she looked into her Mom's sad blue eyes.

After dinner, not the slightest hint of a second date was on the horizon. To Jill, it was nothing more than a 'nice to have met you gesture.' The door closed. This man or doctor stood no chance of interfering with her extremely personal dreams—the ones she refused to share with anyone other than her close friend, Vivian.

As she climbed into the car, Wendy, cursing to herself, had hoped her Mom's surprise blind date would spark an interest, but the insidious look in Jill's sad eyes said otherwise. She prepared herself for the lecture she knew was on the tip of her mother's tongue.

"I cannot believe you would attempt to do such a thing without discussing it with me in advance. And yes, Wendy, I know this was your idea, not James'."

"But Mom!"

"Don't 'but Mom' me. I am really disappointed with you!"

"Okay, I know it's your life," Wendy said, "and I shouldn't have stuck my nose in it. I was only trying to help. I feel sorry for you Mom... the dull lifestyle you are leading since you and Dad divorced."

As the argument reached a higher level, James attempted to intercede... to no avail.

Wendy continued, "I also doubt if you have any concern for Tony and Joe feeling that you abandoned them."

With that comment, Jill became furious. "Take me home... Now!"

Not a word was spoken on the way home. When the car arrived in front of the apartment building, Jill, almost stumbling, was out as soon as it stopped, slamming the door behind her.

Wendy had tasted the wrath of her mother before, but never to this extent. Her comment about her brothers had stung the worst, especially since she knew this was an outright lie. Both Tony and Joe had strongly supported their mother's decision to leave.

James, seeing the sadness in Wendy's eyes, dared not say anything. He shook his head and drove to his apartment, where the two would spend the remainder of the night.

The following day Wendy returned home after work. On the kitchen counter was a brief note, "Sorry about last evening. I'll be home Monday evening. Love, Mom."

As the Marines would say, Jill was AWOL. She would not be seen nor heard from over the next three days.

Chapter 25

New York—JFK Airport

After retrieving his luggage, Clayton got in line for his final inspection by U.S. Customs. He had not dared remove the money envelope from his briefcase. His luggage had made it through, and his only remaining hurdle was presenting both his passport and briefcase for a final inspection.

As routine, the customs agent checked his passport and asked a few questions about his month's stay in Italy. The agent then stamped his passport and said, "Welcome back home," as he motioned Clayton to proceed to the luggage area for the last official inspection. "*Once my luggage passes this checkpoint, Baggage Claim 2 will be its final destination, and I am home free,*" Clayton thought.

As expected, upon arrival at Baggage Claim, Arthur was waiting by the conveyor denoting Clayton's flight number. Arthur, knowing the ins and outs of JFK airport's protocol, had already secured a luggage carrier. With greetings out of the way and briefcase in hand, Clayton said, "I need to give Guy a quick call."

After speaking with Guy, he learned that all arrangements had been taken care of, including reservations for a long-term room at the Plaza Hotel and that Myrna had booked a flight the next morning flight to San Diego along with a room at the Hilton.

Guy next delivered a message Clayton hated to hear, "Taylor is driving Marsha up the wall. She now calls two or three times a day, wanting to know how she can reach you." Clayton's only response was, "I'll deal with that later. Thanks for everything, Guy."

Looking at his watch, Clayton again used his credit card to place a person-to-person call to the MCRD's 'business-only' telephone number.

A smiling Clayton rejoined Arthur. Surprisingly, he had left the Caddy at curbside in the 'Arrivals' area. Clayton asked, "How did you pull this off?" Arthur responded, "Boss, you really don't want to know,"

Headed into the City, their first stop was the Plaza Hotel, and Clayton's check-in was quickly finalized. The bellman removed the luggage from the car's trunk and delivered it to the eighth-floor room that was to become Clayton's temporary new home.

The next stop was Citibank to deposit the $20,000 in cash. From there, a short trip to his Park Avenue office, where Clayton and Guy would have a working lunch, once Marsha finished venting about Taylor's unwanted calls.

From Park Avenue, Arthur drove to Clayton's most dreaded stop, the apartment building located on the corner of Seventy Seventh and York, where Clayton and Taylor Lee shared a two-bedroom apartment. With no response at the door, Clayton entered using his key.

As previously discussed with Taylor, Clayton found that she had neatly moved all of his possessions into the spare bedroom. Clayton called the garage and asked the attendant to send Arthur up to help remove his belongings. Within a matter of fifteen minutes, all of Clayton's things were in the trunk and backseat of the Caddy.

Taking a final check of the apartment, Clayton noticed a bundle of mail addressed to him on the desk and picked it up. However, in his rush, he failed to see yesterday's mail, including the office's telephone bill lying under the newspaper on the dining room table.

He scribbled a quick note, "Taylor, as you can see, I have taken my things and will speak with you sometime next week. Also, as promised, I have left a check for three months' rent for the apartment. I am still unsure why you asked for three months' rent payments. I know your income from your Dad's trust easily takes care of any expenses you may have. Thanks for gathering up my stuff. Sorry things didn't work out. My key is on the dining room table. Take care, Clayton."

Before leaving the apartment, Clayton let his curiosity get the best of him. He walked into the master bathroom, and there was that damn diaphragm setting on the shelf where it shouldn't have been.

Smiling, he muttered, *"Good time to get the hell out of here."*

Chapter 26

As the flight information screen posted the on-time arrival of Clayton's plane, Jill moved quickly from the concourse's waiting area and headed directly to the arrival gate. She politely negotiated her way to the front of the small crowd waiting to meet passengers. Clayton would later tell Guy and Marsha, how beautiful Jill looked in her fashionable blue blouse and white pants, and how excited she appeared to be as he stepped into the terminal.

He mused, "*I will always remember the joy in her face.*" Smiling, "*It feels great to be truly loved!*" For this short weekend stay, everything Clay brought was in his carry-on bag; no need to stop at the luggage carousel.

On their way to the hotel, Jill playfully announced, "I stopped by a mini-mart and bought four bottles of Mondavi Chardonnay, two packages of Hickory Farms, an assortment of crackers, and guess what... two nice plastic wine glasses. Between this and what room service has to offer, Clay, we are set for a grand weekend. Let our party begin!"

With the assistance of the hotel's luggage carrier, everything arrived safely in room 415. Leaving the carrier in the hallway, Clay made two trips to the ice maker, storing the extra ice containers in the freezer of the small refrigerator. In one final move, he hung the *Do Not Disturb* sign on the door.

As Clay was getting ready to open one of the wine bottles, Jill, aware of the short amount of time they will be together, jokingly said, "If you would rather seduce me now than have a glass of wine, just say the word." The two laughed, hugged, and kissed. However, Jill's words excited Clay. Without speaking, he gently took her hand and led her over to the king-size bed. "*The wine be damned,*" he thought.

"Hold on," she said, "We're not going recreate one of those daytime soap scenes where both characters, in a love-making frenzy, rip off each other's clothes. I'll be back in a minute." Jill headed for the bathroom.

Meanwhile, Clay, taking the hint, started undressing. He neatly placed his shirt and pants on hangers and hung them in the closet. Jill, undoubtedly hearing or sensing what he was doing, cracked the bathroom door and said, "While you are hanging up your things, do the same with mine. Here they are. Also, do you have an extra pair of PJs I can put on?"

"Sorry, I only wear undershorts and tee shirts; you are welcome to them."

"Forget it; I'll make do." As she walked out of the bathroom, wearing only her bra and panties, her body began to quiver in anticipation of what was ahead.

Clay sensed his groin stir with arousal, as his eyes feasted upon the beauty of her scantily-clad body. Her skimpy pastel bra revealing the swell of her breasts beneath, and below her navel, the transparency of her matching lace panties caused his heat to reach a near boiling point. With his abstinence from sex for over a month, Clay's lust was ready to explode.

He took her hand and gently pulled her onto the bed, with its spread now on the floor, and the top sheet neatly folded at the foot. Turning onto her side and looking into his bright eyes, *"I knew he wanted me so badly our last evening together before he left for Italy, and then I told him there would be no sex. But tonight is different."*

Jill hungrily thought, *"I love Clay so much! And tonight, I am going to please him."*

"Clay, I love you so much!" Hearing her whisper those words, he wrapped his arms around her and held her close for a long time. As he was reaching over to turn off the bedside lamp, she noticed Clay's erection within his shorts.

Taking a deep breath, Jill thought, *"There are those tingling warmth emotions again. This time, they are stirring throughout my body."*

Another deep breath... His first move was to kiss her on the lips. Returning his kisses, she slowly moved her right hand upward to the back of his head and started to run her fingers through his hair. As their tender kisses became more and more passionate, he removed his shorts and let them fall alongside the bed. As she leaned forward and kissed his chest, he reached behind her, unhooked her bra, and tossed it aside.

Jill gently guided his head downward and led his lips onto her breasts. He heard her moan as he tenderly moved his tongue back and forth between her nipples, chest, and downward to her bellybutton. Clay slowly eased his hand down and inside the elastic and discarded her panties.

Looking up, with only a dim light filtering from the partially open bathroom door, he saw Jill staring at him. His tongue gently reversed and moved upward, touching her most arousing parts until he begins to kiss her on the lips passionately. From her lips, his mouth moved to her neck, and then he lightly breathed into her ear. His hand moved downward, slowly parting her legs.

Her hips began to move upward as she felt the moisture from his mouth that his tender kisses had left as he worked his way towards her navel. In anticipation of what was to come, her heart skipped as his tease intensified. With their heated bodies now touching, Clay moved on top and began kissing her on the lips as he entered her with a slow, but firm, thrust.

The rhythm of her hips matched his, as she felt that incredible swell of him inside. With a slightly audible moan from Clay, she felt his warm semen penetrate at the exact moment she reached her orgasm. His body stiffened as he released another long low moan. He pushed once more to go deeper inside of her. With that final thrust, he collapsed onto her body and wrapped his arms around her.

Jill, with pleasant thoughts, marveled at how natural it felt to be cuddling in bed with Clay. Everything felt so right, so perfect. Yet, she was uncomfortable as she sensed...

Something is amiss... what is causing this uneasiness?" She dismissed this strange feeling... *"Not this time. No destructive thoughts allowed."*

When Jill raised her head off Clay's shoulder, her face was wet with tears, and while looking at him, she said, "Clay, I feel guilty for what happened the other evening between my daughter, Wendy, and me. I need to call her and apologize. Please forgive me. I won't talk long."

Chapter 27

Wendy picked up the phone on its third ring, "Hello."

The female voice on the other end responded, "Hello, my name is Taylor Lee, and I am trying to contact Clayton Clarkson. This is an emergency and involves his former wife, Lorre."

"Sorry, you must have the wrong number." "I don't think so. Clayton has called your number several times between January and February."

"As I said, I don't know anyone by that name. This number is ..." Wendy was interrupted before she could give her number.

"Sorry for cutting you off, but I know I have the correct number. Your number is listed on Clayton's telephone bill.

Do you have a roommate or other person living there he could have called?"

"Only my Mom; she has never mentioned anyone by that name. To be safe, I will give her your information. What is your name again, and your message?"

"My name is Taylor Lee, and I am calling from New York.

If she knows Clayton Clarkson, please have her ask him to call Taylor Lee in regards to Lorre. He knows my number. Thank you."

As she replaced the phone in its cradle, Wendy's gut told her this call could likely mean trouble for her Mom. "*Hmmm... that woman on the phone knew exactly what she was doing. No hesitation about possibly dialing a wrong number. Oh God, I hope Mom has not gotten caught up in some love triangle!*"

The phone rang again. This time it was precisely 6:32 p.m.

"Hi, Honey."

"Mom, is that you?"

"Honey, yes, of course, it's me."

"Where are you?"

Jill, ignoring Wendy's question, said, "I wanted to call and tell you how sorry I am about what happened the other night."

"Mom, I am also sorry. I love you so very much. Where are you?"

"Wendy, I love you and the boys so very much. Well, I just felt I needed to call. I'll explain when I get home tomorrow."

"Mom, before you hang up, you need to know that I got a bizarre phone call about an hour ago from some woman in New York. Do you know a man named Clayton Clarkson?"

Hearing that name, Jill's face flushed as she began to stammer and almost dropped the phone on the floor directly in front of where Clay was now seated on the bed.

"What did you just say?" Wendy repeated the name and short message. "Mom, you do know this guy!"

"Yes, I do."

"What's between you and this... Clayton?" Before Jill had a chance to respond, Wendy followed with a comment that nearly tore Jill's heart out. "I think you may have gotten involved in a love triangle. Oh, Mom!"

Jill stood stunned, not knowing what to say. After gathering her thoughts, she said, "Wendy, I promise to tell you all about me and Clayton Clarkson," as she angrily emphasized his name, giving Clay an '*If looks could kill*' stare..."When I get home. Bye, Honey."

Her first instinct was to throw the damn phone at him but decided against such a violent act. "Who in the hell is Taylor Lee?" Before he had time to respond, she yelled, "You bastard... liar! I gave every bit of my heart and soul to you, and you do this to me."

"God, Jill, please do not judge me before I have a chance to explain. Yes, I told you a couple of lies, but I only did so out of fear of losing you. Please give me a chance to explain."

"You son of a bitch! I'm out of here as soon as I get my things together!"

♥ ♥

Chapter 28

As the apartment's door flew open, Wendy, in a startled voice, said, "Mom, I thought you said you would be home tomorrow."

"I did." With tears streaming down her cheeks, Jill, with a hurtful look on her face and in a trembling voice blurted out, "My world just fell apart."

"Oh, Mom... Clayton Clarkson?"

"Yes, that SOB!"

"What happened?"

"Well, bring that open bottle of wine from the refrigerator, I'll get two glasses from the cabinet, and we'll sit down, and I'll tell you all about that liar... Clay Clarkson."

Wine poured and uncontrollable tears flowed, Wendy moved the tissue box from the counter onto the kitchen table and handed Jill three tissues.

"Okay, Mom, have at it."

"Honey, I wanted to fall in love with ..." Before she could

complete her sentence, the telephone started ringing.

"Don't answer it. It's him calling."

"Mom, you don't know it's him. It could be James." "Okay, but if it's him, tell him to go to hell!"

"Hello, yes, she's here, but she doesn't want to talk to you."

In the background, Jill shouted, "Never again!" Without another word, Wendy hung up the phone.

"Mom, back to our conversation, you were saying that you wanted to fall in love..." Wendy listened intensely to every hurtful word flowing from her Mother's mouth, and she could almost feel the horrible pain herself. To Wendy, the kitchen's atmosphere was filled with hurt and sadness.

What she was witnessing reminded her of seeing her best friend's family in mourning at the funeral services of a younger brother who was killed in a car wreck. At a loss for words, Wendy stood up, took both of her Mom's hands, and gently pulled her upright; the two hugged tightly for three or four minutes.

In tears, she thought, "*My Mom took a chance on love, and now she is devastated. Sometimes love can be so cruel.*"

A couple of hours later, another call. "Don't answer. Let it go to the answering machine."

"Okay, Mom." As Clayton Clarkson started speaking, his sad voice reminded Wendy of a call from James apologizing after the two had a stress-filled argument a year ago.

Brokenhearted and pleading to let him explain, Clay said, "Jill, I beg you just hear me out. There is no other woman. I only love you... Please let me explain." The message then ended.

Jill knew Clay could only reach her by telephone. He did not know the location of her apartment. And, surely, he wouldn't try to see her at MCRD, even if he could talk his way past the gate guard. It was too risky that one of Colonel Cooperswaite's staff would spot him.

Time was also against him. Clay had mentioned in addition to his consulting projects, his schedule included presenting a series of nationwide seminars for a major New York publishing company. He wouldn't have the time to seek her out.

Jill did not erase Clay's message and played it again, once Wendy was out with James. In a moment of weakness, she became tempted to make that call. But reminded herself, *"Clay has been caught lying to me at least three times.* With that, she thought, *"He's not worth this kind of heartache."*

♥ ♥

Chapter 29

To Jill, not hearing from Clay was a sure sign that he had put the past behind him, and that she should do the same. *"Get a life and move on,"* she scolded herself while recognizing that any attempt to apply mascara between the teardrops was a losing battle. However, for some unknown reason, she was unable to dismiss him from her mind, at least not right away. *"Vivian may have been right when she first told me that he might be as phony as a three dollar bill. But God, I really loved him,"* she thought, *"I'm heartbroken, and my life feels so empty. "*

Thinking and trying to put all of Clay's lies into a single bucket, just as she had done in consolidating Roy's shit list. Jill wanted to convince herself that she had to escape from the mental prison that was keeping Clay and their beautiful memories in her life. *"God, I just can't believe I was so gullible as to accept whatever he told me as the truth."*

That night as she tiptoed from the bathroom to her bedroom, taking precautions so as not to wake Wendy, Jill dropped her robe on the closest chair, and without hesitation, plopped onto the bed, grabbed her pillow, and buried her head in it.

"This moving on crap isn't easy. No matter how hard I try to push away from those memories of Clay and our fun times, although brief, he consumed my life and dreams of love and happiness." Sobbing into the pillow, she mused, *"I can't believe he was such a smooth con artist. God, this guy was good... a real fraud."*

Remembering how impressed she was once she learned that Clay had a deep appreciation of art and her artistic talents, she smiled thinking, *"He loved my paintings, and went bonkers over the oil I cherish most; the old Indian lady holding her grandchild on her knee while working at a spinning wheel. I remember telling him..."* Pausing, she whispered, *"It is my Mona Lisa...."*

Caught in a state of bewilderment she took a couple of calming breaths, as she looked back on the day she listened intensely as he talked about his visits to the Uffizi Gallery in Florence, Italy; the Louvre in Paris, France; Museum of Fine Arts in Boston; the Metropolitan Museum of Art in New York City and, as a teenager, making several trips via a streetcar from his family's apartment in South East Washington to the National Gallery of Art in the Northwest section.

"Oh my, was I impressed?" Answering her question, *"You damn right I was. If he was faking, he sure as hell held his own when I brought up Rembrandt, Michelangelo, Monet, Van Gogh, da Vinci, Picasso, and Dali. But when he started naming off American artists like Peter Max, Thomas Kinkade, LeRoy Neiman, Norman Rockwell, Andy Warhol, and even the lesser-known, Nanette Willey Kinkade... I was truly impressed. But who wouldn't be?"*

Jill's curiosity about Clay's artistic expertise began to heighten as she wondered how the son of a poor West Virginia coal miner could have developed such an appreciation. *"Had he studied art in school?... his answer was, 'No.'"*

Not one to avoid asking sensitive questions, especially when all pieces of the puzzle didn't fit, she began sensing that he did not want to explain from where this diversity of knowledge came. Jill received a warning signal but chose to ignore it. She also remembered, *"He hadn't been this evasive since that night at the Rubin E. Lee restaurant when I asked him about those telephone calls."*

The more Clay attempted to provide unrealistic explanations to what should have been easy answers, the greater Jill's fear increased. *"He's not truthful; it is showing in his eyes, voice, and body language."*

Clay had talked about having contacts in social circles who introduced him to New York's art scene and managers of prominent art galleries. He also said he had attended auctions at Christie's and Sotheby's, but never purchased any works of art. He simply said, "Too rich for my blood."

Tossing her tear-soaked pillow onto the floor, a sobbing Jill sprang up and sat on the side of her bed, reaching over to the nightstand, she grabbed a tissue. *"Oh God, please... please help me! Every instinct tells me he is trouble. But why, oh why, do I still love this lying bastard?"*

♥ ♥

Chapter 30

About nine days later, Jill, expecting a call from Wendy that evening, picked up the ringing telephone.

"Jill, this is Guy Devine. I hope you remember me."

"Yes, you are Clay's partner."

"Please don't hang up. You need to hear a few things about Clay, and I promise I will always tell you the truth, no matter what you ask.

"Okay, I'm listening. Surely you know he lied, and the only way I found out was a phone call from some woman in New York."

"Taylor Lee."

"Yes, I believe that was her name."

"Jill, Clayton doesn't know I am making this call. I am at home in New York, and it's after midnight here." With a slight laugh, Guy said, "I guess you could say that I am playing cupid, and trying to patch up a true love affair that has slid off the tracks.

Clayton loves you very much, and he never meant to hurt you in any way. If you have any feelings left for him, you owe it to both yourself and Clayton to set aside a couple of hours and let him explain."

"I'm listening, but promising nothing."

"Jill, he loves you deeply; that I am positive. If you listen to what he has to say, I will make him promise to tell you the truth. And once you hear why he chose to tell you one lie after another, you'll understand his reasoning for doing such dumbass things."

"I doubt that, Guy."

"Well, he is scheduled to do a two-and-a-half day seminar in San Francisco this coming Wednesday. Earlier this afternoon, I had our travel agent check for a timely hop between SFO and Lindbergh Field. He could be there by seven or shortly after, but must leave no later than 10:30, because of flight restrictions."

"Yes, I am aware of the 'no planes take off past 11:00 p.m. law.' How do you know he will come?"

"Believe me; he will be there. He's devastated and needs to know I talked with you, and that you agreed to meet and listen to what he has to say. Keep in mind; he can only spend around two and a half hours with you."

"Guy, I guess I have nothing to lose. Besides, I would like to hear him try to explain his way out of this mess. Okay, tell him I'll meet him at the bar in the Hilton at 7:30 p.m."

"Done, I guarantee he'll be there. Jill, he's really a good guy. If you have any love left for him, he's worth taking a chance."

Chapter 31

Jill walked into the Hilton bar slightly ahead of the 7:30 p.m. meeting time. Clay was already seated at what she used to refer to as 'our favorite table.' He immediately spotted her, slid his chair aside, and after taking several steps forward, reached out as if he wanted to greet her with a hug. She politely held out her hand. He got the message and shook her hand.

She callously looked at him and said, "Hello, Clay."

He returned the unemotional greeting as the two took their seats, one across from the other, at the table. The waitress came, and Clay looking at Jill asked, "Chardonnay?"

"No, thanks. I'll have a glass of water."

"Bring a Chardonnay for me, and also the check."

"Okay, I'm here to listen to your excuses for lying and deceiving me. Guy told me you have only a short time before you must fly out."

"That's right; my flight leaves at 10:20."

"Okay." Jill WAS determined not to show the slightest sign

of caring. Her body language and tone of voice were on the verge of being rude, a Jill Simpson he had never seen before. *"God, if she wants me to crawl, I am ready to crawl… I cannot screw this up. She is the love of my life."*

"I don't know what Guy told you, but I am so thankful that he called, and you agreed to listen to me."

"You hurt me more than I could ever say. Please, I am not here to talk about me. I am here mostly out of curiosity, and to hopefully learn something that will help shield me from such a dreadful thing in the future. 'Enough,' as Wendy would say, so get on with it!"

"Jill, my personal life has been an unbelievable mess for what seems like a lifetime. I have been married and divorced twice. My first wife was my high school sweetheart, and we have a daughter from that marriage.

"Was she pregnant when you got married?"

"No, we were both nineteen years old. My parents loved her, and her parents made it known they felt the same about me. We both had good jobs with the federal government, and I was attending college at night. Everyone expected us to marry. I also felt we were destined to marry.

"After our daughter was born, we tried to make it work, but we didn't mesh. Finally, we reached the point we couldn't stand each other. I decided to leave so as not to subject our four-year-old daughter, Lynn, to our constant arguing.

"Because of Lynn, my ex and I continued to remain in contact, although to this day, I cannot stand her husband. When I would go to pick up Lynn for our times together, he made those few minutes I had to wait at their house while she got dressed, as unpleasant as he could.

"He never spoke directly to me. It was the things he would do or say to someone else. My ex, Cindy, was also rude. She would lay down her rules for Lynn's return; many were unfair. I think they were trying to sever the relationship I had with my daughter. As Lynn reached middle school age, Cindy asked me if I would let them legally adopt her... the reason given was that they were going to move and Lynn would be attending a new school, and since they also had two other children, they thought it best if Lynn and their other two kids had the same family name. They assured me that my visitation rights would remain the same.

"As an additional incentive, I was told my weekly child support payments would cease. We agreed, and the adoption was formalized. However, if they thought this would be the wedge that would break up our growing relationship, it didn't work. Even when I moved from Washington, D.C. to both Boston and New York, Lynn's and my love for each other never faltered. Someday, I hope you will get to meet her.

"About a year after the divorce from my first wife, I met Lorre. She was a beautiful and intelligent corporate accounting manager for a large pharmaceutical company. We were married for over ten years. During those years, I held executive positions in Washington, D.C., Boston, Massachusetts, and New York City. Lorre hated having to relocate, even though each move brought with it several perks and lifestyle upgrades.

"When we left Washington, Lorre made it clear that if we moved, she would never work again. I had no concern about her making that pledge. We moved three times, and she held to her word. After our separation in New York, she told a friend, she was puzzled about what makes me so determined to be successful. And that she preferred to be married to a minimum wage earner who would provide the comfort and security of staying in one place.

"Three years ago, I separated from Lorre, but as of today, that divorce is still not finalized. Unfortunately, she is a hopeless alcoholic—in and out of multiple treatment centers—and refuses to acknowledge she has a problem.

"Even though we departed ways some time ago, she still lives in the house we jointly own. I never pursued filing for divorce and continue to support her. Also, I would go to our house on Long Island and check on her every so often—no love or romance—I just felt sorry for her since her only living relative, a sister, knew about her drinking problem and stayed away.

"Jill, you may wonder why I did not follow through with the divorce. Perhaps, it was guilt. Did I drive her to drink? I don't know, but maybe so. I could not just walk away and abandon her.

"One day I drove to our house in Rockville Centre, and when she didn't answer the door, which was not unusual, I used my key to go inside. I found her at the bottom of the lower-level steps unconscious. She was transported by ambulance to the hospital. She had had a stroke.

"I called her sister—no help there. So, you might say the ball was in my court. After spending three weeks in the hospital, she was scheduled for release. I again called her sister for help, and she offered none. She made it clear that I was the one responsible for taking care of her sister.

"Lorre and I were separated for three years, and there was no love left in our relationship. I was well aware that if Lorre was able to return home alone, she would be hitting the bottle in nothing flat. So, what could I do? Return home? Not an option. Drop her at her sister's doorstep and insist she is her sister's family's responsibility... No!

Finally, I came up with Lorre's best alternative. Without hesitation, I was on the phone calling my mother."

"Your mother?"

"Yes, you heard right... my mother. She lived alone in a house on Solomons Island, Maryland. Mom was well aware of my predicament. I had kept her updated as to Lorre's condition and what was going on.

"Let me give you a little background that'll help you understand why I looked to Mom for help. Shortly after Dad's death, Lorre and I convinced Mom to quit her salesperson job in downtown D.C., and come live with us in Prince Georges County, Maryland. Lorre and Mom always got along great.

"Back then Lorre had a full-time job, so most of the household duties were taken care of by my Mom. She lived with us for nearly four years—up to the time I took a job in Boston. Mom did not want to relocate, so I bought her the house where she now lives before we moved away. Mom loves Lorre, and she welcomed having Lorre come live with her.

"From my point of view, the two best things about this 'off-the-wall resolution were that the closest liquor store was ten miles away, and my mother would not tolerate drinking. Lorre wasn't always a big drinker. I could cop out and say that life had thrown her one curve ball and then another, and she couldn't handle the boredom of sitting home without a hobby or close friends nearby.

"My mind was not on Lorre's needs. I was too busy trying to prove that the son of a coal miner could achieve financial success.

Jill, I was most likely the one responsible for her downfall, and I couldn't walk away from Lorre and leave her to fend for herself. Jill, most of my friends still find it strange, to say the least, that I would bring my 'former wife' to live with my mother. Weird yes, but I still believe this was the best alternative to keep Lorre from destroying herself."

Finding his story more believable than expected, Jill said, "Oh God! Tell the waitress to bring me a nine-ounce glass of Chardonnay."

Chapter 32

"Jill, now I'll tell you about Taylor Lee, the woman who spoke with your daughter Wendy. I met Taylor approximately one year before Lorre moved in with my Mom. Initially, Taylor and I got along great. She is an attractive, thirty-five-year-old woman who always travels in elite circles and likes to be invited to snobbish parties.

"Taylor, a true socialite, enjoyed teaching me the ins and outs of social scenes. She taught me the most about art and upper-class art galleries. She's why I stayed away from telling you how I learned so much about the art scene. I always admired the work of the masters and a few American artists, and I did visit those galleries I described.

"Taylor certainly added to my knowledge, and we enjoyed attending art shows and listening to a bunch of phonies who didn't know crap about fine art. But a few tried to pass themselves off as experts. We traveled in elite circles where there was so much phoniness; it was sickening. However, the lifestyle she was living was very appealing to me.

"Bottom line, both Taylor and I were using each other. For her, I was nothing more than a temporary Sugar Daddy. While the majority of her financial support was provided through a trust set up by her wealthy parents, I paid the monthly rent, other incidentals, and those expenses we incurred during our time together. For me, she taught me a great deal about the lifestyles of those fortunate enough to live on the upper Eastside and Westside of Manhattan.

"Before I met you, Taylor and I were having serious problems. She was cheating on me, and I was doing the same. We both knew our relationship was on its last days of survival. I moved out the day I returned from Italy. I had planned to tell her about you once I get settled back in Manhattan."

"Clay, I appreciate you sticking with your promise to try to explain your reasoning as to why you chose to lie to me about your personal life, and for not using this time to try to make up."

"Jill, I am so sorry that things have taken the course they have. I do hope you can see and feel the love I have for you. I have given you the whole truth about those things I tried to conceal from you.

"All I ask is that, if you can, after hearing what a mess my life was, please try to put yourself in my position of having met someone you are confident is the love of your life, and believing it is likely that if you tell that person this screwed-up story, they will want nothing to do with you. Or do you—as I did—take a chance and avoid telling the truth about your past. Jill, what would you have done?"

Staring into her glass of wine, Jill winched at the thought, and replied, "I don't know. I need to think about this before I answer you."

Looking at his watch, Clayton said, "It's time for me to pick up my bag at the valet desk and catch the shuttle to the airport. Thanks again for hearing me out. I hope to hear from you soon. I know you have my office number, and if I am not in town, leave a number for me to call with either Marsha or Guy... Jill, please don't give up on me."

While he was standing at the lobby door waiting for the shuttle, Jill walked up and said, "Clay, grab your bag. I'll give you a ride to the airport."

♥ ♥

Chapter 33

It was four-thirty in the morning when the phone rang, "Hello," Clayton excitedly said.

The voice on the other end responded, "Sorry, wrong room."

Clayton, not disturbed by the call, wasn't asleep. He had been awake all night, praying that she would call. Rolling out of bed, he headed for the bathroom to pee. Returning to bed, Clay wondered how long he could resist that overpowering urge to pick up the phone and call California.

Six-forty-five, the phone rang again, but this time it was his wake-up call. By seven-thirty, he had shaved, showered, dressed, and was downstairs in the dining room drinking coffee, having two eggs over easy, two sausage patties, and a plain bagel with a smear of cream cheese.

The waiter, as customary once the meal was over, placed a folded *New York Times* on the table. Skimming for articles of interest, Clayton paused to read about two pipe bombs being mailed to separate diplomatic offices in Manhattan, which were defused by the Police Department bomb squad. '*The bombs, mailed to the United States Mission to the United Nations and the Honduran Consulate, were similar to one that had killed a man early Saturday morning at Kennedy International Airport.*'

The next article, about the United Mine Workers Union in negotiations to avoid a strike, brought back memories of his Dad, and his childhood in that godforsaken place where he had lived until the age of eight.

On his short walk from the hotel to his office at 277 Park Avenue, Clayton was growing more depressed and testy by the day; three days and not a word. He was sensing that any hopes he had of rekindling his nearly lifeless romance were likely dead.

He began to think as he had done in the past. "*The cure for being ditched by one woman is to find another and get laid, an easy solution in Manhattan. You dumb bastard, even to let that thought enter your mind is shameful,*" he muttered as he headed over to Park Avenue. "*Giving up is not in my vocabulary, and no way in hell am I going to sit idly by and end up losing her.*"

As a young boy in that small coal mining town in West Virginia, Clayton had learned firsthand that good things rarely, if ever, come your way if you are silent or fail to make your intentions known. He had used this philosophy successfully throughout his childhood and teen years, and several times as an adult.

Clayton knew what he wanted; her name was Jill Simpson. And every instinct was signaling that if he stood idly by waiting for a response from the love of his life, he would end up heartbroken. He knew exactly what he had to do...

Chapter 34

Vivian had not treated Jill's need for advice lightly, especially since her earlier plea for Wendy's help had fallen on deaf ears. "This is no place to talk," Vivian said, getting up from the table on the porch. "We can always grab a snack later. Honey, you need to be able to freely talk without having some jarhead Marine bursting his balls trying to listen in."

"Makes sense."

"Let's go over near the Mess Hall," Vivian continued, "There are always unoccupied benches around there and plenty of space in between."

Jill, smiling, said, "Even Superman, with his extra sensitive hearing wouldn't be able to listen to what we are talking about."

"Silly girl, I'm glad to see that you have perked up."

"So Viv, what advice do you have? And, don't tell me you are going to cop out like my daughter did."

"No honey, that I am not doing. But I do believe the advice she gave you made good sense. But, just like with Wendy, you're not going to like what I have to say.

"Let's look at what you now know about Mr. Clay Clarkson. You know he had two wives and a live-in girlfriend, and you have only heard his side of the story. You know he's a smooth talker, and if he weren't, he wouldn't be in the business of selling himself as a consultant. He's fun to be around; I suspect he's also exciting in bed, and like I have told you before, just like a sailor, Clay most likely has a sexual partner in every city where he works. Honey, you know, from your experiences, he's a proven liar and heartbreaker."

"God, Vivian, that was cruel and hurtful."

"Oh, honey, I am so sorry! But you asked for my opinion, and I am giving it to you. So, now you've heard what Wendy and I had to say. Now you must weigh your alternatives carefully and decide what is best."

Vivian saw real pain in Jill's misty eyes, and she wished she could take back the four or five minutes of advice she had just dished out. Jill shook her head, trying to push the hurt into a place where no one would able to penetrate.

"Oh, honey."

"Don't, 'oh, honey' me. You don't know how it feels to have someone you really care about—someone you trusted—and then find out they had lied to you, not once, twice, but at least three times."

"Jill, dwelling on what you had with Clay is not good... forget him!"

"Forget him... forget him! Oh Viv, this is the first time since my marriage years ago, that I genuinely cared about someone. I wanted this relationship to work."

"Honey, I think you will be taking one hell of a chance if you are thinking of reconnecting with this guy," Vivian scolding her sensibly.

"You don't know who he is, except for what he has told you."

Jill was quick to defend Clay, "He's a gentleman and a very respectable man."

"There's no such man," Vivian replied in a suspicious tone. "Forget what Colonel Cooperswaite told you. He can only vouch for his business image and façade. But, if that's the way you feel, just be careful, for God's sake."

"I will, and I'll be fine."

It was evident to Vivian that she was on the losing end of this argument, and if not careful, she could be destroying a highly valued friendship. Vivian said, "Honey, I hear it in your words and see in your eyes, that you have made the decision your daughter told you to do in no uncertain terms; you must resolve this yourself and not follow what others think."

Vivian paused briefly, looking directly into Jill's eyes, took both hands, and said, "Honey, you should never be afraid to take a chance on love, if that's what you feel in your heart."

Surprised at Vivian's last comment, Jill responded, "First, you practically call me a moron, and now you are encouraging me to go for it. Oh Vivian, thank you, thank you... thank you!"

Both ladies, with big smiles on their faces, headed back to work. Neither had any sense of what the future would hold.

Chapter 35

Finishing up his work, Clayton noticed the clock indicated it was four-thirty-eight. *"Damn, I had better make a decision within the next ten minutes, or I will be shit out of luck in dealing with Friday's schedule,"* he thought.

"Marsha, drop whatever you are doing and come in here." When she didn't appear immediately, he called again, but this time used a more pleasant tone, "Marsha, please come in here and bring me this Friday's appointment calendar and Myrna's telephone number."

"Clayton, didn't you see that I was on the phone?"

"Oh, sorry, I forgot to look at the phone light button. How heavy is my schedule for Friday?"

"You and Guy have an eight o'clock for a status update on three client projects. Nothing else for the rest of the day."

"Great, let Guy know that our meeting is still on. Also, tell him I am going to San Diego, and I'll need a ride out to JFK."

"Nice," Marsha said smiling. "So you aren't going to wait for that California phone call?"

"No, I am going to resolve this situation... in person."

"Speaking as a woman, I think she has been hurt and needs her knight in shining armor to ride in on his white horse and rescue her from all of her heartaches."

"What are you saying... how did you know?"

"Ah, come on boss, you surely know that Guy and I talk."

"Okay, I do appreciate your input, especially in believing I need to take this trip. Do you have Myrna's number?"

"Here's the number. She leaves her office around five-thirty to six."

"Thanks, I'll call now. Have a good evening, and I'll see you in the morning."

"Thanks, boss. See you tomorrow."

After putzing around in the silent office, Clayton, now bored, looked at his watch for about the umpteenth time, thinking, "*It's now only quarter past three in San Diego. Damn, another three and a half hours before I can call her at the apartment. Or, do I risk calling the office phone where she works? "What if I get her in trouble for taking a call at work? Or worse yet, what if she refuses to take my call? Embarrassing, you bet your ass. Think! Do the right thing.*"

Clayton got up from his desk, grabbed his topcoat, turned out the lights, went into the hall, and caught the elevator down.

"*Dinner, that's what I can do. I can kill an easy two or so hours there, depending upon where I go ...hmmm, TGI Friday's over on First Ave could be a good choice. Always crowded, and a wait is virtually guaranteed.*"

Clayton had guessed right. The hostess was taking names. "One, please."

"Just you?"

"That's right, just lonely old me."

"I can seat you immediately at the bar, or you'll have an estimated thirty to forty minutes wait for a booth or table."

"I'll wait; I prefer a booth."

"You're on the list."

"Thanks."

After a long and leisurely meal and taking what appeared to the waiter to be forever for Clayton to finish his second glass of wine, he finally asked for his check. Well aware that his stalling was costing the waiter additional earnings from tips, Clayton smiled at the waiter as he was leaving; his smile not returned.

"I bet his attitude towards me changes when he finds the tip that I left under the plate. When I get back to my room, Jill should be home. Mission accomplished."

San Diego

At six-forty, the telephone in the apartment started ringing; four times in all, before Jill answered.

"This is Clay, and I'm coming to talk with you on Friday evening."

Bracing for a barrage of reasons for not seeing him, she said, "We've talked."

"Jill, I'm not referring to my confessional meeting. I need to talk... face-to-face."

"What've we got to talk about?"

"Us...our relationship, and where we go from here. Don't you get it? I cannot see my life without you... I love you!" Silence took over the phone line. At first, Clay thought she had hung up. *"No dial tone, so I'm still connected."*

After what seemed like an eternity, Jill, obviously crying, blurted out... "and I love you too! Oh, Clay, I really miss you. What time will your plane arrive? Give me all the particulars, and I'll be at the gate waiting for you."

"Thank you, Jesus, God; thank you!" Those words were quite unusual coming from a guy who rarely attended church except for a wedding or funeral.

"Don't make a reservation at the Hilton. You're staying at our apartment. It's time for you to meet my daughter, Wendy, and her fiancée, James. If you behave yourself, I may also introduce you to my two sons, if they are around.

"Clay, I'll be waiting at the arrivals gate... as I have heard you say, 'you can take it to the bank.' Goodnight, my love, I'll see you on Friday afternoon. Bye."

♥ ♥

Chapter 36

"Don't forget, gentlemen, you two have a 10:00 a.m. with Earl Williams at his office," said Marsha reading from her appointment book.

"Gentlemen?... Marsha, I like the formality," responded Clayton.

Guy joined, "I have never heard you call us that before. What gives?"

"Well, a half hour ago, I received a very formal reminder from Williams' secretary about your meeting. So, I thought since we're also located in a high-overhead area, I would practice our snooty Park Avenue manners."

As Clayton and Guy walked into Earl Williams' office, the secretary greeted them, and politely said, "Mr. Williams is expecting you, gentlemen." She used the intercom to let him know they were in the reception area.

"Send them in." Williams suddenly appeared in the doorway and turned to introduce Edgar Smythers, CEO of PMP Motion Picture Studios.

Wasting no time, Williams explained the purpose of this meeting and stressed the need for total secrecy regarding what will be discussed. It quickly became evident this had to do with the crime of embezzlement.

Williams, directed his remarks to Mr. Smythers, reinforcing his belief that there are very few audit firms, including his, that have the expertise to investigate suspected embezzlement and internal fraud matters. "Clarkson International has a proven reputation within this critical area." Edgar Smythers smiled and nodded in agreement.

Unknown to both Clayton Clarkson and Guy Devine, a comprehensive background investigation had already been completed on Clarkson International and its staff. They had passed with flying colors. With the active support of Earl Williams, the selection of Clarkson for this sensitive project was a foregone conclusion.

The briefing by Smythers and Williams had taken slightly over one hour. As the two men were leaving, Williams reminded Clayton his need to have the proposal in hand no later than tomorrow afternoon.

After leaving Earl Williams' office, Clayton and Guy stopped by the coffee shop next door to their old Fifth Avenue building. Clay bought three cups of coffee, two black and one regular for Marsha. Once inside the office, he handed Marsha her coffee and left instructions that under no circumstances were they to be interrupted, including no phone calls.

"Not even a call from area code 714?" Marsha said.

"Well, that's the only exception," responded Clayton.

Before getting down to the nitty-gritty of writing the proposal, Clayton said, "Guy, sorry to do this to you, but I need to fly to San Diego on Friday, and I will be back early Monday morning... I promise."

"Female problems can be a real bitch, especially when you keep screwing up," Guy quipped.

Clayton responded, "Funny!... very funny."

"This means we must finish the proposal no later than tomorrow morning," Guy remarked.

"That's right, and then Marsha can deliver it to Williams' office. With the door closed, the two men went to work. Clayton whispered, "Can you believe it? One of the candidates for President of the United States—a popular one at that—and a highly talented female executive may be connected to a multimillion dollar embezzlement scheme in PMP's subsidiary studio."

♥ ♥

J L Hayes

Chapter 37

Guy pulled into the 'No Standing Zone' in front of their office building, and Clayton quickly tossed his small bag on the back seat and hopped in on the passenger side. Off they went before a cop spotted the illegally stopped vehicle. Both were quiet on the way to the airport, even though there was much to be said. Guy had told Clayton over and over, he was making a big mistake in lying to Jill. Now his lies had caught up with him... still no words, just silence.

Over the years, the two had always been there for each other; sometimes, the unspoken word is best. As Guy pulled up to the departure terminal at JFK, he said, "Call if you need me."

"Thanks, my friend. Pray that you don't hear from me until Monday morning. I'll be taking the red-eye back. Marsha said she gave you the flight information."

"That she did." Clayton reached in the back seat and grabbed his bag. The two men shook hands as Clayton opened the car door. With a pause, Guy said, "Good luck!"

Clayton, standing on the curb, leaned in and said, "Thanks! I will need it." He closed the door just as the traffic cop approached. Guy drove off in a flash.

Once the plane was at the gate in San Diego's Terminal 2, Clayton was the fifth person off. There, as close to the passageway door as permissible, wearing a yellow blouse and white jeans, stood a highly excited Jill Simpson.

Before he could reach her, he thought to himself, "*I cannot ever remember seeing anyone being as excited about seeing and greeting me than she is tonight.*"

Their hugs, kisses, and show of affection caused one male passenger to comment, "I wish my wife would greet me like that!" Another spoke up saying, "Bet they are not married." Clayton, smiling, turned and winked at the men.

"This bag is all I have. No need to stop at baggage claim."

"Good, I am in short-term parking." As the car exited the lot, Jill said, "Let's grab a quick dinner... anywhere in particular?"

"Wherever, you pick. All I had were peanuts, cheese, and crackers... the gourmet food of the economy class."

"What happened, I thought you said you always fly First or Business Class?"

"Well, when you make a reservation in less than twelve hours before departure time, you take what you can get."

"So, you are hungry. Let's go Mexican. How about El Torito's in Old Town?"

"Great. I have never been to Old Town."

After dinner, Jill asked, "Well, what did you think?"

"Great meal, and I enjoyed the margarita, and you?"

"Their tacos are always my favorite, and like you, their

margiritas always rank high on my list."

"How far is your apartment from here?"

"Oh, less than fifteen minutes, why?"

"Well, I'd be lying if I didn't tell you that I am nervous about meeting your daughter, Wendy."

Laughing, she reached over, touched his knee, and said, "You're in luck tonight. Wendy knows you are coming. So she is staying over at James' tonight. The two of them will meet us at nine o'clock for breakfast at Marie Callender's... ever eat there?"

"No, but I recognize the name, a franchise, I believe."

"Well, here we are," with a smile, she said, "Are you able to carry your luggage, or do you need help?"

"Funny!"

"You men are amazing. If a woman is going away for the weekend, we wouldn't dare leave home without at least two or three pieces."

♥ ♥

Chapter 38

Unlocking the door, Jill paused, turned, and said, "Please Clay, no sex tonight. I just want to sit, talk, hug, and enjoy being back together."

"I understand... believe me; I am thankful that we are together. To hold, hug, and kiss you is fine with me."

Once the two were ready for bed, Clay walked into the living room wearing a tee shirt and pajama bottom. Surprised at what she was seeing, Jill said, "I didn't think you wore PJs?"

"I don't, but when you told me not to make reservations at the Hilton, and that I would be staying here, I ran out and bought them at Saks. I didn't want your daughter to see me in undershorts."

"Well, I have a nice surprise for you." With that announcement, Jill opened the refrigerator and took out a bottle of Chardonnay and placed it on the table. She then returned to the fridge, and when she turned around, she was holding a small platter of Hickory Farms snacks. "Remember, our Hilton survival kit?"

"You bet I do."

"I even have an opener and real wine glasses. You open and pour, and I'll get a couple of small plates for the sausages and cheeses."

With the wine poured, Clay, handing Jill her glass, picked his up from the table, and raising it into a toasting position said, "No woman has ever affected me the way you do. I love you so very much." They touched glasses, and each took a sip.

Even after hitting a big pothole in their road to romance, the blossoming of their love once again seemed so right. Jill said, "My turn," as she raised her glass and softly said, "All I want is for our love to last."

In bed, Clay honored Jill's request. He held her tightly, kissing and cuddling until they went to sleep. The next morning they met Wendy and James for breakfast at Marie Callender's.

This get-together was the first meeting between Jill's daughter and her future son-in-law, and Clay. The introductions and breakfast went smoothly and, as expected, Clay picked up the check. Outside the restaurant, Wendy told her Mom, "James and I are going over to Coronado, and I won't be home until late Sunday night."

"Oh, that means you won't see Clay again until his next trip. He's returning to New York Sunday evening on a nine-forty-five flight." With that bit of information, Wendy, James, and Clay said their goodbyes.

In the car, Wendy asked James, "Well, what do you think?"

"I don't know. From everything I've heard, they barely know each other, and that shit you told me about his history sucks. But in listening to your Mom talk, she has been completely swept her off of her feet. Wendy, I believe she is madly in love with him."

"I agree, and what I find amazing is that Mom has never been impulsive before. I can see he's a man with determination and passion. Crap, I can't believe my Mom is deeply in love with a perfect stranger, a man with a deep dark history."

"Wendy, I am suspicious of Clay Clarkson. I will pray that I am wrong and that your Mom doesn't end up with a broken heart."

Wendy using her finger, wiped away a tear as she said, "Oh God! Poor Mom!"

♥ ♥

Chapter 39

After returning to the apartment, Clay asked Jill to see her paintings.

"Oh, I'm surprised you remembered me telling you about them."

"Are you kidding? I adore art. You can learn a great deal about the artist by studying their work. So, I am ready..."

"Okay, but just don't laugh."

"Never! I would never make a joke about someone's art, even those pieces revealing the artist to be lazy or unexciting."

"Good, because I always try to pour my heart and soul into each piece. Now, here's my most favorite." With that introduction, Jill removed the cloth covering and held up the framed piece.

With a surprised look on his face, Clay said, "Wow, wow... unbelievable!"

Jill appearing somewhat nervous, said, "I call her the 'old woman.' She has no formal name."

"This is an oil, isn't it?"

"Yes," she replied, "it's an oil."

Eyeballing it, Clay estimated the size to be twenty-six by thirty-four inches. "Where did you find the model?"

"I took her from a magazine several years ago. The woman, obviously working with yarn on a spinning wheel, is likely of European Indian descent. I like to think the child sitting on her lap is her granddaughter."

"Magnificent! Show me more."

"Ok, give me a couple of minutes to get them out of our three closets. I also have several others in our house that my two sons and ex-husband now occupy."

"Your talents are much better than I expected. Your paintings' originality, rich colors, texture, brush strokes are right on. No bullshit Jill, your art jumps out at me. I need to spend some time thinking about where your talents are most beneficial. I will talk to a few people when I get back to Manhattan. No promises that I can help promote your talents, so please don't get your hopes up."

"One favor, please."

"Sure, what?"

"Don't get your friend, Taylor Lee, involved."

"No Taylor, I promise. But she does have several good contacts."

"Clay, No! I mean absolutely not."

After Jill's art preview ended, and while replacing her paintings in the closets, she began thinking about how much she loved Clay, and how those hours together made her world seem so dreamlike. With tears in her eyes, she wrapped her arms around him.

"Tomorrow night, you'll be gone; that blasted red-eye flight taking you from me." She looked into his eyes and said, "Last night, I told you no. This morning, I am more than ready to enjoy making love with you."

He gently lifted her into his arms, kissing her as he walked towards the bed they had shared last night. "I love and adore you," he whispered as he placed her gently on the edge of the bed.

Saying nothing more, they began removing their clothes. Clay was naked by the time she had removed her shoes, skirt, and blouse. Driven by an overwhelming desire, he stretched out on the bed, reached over, and pulled her down alongside him.

"Clay. I love you so very much..." She finished her sentence by uttering in a quiet voice, "I promise to make you so very happy!"

"Thank you for saying what you just said," he responded.

"Clay, I mean it."

He thought, "*I have heard several women say all types of things while making love, but this time I believe she really meant that promise.*"

Drawing her closer to him, he reached around her back, unfasten her lacy bra, tossing it aside. It was she who pushed her panties past her hips, down her legs, and onto the floor.

Naked, she now lay flat and appeared relaxed as she waited for his foreplay to begin. His kisses tenderly touched her lips as he teasingly started with a couple of light smooches, and increased the intensity of each kiss, and followed by hungrily brushing the intoxicating moisture of his tongue against her's.

Moving downward, he softly blew his warm breath into her ear, first the left, then the right. His kisses tenderly touched her neck, and from there, his tongue moved slowly and deliberately, skimming across the nipple of each breast until it was hard and ripe with arousal.

She made an erotic purring sound as her body relished the points of arousal as she succumbed to the artful foreplay of his tongue.

Sensing his primal instinct to thrust and crave the pulses of pleasure of being inside her, she nudged his body upward until he was lying on top. The two spent the remainder of the morning and well into the evening making love.

Chapter 40

Clay slept poorly on his final night at the apartment. But he was not uncomfortable; she was snuggled by his side. He would not allow himself to surrender to sleep as he was too busy replaying in his mind the last two days they had spent together.

He also reminisced about the first time he spotted her at MCRD, and not understanding why he was so convinced their paths had crossed somewhere in the past... but where remained a mystery.

He thought about their first date and dinner together and how he almost blew it by telling his lies, their nights together at the Hilton, and joking about surviving on those Hickory Farms snacks. So many pleasant memories of their time together, although brief, caused him to try visualizing when he first began to realize how much he cared for her.

"I am deeply in love with Jill, and even though I nearly destroyed our relationship by making a few dumb decisions, I can't imagine not having her in my life. Don't go there," Clay told himself, as he attempted to steer clear of the unpleasantries he had generated or encountered.

He knew that if he gave even the slightest thought to a single one, his pleasant memories would quickly turn into a restless nightmare. The hours were passing slowly as his mind kept battling to bring back those disturbing realities. "*I should just get up,*" he thought. He looked over and could see Jill was sleeping peacefully.

When she awoke, Clay was not in bed. Gathering her thoughts, "*Today is Sunday, the day Clay is to fly back to New York.*" Walking into the kitchen, she found him sitting at the kitchen table drinking a cup of instant coffee.

"Hey, you! You shouldn't be drinking that crap. Wendy only makes it when she's rushed and forgets to prepare the coffee maker the night before. Pour that out, and I'll fix you a real cup of coffee."

When he turned to face her, she saw his eyes were bloodshot. "*He's been crying.*"

"Good morning," he responded. "I couldn't sleep, so rather than disturb you, I decided to get up. And yes, I'll take you up on the coffee."

"Coming right up." As she was preparing the coffee maker, Clay stood, and while moving towards her, he said, "Well, what have you planned for today?"

"Let's go out for breakfast and then spend the day at Balboa Park. Have you been there?"

"No, I know nothing about it. Say, isn't it well known for the TV show, 'Zoo Parade' and a guy... I believe his name was Perkins, Marlin Perkins?"

"Sorry, Clay, but you are thinking about the Lincoln Park Zoo in Chicago. However, our park is also filled with all sorts of interesting things: a nice zoo, several cultural sites, including the Museum of Art, and a variety of modern international gardens.

Or, we could bring a blanket, something to drink and snack on, and just enjoy relaxing and being together."

As he reached to hug her, he heard her sigh deeply as she turned away. "What's wrong?"

"I'm okay," she said as she reached into the cabinet for a cup.

"You aren't acting okay."

"Clay, I'm sad. I can't help it. I don't want our perfect weekend to end."

"Neither do I, but I have to get back to New York. Just remember, Guy and I'll be back here shortly to work at MCRD."

"The coffee is ready; let's have a cup to cheer us up. Afterward, we'll shower, get dressed, and head out to breakfast. If it's OK with you, it looks like it's going to be a beautiful day, and since we are in no rush, we can walk to Marie Callender's, and come back for the car."

"Sounds like a plan."

After spending the day at Balboa Park, they returned to the apartment, and picked up Clay's piece of luggage. Seeing his carry-on bag brought a laugh from Jill as she again made fun of him carrying such a small bag on a three-day trip.

He replied, "You're just jealous; that's all."

Their next stop was San Diego International short-term parking lot. This time Jill was sure she wasn't going to miss seeing him off. In the lounge, the two kissed, hugged, and held hands. She stayed with him every minute until the final boarding call to New York's JFK Airport was announced.

As the attendant moved to close the walkway, only then did she move to the large window where she could see the plane as it was pushed back from the gate to take its taxiing position for takeoff. Once the aircraft was airborne, Jill turned to leave, dabbing tears from her glossed over eyes as she made her way out of the terminal.

"*He will be back in two or three weeks,*" she told herself.

♥ ♥

Chapter 41

While preparing to be seated in the first-class section of the plane, Clayton removed a pad of paper and a pen from his overnight bag before placing it in the overhead and closing the compartment door. Comfortably seated and alone in his row, Clayton, a discreet and undeclared pragmatist, began to jot down a few characteristics that he considered essential in making any successful relationship work.

Consciously retracing a variety of events connected with his past, he was resolved to not making the same mistakes he had made in prior relationships, including those associated with his two former wives and his live-in girlfriend.

With his list assembled, one by one, he focused on each of the three women and identified what he believed were their best and weakest traits, and each of those characteristics was carefully analyzed. The word 'beautiful' was troubling, and Clayton decided that, based upon his experiences, it would be more accurate for him to divide this characteristic into two separate categories;

'outer' and 'internal.'

Clayton had learned the need for this division because of his relationships with both Lorre and Taylor. As for external beauty, both women would score a five on his scale of one-to-five.

But on the internal beauty rating, he gave Lorre a four and Taylor a miserable two. At this point, he did not rate Jill on either. She would come later, once he was satisfied with the scale he was creating. However, he was discovering that the more in-depth he went in analyzing each of his three women's trait components, he subconsciously began to rate himself. "*Not good,*" he thought.

"*No wonder my track record sucks. Much of the blame for my failed romances can be placed directly at my feet. I don't know how to pick the right woman.*"

"Sir, can I get you anything?"

"No, thanks."

"We'll be serving breakfast in about a half-hour."

"I'll pass on that also. Otherwise, I won't be able to complete this important task while onboard."

Clayton, knowing full well that once he is off the plane and involved in the City's daily hustle and bustle activities, he will lose the quietness he needed to think clearly and possibly make a life altering decision. Once his list of a dozen personal relationship characteristics was completed in no particular order, it read:

- Beautiful/Classy
- Internally Beautiful
- Truthful/Honest/Loyal
- Commitment/Sexual Faithfulness
- Punctual/Dependable
- Good in Bed

- Common Sense /Smart
- Affectionate/Supportive
- Forgiving/Patient/Empathetic
- Independent/Confident
- Selfless/Non-Materialistic

After studying those characteristics he had chosen for the third time, he decided to add one other:

- In love with me.

After noticing his list had grown too long to manage at this time, he scratched out: ~~Maturity~~, ~~Openness~~, ~~Pleasant~~, ~~Generous~~, ~~Humility~~, and ~~Well Groomed~~.

Now comfortable with the list of attributes, one by one, he scrutinized those ratings he had assigned to each of his three ladies.

Once again, the efficient flight attendant smiled and said, "Are you sure I can't bring you something to eat or drink?"

"No, but thank you for asking."

Back to his project, Clayton knew he had approximately two hours before he would hear that 'prepare for landing' message spread throughout the cabin.

"I need to finish this thing and think about making a hard-and-fast decision. This time no bullshit. My brain, not my heart, is going to decide what is best for my future. Jill, oh Jill... I hope she will forgive me."

♥ ♥

Chapter 42

Jill made herself stay strong as she readied for work Monday morning. Clay was gone, although his familiar smell remained and brought back vivid memories of the spectacular weekend they had spent together. But for some reason, she couldn't stop having an insecure feeling about their relationship; she winced at the thought of it failing.

"Oh, Wendy, you're here. I didn't hear you come in last night," Jill said.

"Well, I guess that's because I didn't come in until after twelve, and I tried to be as quiet as a mouse," Wendy quipped.

"Well, I guess you are dying to tell me what you and James thought about Clay. Correct?"

"Yes, Mom, but do you want to talk about this right now... you have to leave for work shortly?"

"Okay, this evening when we get home. I'll also have a little something we can drink and munch on while we talk."

"It's a date, Mom. I'll be back here by seven o'clock."

Throughout the day, Jill's curiosity about what potential positives and negatives she will hear from Wendy drifted in and out of her mind. As Jill unlocked the apartment's door, she thought, *"I'm as ready as I'll ever be to hear her out."*

"Hi honey, I just beat you home by about ten minutes."

Showing a big smile, Jill looked at her daughter and said, "I didn't even have time to change into my evening attire; just kidding."

"Mom, if you don't care, I'd rather sit at the kitchen table if we are still going to have those snacks you mentioned. I hate to drop crumbs on the living room rug."

"That's fine with me, honey. The kitchen, it is." Jill's first move was to open the refrigerator. She took out a medium-size and partially opened tray of sausages and cheeses, followed by a full, unopened bottle of Chardonnay. "Please hand me the opener. It's on the counter behind you."

"Sure thing, Mom."

With the snack tray placed in the center of the table, Jill opened the wine and poured two glasses. "Okay, I am now ready to hear what you and James have to say about my relationship with Clay. And Wendy, please don't call it some fling."

Mom, get a grip! Have you already prejudged what I am going to say?"

Jill's eyes dropped ever so slightly as she fingered the stem of her glass. Somewhat embarrassed, she said, "No, but knowing both you and James, and that you already know about his history with those women, surely you can't expect me to think otherwise."

"Mom, think back to that evening when you first ask for my advice, what did I say?"

"Well, you hurt me because you refused to offer any advice

when I needed your help so much."

"But Mom, I distinctly remember what I said, "This is something you and Clay have to resolve yourselves.""

Jill nodded but didn't speak. She paused, thinking, and then said, "Okay, the guy's a double-timing cheater. You heard it firsthand when that woman, Taylor Lee, called from New York. A scorned lover if there ever was one."

"*Clay is an admitted liar and cheater. And that's one thing Mom was having difficulty in handling.*"

"Mom, sometimes it's not easy to forgive someone for the hurt they have cast upon us. Yet, being in love is crazy. Mom, you need to ask yourself and honestly answer these two questions: Do you really trust him? Do you love him?"

♥ ♥

Chapter 43

Walking east on 48th Street away from his parking lot, Clayton stopped at the corner of Fifth Avenue. Waiting for the light to change, he looked across the street into the glass-fronted lobby of his former office building, and thinking, "*What a great location to have found my first office there... on Fifth Avenue in the heart of Manhattan. And I am even more pleased now that we have moved to our prestigious new office at 277 Park Avenue.*"

Stepping off the elevator on the twentieth floor, Clayton mused, "*What a difference three days away from the office makes.*" A wave of guilt passed over him when he thought about the extra burden he had placed on Guy, who was trying to juggle and schedule business projects while Clayton focused on his personal affairs with the ladies.

"*But, I did get to accomplish two important things by being away from the office: My relationship with Jill is back on firm ground and I have a good idea of which direction I should go in picking a soulmate.*"

Clayton had reached his decision regarding his list. Even

though he fought hard not to give any edge to Jill, both his brain and his heart had declared her 'hands-down' the overall winner. *"This time, I have learned a tough lesson about both my actions and how to find the best woman. I am not about to let anything, or anyone, interfere with our love and happiness."*

Following close behind and as he was about to close the door, Guy called out, "Sorry I'm late. It took forever to get our coffees. The line was practically out the door."

Almost in unison, both Marsha and Clayton responded, "Thanks."

Clayton followed by saying, "I'm buying... how much?" "Four-fifty will cover it. And boy, do I have some good news for you!"

Taking the lid off of his coffee cup, Clayton looked up, and smiling said, "Let me guess. Taylor Lee got married and left town?"

"Dream on! No, it's business-related."

"Now that's what I like to hear."

"While you were traipsing around in San Diego on Friday, we received a desperation call from Earl Williams about that motion picture studio in Los Angeles. Well, they accepted and signed our fraud audit proposal, and are sending a signed copy along with a check for one-third payment by FedEx.

"Smythers wants us to come out ASAP. Since this involves our returning to Southern California, I called Colonel Cooperswaite and suggested he may want us to finish up during this trip. I told him that combining the two visits into one would result in good savings in airfare, rental car, and a couple of other incremental expenses for the Marine Corps. The colonel loved it. He also agreed to allow us flexibility in our work schedule."

"Great!... really great, Guy. The timing of this trip can help me with my personal life more than you know. Have you scheduled us?"

"I did tentatively. All I need is your okay, and I'll call Myrna and give her our itinerary. It's already worked out. All she has to deal with is the flight, rental car, and hotel reservations for San Diego. And the hotel will be the Hilton. In L.A., we will be staying in a company-owned apartment near the studio."

After hearing the news that Clayton is leaving on another long trip, Marsha said, "I know this is none of my business, but you must be spending megabucks on your room at the Plaza; you are rarely there."

"You are right. It is ridiculous, and I need to move out."

"Why not the house you still own in Rockville Centre," she said, "or the one up in Rhinebeck?"

"Too many bad memories in Rockville Centre. I need to put that damn jinxed house up for sale and settle up fair and square with Lorre. The house in Rhinebeck is my best alternative. Thanks for the advice."

Chapter 44

After three rings, Jill answered the phone, "Hello."

"Hello, beautiful."

"I thought it would be you, Clay. You always seem to call me at eight."

"Just like clock-work, and to be truthful, I plan it that way," he said, "I know you will be ready to leave for work in about twenty minutes."

"Clay, hold on, I want to turn the radio's volume up... listen."

"Hey, that's Neil Diamond."

"Right, and the song he is singing is *Hello Again*. Clay, let's make this our song."

"Why not, it's most appropriate for the two of us. But, Jill, aren't you curious about why I am calling this morning?"

"Yes, but you generally call around this time. So, for you to ask that question, I feel you have some good news." Clay wasted no time in telling her about the new project in L.A.

"Oh Clay, you'll be here for Mother's Day, won't you?"

"I hadn't thought about that." Looking at his desk calendar, he said, "Yes, we'll be out there for at least three or four weeks."

"Good, I want you to meet my two sons, and Mother's Day would work just fine."

"I have an idea; you have often mentioned that very nice restaurant on the water in La Jolla, The Marine Room."

"Yes, that's it."

"Please ask Wendy to call right away and make reservations for all six of us."

"But there's only five."

"Now, Jill, do you think I would leave James out? Caution her to call today while we are not under pressure. Mother's Day reservations come at a premium in most upscale restaurants."

"Believe me, she'll love making that call, so don't worry. Clay, I've got to go."

"So do I. I also have a lot to do this week, and I only have five days to get it done. Bye love!"

"Bye Clay."

Clayton reached into his closet, removed a large portfolio case, and within twenty minutes, he was walking through the front door of a five-story brick townhouse located near the corner of 72nd and York. This elegant old gilded-age building now served as one of the City's premier art galleries.

With an estimated one thousand-plus art galleries spread throughout Manhattan, The Bronx, Queens, Brooklyn, and Staten Island, he had chosen this one for two reasons: It was one of the ultimate art venues within the five borough catering to New York's elite. And, most importantly, he had developed a friendly relationship with its owner, Jules Edwards, while in the company of his former girlfriend, Taylor Lee.

Clayton was well aware that Jules was not only one of the best corporate art consultants in the country; he also had a following of numerous contacts throughout the art world. In Clayton's mind, if he was to help Jill with her art career, Jules had to be his best starting point.

Before Clayton had a chance to mention severing his relationship with Taylor, Jules said, "I ran into Taylor at a recent gallery party over on the West Side, and she told me about your breakup. Actually, I was surprised she didn't put you down. Clayton, she may still have the hots for you."

"It's over, Jules. Let's talk about my discovery of a promising West Coast artist."

While unzipping his leather portfolio, he said, "I have a few examples I would appreciate you taking a look at," as he removed four color pencil sketches and four finished pieces of art; watercolor, acrylic, and oil.

Without hesitation or asking permission, Clayton meticulously spread the pieces across the large uncluttered antique oak table, likely used for such purposes.

Jules massaged the back of his neck as he moved from one print to the other. "First, let me say, overall, her artwork is powerful and thought-provoking. I see the talent, and I particularly like her composition and color values. However, these samples are lacking the depth and interest I would expect to find in the work of an accomplished artist."

"I told you she's not an accomplished artist... at least, not at this time. She's never had any formal training. Over the last twenty-plus years, she's been a housewife and raised three children."

Jules changed the subject by saying, "Clayton, I know you well enough that I bet I can describe your newly discovered artist. She is beautiful, a blond or brunette—but come to think about it... Taylor is a redhead—so I better add the possibility she may be a redhead. She's more on the thin side, and a classy dresser. How's that?"

"Not bad, but back to her artistic talents. Jules, I am not kidding you. She showed me an oil that she did years ago that would blow your mind. She has talent. She just needs a break."

"Look, I can't go out on a limb for an unknown. But I am going to help by introducing you to a real player in the corporate art world. This fellow is the Executive Vice President of the Association of United States Retail Merchants; his name is William Gordon Sr."

Clayton said, "I have heard of AUSRM and know it is huge and that it offers all sorts of services and supplies to a wide variety of North American wholesale and retail companies."

"As I said, I can get you in the door, but from there, Clayton, you and your artist friend are on your own. William Gordon is a hard-nosed and demanding New York businessman. So, when you meet with him, you better have something he will be interested in, or he will kick you in the ass and send you on your way. So, where is your lady artist now?"

"She is living in California. But don't think that is a handicap. I'll have her back here within four to six months; I promise."

"Sounds good. I hope you can pull something great out of the hat when you meet with Gordon. Remember, you will have only one shot with him, so make your presentation a showstopper. Just call me when you are ready to meet with him. Oh, by the way, his son is one of the nation's premier news broadcasters."

"I thought I had heard that name before... so, he is Junior?"

"Right, he's junior in every sense of the word."

"Jules, the next time you and Taylor cross paths, I would appreciate you not mentioning me telling you about my visit. She has already attempted to destroy this relationship once. And, she almost succeeded."

"Clayton, there's truth in that old saying by the English playwright, William Congreve, '*Hell has no fury like a woman scorned.*'"

Chapter 45

"Clayton, pick up line two, a Mr. Sawyer. He said he's returning your call from last night."

"Thanks, Marsha." Clayton pressed the line two button,

"Hello Mr. Sawyer. I wanted to update you about our house on Miller Place. You may remember me. I talked with you last December about possibly selling that house."

"Yes, sir, I remember. How is your wife doing?"

"She's okay, but now lives out of state, and we have jointly agreed to put the house up for sale immediately."

"Okay, but I'll need to have an official listing form completed and signed, preferably by both of you since you are both listed on the title as co-owners."

"This could be a slight problem. As I mentioned, she is now living out of state, but I have her authorization to carry out such business transactions. I am leaving New York on Friday and will be away for several weeks. So, what can I do to get this ball rolling... my next step?"

"We need to determine a listing price, and you can sign the listing form and inventory sheet."

"Fine, can we get together at the house this afternoon?"

"Yes, you name the time. Also, I'll pull your file, and it should contain much of what I need. I'll start on it right away."

"Let's meet at the house at six-thirty. It is vacant, so we'll have no problem."

"See you then, Mr. Clarkson."

"Marsha, I'm sure you overheard some of that conversation. Well, I am taking your advice. That was a Realtor from Long Island; I am going to start focusing on putting my life back together. I will put that house up for sale this evening. On Wednesday, I'll check out of the Plaza and move my small load of belongings to my house in Rhinebeck."

"I remember you telling me that house is ninety miles from midtown, she said, "Are you going to have Arthur chauffeur you back and forth?"

"Heavens, no! I can either take the train or drive down the Taconic Parkway. The train takes slightly over an hour and the drive down an hour and a half, at most. When I lived on the Island, it took me an hour and a quarter to drive twenty-six miles; mostly stop and go traffic all the way on the Southern State. As for hassles, parking the car on a day-by-day basis will be my biggest one. And, hopefully, I will have that covered before I leave town."

"How are you going to do that?"

"I was always good to the attendants at the parking garage where I used to live; I hope they will take care of my car daily when I drive in and store it long-term while I am traveling. Besides, they and Arthur also have a good relationship. Nothing different required for them to do. I will continue to pay the daily going rates, and it doesn't matter that I no longer live there."

"That's where Taylor Lee lives?"

"Correct, but she will never notice the car. The garage's entry and exit are in the back. Besides, the garage elevator requires all residents using the garage to have a special key. And, she doesn't have one, but I still have mine. So, if I needed to use the main lobby entrance, I'm all set. Tomorrow, I'll deal with this situation and tell Arthur about the changes."

Chapter 46

Jill was seated at the relatively small kitchen table, sipping a cup of green tea when she heard the front door of the apartment open and close. Simultaneously, Wendy called out, "Mom, where are you?"

"In the kitchen, I'm having a cup of tea. Please join me."

"Okay, Mom, don't mind if I do... I have good news!"

Preparing a cup for Wendy, Jill surmised her daughter's good news was that she got the booking at the Marine Room. "You were able to get the reservations?"

"Yes, I did. We are set for 2 p.m., and I talked to Joe and Tony; they will go together, and James and I will also. Would you and Clay like to ride with us?"

"I think not, honey. I will spend the night at the Hilton, and we will leave from there. His associate will likely use their car, so I plan to drive the two of us.

"Oh, Wendy, thanks so much for calling the boys. That's one less thing I have to take care of."

After taking a sip of tea, Wendy said, "Mom, you look a little pale, are you feeling okay?"

"Honey, I'm good, just tired from spending most of the afternoon doing inventory counts between helping and applying makeup to customers."

"You need to rest."

"That's what I am going to do. But first, I need to run over to the house and pick up a couple of my smaller paintings, and then I need to get ready for the weekend."

"Your paintings? I thought you would have already shown the ones you have here to Clay."

"I already did."

"Well, Mom, what did he say when he saw the 'old lady?'" Jill smiled and started to speak. "Wait, Mom... I bet I can tell you what he said. If he didn't say he was awestruck, I bet he said something very similar. Am I correct?"

"Close, my dear, close."

"Mom, that smile and look in your eyes tells me you are up to something devious."

Jill grinned and shrugged. "*Jesus,*" she thought, "*Wendy really can read my mind.*"

♥ ♥

Chapter 47

S tanding inside the airport Terminal 2 baggage claim area, Jill was closely watching the flight monitor for the touchdown of DL 961 from JFK. Nervously, she kept looking at her watch for what felt like the umpteenth time. Finally, the monitor's screen began flashing, 'Landed. Arrival time: 2251'.

Muttering to herself, *"Damn those airport screens for not simply reading 10:51 p.m. Just because I work on a military base doesn't mean I understand those stupid military hours."*

A flutter of butterflies appeared to be wreaking havoc inside of her empty stomach. "I knew I should have eaten something, even if it was only a quick burger at a Jack In The Box. Oh well, Clay usually complains about those airline meals, so maybe we'll still get something before going to the hotel."

Finally, he appeared at the top of the down escalator. Immediately upon seeing him, Jill, in an almost run, arrived at the escalator's bottom. As excited as she was, he was equally so, if not more. He felt a sensation he never knew existed. Once in each other's arms and hugging and kissing, it took them a minute or so before they realized they were rudely blocking several hurried passengers on their way to retrieve their luggage.

Clay spoke up, "Sorry, we are so sorry."

One of the male passengers looked towards him and remarked, "You are acting like one of those military guys just out of boot camp."

Clay smiled, winked, and responded, "*Semper Fi.*" The man gave a casual, half-hearted salute, smiled, and went on his way.

Jill, looking puzzled, said, "What was that about?"

"The guy was implying that I was acting like a horny serviceman wanting to have sex."

She answered, "Well..."

They both laughed. "Your comeback, *Semper Fi.* I have heard Marines say that, but never gave thought to what it means."

"*Semper Fi* is the Marine Corps motto. It means *Always Faithful.*"

"Were you a Marine?"

"Not really, however, I did spend four years in the Marine Corps Reserve. I was not a good military candidate. I hated taking orders, especially from people I thought were dumber than me."

Again laughing, the two hugged and kissed. He went to the carousel and removed the last piece of luggage that had been circling and circling. Everyone else with their bags in hand had left the area.

"Only one bag?" she asked, "I thought you said you would be working between L.A. and here for up to six weeks?"

"I did. Guy is flying into L.A. on Sunday afternoon with our bags in tow. I don't have to be up there until late Sunday evening."

"Hooray! My car is in the short-term area, so let's go. Also, Clay, I have a confession to make."

"Confession?" he asked, "What kind of confession?"

"Well, I am hungry as heck. I missed lunch."

"I did eat on the plane, and the meal wasn't bad. But no sweat, my lovely lady. We'll stop and get you something."

"Clay, if you haven't sensed it by now, then I'll tell you I am an incurable romantic. Think about it: Our Neil Diamond 'Hello Again" song, Hilton lounge and our favorite table, and our Chardonnay wine and Hickory Farms snacks in your room."

"So, what are you telling me... as if I didn't know? Our next stop is that mini-mart near the hotel... right?"

Walking up to the Hilton reception desk, both Clay and Jill had their arms full carrying two overnight bags, a reinforced bag containing four bottles of wine, and another bag containing a large Hickory Farms gift box filled with sausages, cheeses, crackers, and a few miscellaneous treats.

The clerk took Clayton's information and confirmed that his registration had him staying in room 415.

"Oh Clay, that was sweet. Perhaps I am not the only romantic."

"Guess not, but I couldn't resist. After all, Guy and I are becoming regular customers here, and we are entitled to certain privileges." Turning to face the desk clerk, Clay said, "My man, could we trouble you for three dinner size plates, two knives and forks, a few napkins, and ..."

Jill quickly interrupted, "Not the bottle opener; I have it in my bag."

"Over at the breakfast bar, sir, help yourself," the clerk pointed and said. "Also, if I may suggest, use the rolling rack sitting just inside the lobby door to carry your things. No one is available to help."

"Thank you very much," Clay responded, "Next stop, room 415."

Chapter 48

Once inside the room after retrieving a container of ice, Clay said, "First, let's have a glass of wine and some snacks to help satisfy your hunger, and afterward..." projecting a big smile, he continued, "I'll shower... not that I need to after all that travel."

"Okay with me. You go first, and I'll follow. It will take me a little longer."

Both found the wine and snacks tasty, refreshing, and relaxing. Clay, after his third sip of wine, placed his glass on the table, and Jill did the same. He leaned over and, using both hands, took her in a tender embrace, and while hugging and kissing Jill, he whispered, "I love you more than I've ever loved anyone in my life." The tender and loving ways Clay held her reassured Jill that his warm hugs were as meaningful as those physical intimacy moments they would be sharing before the night was over.

With his shower and bedtime preparations completed, Clay poured another two glasses of wine and placed them on the bedside table. Now wearing only a bath towel wrapped neatly around his midsection, he anxiously waited for Jill to step from the bathroom.

Sitting there and slowly sipping his wine, Clay remembered what it was like when he first joined Jill in bed. To admire her beauty and feel the heat of her body as they made love in ways that reminded him of his teenage years. He closed his eyes briefly, trying to recapture those moments of bliss, as his groin stirred. His urge was nearly overpowering, as Jill stepped from the bathroom, also clad in a large towel covering everything sensuous. Jill picked up her glass of wine and took a swallow and returned it to the table. *"It seems wonderful to be here with Clay; everything feels so right."*

Now seated on the side of the bed alongside Clay, she leaned in, and as they kissed, she gently loosened his towel, causing it to slide inconspicuously onto the bed. Their kisses and hugs continued as he followed her lead and gently pushed her back into a horizontal position. His groin now agonizing, felt like it could explode. She could feel the tension growing in him as he positioned himself on top of her. She affectionately pushed him back just enough to watch the way his eyes searched for hers. Both were looking at each other, seeking the correct words, but none came to mind.

Their dance of love grew heavier; she pulled him closer and brushed her lips lightly across his. With the raw desire she was sparking, Clay's dreams of those earlier moments of bliss faded rapidly. On fire, he answered with a passionately hot and demanding kiss that exploded her senses. Unhurried, more emotional than passionate, the sensual touching and teasing of his tongue ignited a rush of heat within her.

Tonight, the two were destined to revel in irresistible intimacy and enjoyment of their love for each other.

Chapter 49

When Jill awoke on Saturday morning, Clay, propped in an upright position by using two pillows resting against the headboard, greeted her with a broad smile and said, "Happy day before Mother's Day, my love."

"Thank you, honey. I like it when you call me... your love."

"Well, you are my only true love."

Trying and failing to keep her breasts covered with the sheet, Jill leaned over and kissed Clay.

He responded with a hug and kisses and said, "By the way, what's on our agenda for today?"

"I don't think I want another snack of cheese, sausage, crackers, and wine this morning. They are our nighttime and hanky-panky eats," Jill said, playfully teasing.

"Neither do I. Let's shower, get dressed, and go out."

"That's fine with me. Also, it will give housekeeping time to clean the room."

By noon they were in Jill's car and headed a short distance up the coast to a quaint family-operated restaurant situated directly on the beach. "Wondering why I would pick this drive?" she asked.

"Yes, I am curious." "I wanted you to see the beauty of the areas outside of touristy San Diego and Coronado; there's no better time than today. This drive always reminds me of an artist's color palette. It's a wildflower paradise."

"Jill, as you likely suspect, with me coming from New York City, I know very little about flowers unless they are the kind found in florist shops such as roses, daffodils, tulips, and similar types. But... hey, I am willing to learn. After all, as a kid, I spent a lot of time on my grandfather's farm. Wildflowers were everywhere. I just never paid attention."

"With your knowledge of artists and art galleries, it's difficult for me to understand your lack of appreciation as to what nature has to offer."

"Thanks, lady, that comment"... Clay said, laughing, "really hurts."

Momentarily she took her eyes off the road as she looked at him and said, "Oh, cut the crap. But seriously, I did expect you to have a greater appreciation for nature's beauty."

"Only your beauty... my dear."

"Look over there, see those beautiful blooms; no use in naming them, you won't remember. So, feast your eyes on the mosaic of color, many changes take place daily. If I can get you to become an enthusiast on this trip, I promise to take you to a few backcountry roads on the way up to Julian."

Clay mused, "I believe," pointing, "that beautiful ocean and those sand dunes are more my style."

Jill turning the car into the crowded parking lot, said, "We have arrived. I hope you are as hungry as I am?"

"You better believe it." As they left the car and stepped onto the pilings supporting the restaurant, Clay thought, "What an appropriate name for this place... Beach House."

As they were finishing brunch, Clay got a serious look on his face as he said, "Jill, we need to talk about tomorrow."

"Nervous?" she asked.

"Yes, aren't you? Your two sons don't have any inkling about me, right?"

"No, they don't unless Wendy or James spilled the beans."

Clay responded, "That's not what is bothering me. Jill, I am about to drop a bombshell on you."

"Oh, God, Clay... why do you torture me? I am out of here. I'll wait for you in the car."

Surprised at Jill's reaction, Clay jumped up from his chair and followed, saying, "But Jill..."

The waiter in close pursuit and speaking in a delicate tone said, "Sir, you can't leave until you pay your bill."

"Okay, sorry, I am not trying to leave without paying. Something upset my girlfriend, and I don't know what the hell I did."

The waiter replied, "Women, go figure." Clay looked at the tab and threw down two twenty-dollar bills. He turned and said, "That should more than take care of what I owe. You keep what's left." Out the door he went, stumbling as he nearly missed a step on the pier walkway.

♥ ♥

Chapter 50

"Jill, what happened... why are you so upset?"

"Why, why am I upset? You've got to be joking. First, we are spending a really nice morning together, and then you tell me your bomb is going to destroy our relationship."

"Oh, Jill, that's nothing of the kind! Surely you know that I am madly in love with you; I could never hurt you in any way. My words, that's it—it was that word 'bombshell,' wasn't it? Please calm down and let me explain."

She stopped and said, "Okay, I'm listening."

"First, I must ask, do you love me?"

"Yes, you know I do, and haven't I proved it in every conceivable way, including in bed?"

"Yes, without question. I also thought I had proven my love for you."

"Well, yes. At least I thought so."

"Jill, what I was trying to get across was that I know you love your kids very much and that you also enjoy your job and lifestyle here in San Diego. Even though my words were poorly chosen, the point is that I want and need for you to move to New York, hopefully by the end of August."

"Oh, Clay, are you serious?"

"Yes, I am damn serious. What I hadn't told you was that while back in the City, I spent some time trying to identify one or two job opportunities that will complement your artistic talents. One of my contacts is prepared to help us get our foot in the door with the executive vice president of a major organization. This opportunity could pan out for the two of us."

"Are you implying we would be working together?"

"Yes, under the Clarkson umbrella. I see much more talent in you than just your sketching and painting abilities. I have watched and listened to you carefully. You have a variety of business-related skills that I find most impressive—inventory control, accounting, and a proven salesperson. You also have what I like to call that 'fire in the belly' drive to be a winner."

With a big smile and joking, he said, "I also give you high marks on your positive attitude, except for those few times you flew off the handle and showed your distrust of me."

"Yes, but you brought it on yourself. I trusted you, and then I caught you in not one, not two, but in at least three lies about your personal life."

Clay looked into her eyes and replied, "Touché."

With that, Jill smiled and appeared to be warming up and forgiving, and she said, "Clay, I apologize for letting my mind think the worst. I couldn't stand not having you around. I love you more than I have ever loved any man in my life; this is frightening."

"Look, Jill, I am a good judge of people, and we have the

synergy to make positive things happen, whether it's in our personal or business life; mark my word. As for your salary, I'll start your pay at triple your current salary. So, will you join me in New York?"

"Let me digest what you just said. I will give you an answer no later than tomorrow morning."

♥ ♥

♥ ♥

Chapter 51

On the drive back, Jill was more silent than usual with Clay. He also remained quiet and closed his eyes while thinking that she was likely evaluating his offer. He was correct... she was doing just that.

"Hmmm, I love Clay very much, and if I don't go back with him, I know that our relationship will collapse. So, what do I have to lose? Other than being away from my kids, not much. I know Wendy and James will be moving up to LA once they marry in July. He has a job lined up, and I know they have already started apartment shopping. Who knows what the boys will do after college. If I try living with Clay and it doesn't work out, I haven't lost much. I can always return to San Diego and get a job here."

Suddenly, Jill saw the 'rest area one mile ahead' sign and moved into the right lane. In nothing flat, she pulled into one of the numerous available spaces and came to a stop.

Waking up from a light nap, Clay suddenly looked up and said, "What's wrong!"

"Nothing, but I've made a decision that will affect the rest of our lives. Not giving Clay time to digest what he heard, she said, "Tomorrow, we are going to tell the kids that I am moving to New York to live with you. Now, Clay, that's what I call… dropping a bombshell."

Clay suddenly jumped out of the passenger door, ran around to the driver's side, opened her door, reached in, took Jill by the hand, and gently pulled her out. They kissed and hugged as tears trickled down each of their cheeks. Startled eyewitnesses looked on; the couple parked alongside clapped, not knowing for what. Those in the other four or five cars waved, and the drivers' beeped their horns as they passed alongside.

"You'll never regret this decision, Jill," Clay happily announced. During the drive back to San Diego, for some unknown reason, he was able to see the beautiful medley of colors of those sprawling wildflowers along the road.

After a day spent eating, sightseeing in Balboa Park garden, visiting a variety of cultural exhibits, and winding up the day by talking about finding a decent place to eat again, Jill said, "I want to take you to the type of restaurant you will never find in Manhattan or one of those trendy tourist places in other cities. Today, I feel daring, and we are going to *Las Cuatro Milpas,* a small, fun, and authentic Mexican place operated by a third-generation family in the Barrio Logan area.

It's not in one of the safest places in San Diego, but the food and its low prices are great. Besides, have you ever seen a Mexican place that does not serve margaritas, beer, or wine?"

"Never, not even in my wildest dreams," he responded.

"Well, get ready for your first sighting."

"I'm ready."

"Clay, do you like real tacos, not the Taco Bell kind... real Mexican tacos?"

"I don't know, but I doubt if I have ever had any tacos outside of a tourist area."

"Whatever they serve is very good, that is if you like hot spicy things."

"Jill, you know I love hot... and spicy things."

"Okay, watch your thinking buster; keep it clean."

Clay mused, "I promise."

"Here we are, and not a parking place in sight." Suddenly, Clay pointing, says, "Over there. Follow that guy carrying the large bag."

She responded, "I see him, and I'll make sure no one cuts me off."

Once parked and inside, the two joined the fast-moving line. It was at this point Clay learned this place had no menus.

Jill said, "You order off the menu sign," pointing up, "the one over the counter. Not much seating room, either."

"Jill, let's order takeout and go to the room. There we can have our wine and celebrate your anticipated move to New York."

"Good idea, since you don't mind spicy foods, let me order for the two of us. Oh yes, they only take cash; no credit cards or checks. The food here is cheap, so we should be able to come up with the cash."

"Very funny, I'll take care of it."

"Don't pull out a hundred or fifty-dollar bill. If you do, we might get mugged before we make it to the car."

"I love it. Just like a few spots up in the Bronx."

"If it's okay with you, here's what I'll order: four tacos, an order of *chorizo,* and an order of rice and beans."

"Sounds good to me." Within a couple of minutes after Jill placed the order, it was ready. Clay handed the cashier a twenty-dollar bill, and she gave him both a large bag of food and his change.

Back at the hotel, after the two had consumed their food, Clay reached over and took Jill in his arms, chuckled, and said, "Now this is living—a beautiful woman, a full stomach, and a couple glasses of wine. What more could a man ask?"

Once in bed, they talked about their dreams and marveled over their thoughts and feelings that had led to this moment. They made love, and as Clay had previously done, he embraced her tenderly, letting her know that their physical lovemaking was secondary to his true passion for her.

Both spoke briefly about the importance of tomorrow, Mother's Day.

Jill's last thought as she closed her eyes, *"Oh God, I pray that what we are doing is the right thing and that all three kids will understand and accept my decision."*

The two, cuddling together, went to sleep.

♥ ♥

Chapter 52

"Mothers Day," the first thought to enter Jill's mind as she opened her eyes. "*I wonder if I should be concerned about how the kids will react when we break the news about me leaving San Diego?*" Jill answered herself by muttering, "*I met and fell in love with a stranger in less than one week. If I don't go away with him, I may never find true love again.*"

Upon seeing her awake, Clay, without saying a word, snuggled closer as he raised her hand to his lips and kissed her fingers before returning it to its normal position. He whispered her name and professed his love. She moved as close to him as humanly possible, feeling the softness of her body intermingling with the ruggedness of his. They kissed for a long time, and she felt the touch of his tongue against hers.

He slowly moved to kiss her cheek and neck, his hot tongue lightly brushing her skin as it tenderly worked its way down to her navel and beyond. Her heart fluttered as her body trembled with sensations. They made love slowly. Afterward, Clay lifted his head and kissed her, and as to what was becoming a ritual, he whispered in her ear, saying how much he adored her. Jill took pleasure in knowing she was a well-loved woman.

"We don't have all morning to spend in bed," she said.

"Oh, how right you are. But while we are not in a rush, let's go downstairs, have coffee and sample that buffet breakfast before it closes,"

"Good," she said, "We can get dressed afterward."

After two cups of fresh coffee, and a so-so meal consisting of scrambled eggs, slightly over-crisp bacon, hash browns, and French toast, the two returned to their room just as the housekeeper was leaving.

"Mind if I use the bathroom first?"

"Just don't take too long."

"Ah, Jill, you know it doesn't take guys long; we just do the three 'S's.' I'll be out before you can pick out the clothes you are wearing." True to his promise, it appeared as if Clay was in and out before Jill had laid her wardrobe on the bed.

"Your turn."

Wearing only her panties and bra, she placed the outerwear she had worn to breakfast on hangers and hung them in the closet. As she entered the bathroom, she turned to Clay and said, "Don't worry, taking a shower is nothing. It's putting on all the makeup, fixing my hair, and getting dressed are what takes so long."

Leaving the bathroom in Jill's care, Clay turned on the TV and seconds later, turned it off. He then walked over towards the window, moving the floor lamp and maroon drapes aside, he gazed outside. There in the parking lot below sat Jill's 1979 orange Datsun. Somewhat surprised, he realized his room was directly above the front entrance. This mundane discovery meant nothing to him since he hadn't opened the curtains since they had checked in.

Now squinting from the bright sunlight that was flooding the room, he quickly closed the drapes. *"What the hell is wrong with me, and why am I so fidgety... could it be her kids? There will always be doubters when it comes to our quick romance, and I suspect her kids may be at the top of the nonbelievers' list. I've got to convince them that, while I can't guarantee we two will have a happy and successful life together, their Mom should not be put into the tormenting position of trying to answer the* "What if I'd followed my heart" *question, and that she could likely carry that doubt to her grave without ever really knowing the answer."*

His attention shifted when the water in the shower shut off with a thud noise likely coming from the water pipe or faucet. After what seemed like several minutes, the bathroom door opened, and Jill stepped into the bedroom wearing only a large, white towel wrapped around her body.

"I'm not finished," she said, "I need for the steam to leave the mirror, so I can make myself presentable."

"Presentable? The correct word is beautiful."

"Okay, okay, whatever. I still need another five minutes once the steam clears. My hair, you know."

She later used the blow-dryer, and when finished, she was pleased with the result.

Chapter 53

Once dressed and standing in front of the closet mirror, Jill looked herself over once more. Clay, wearing an open collar Brooks Brothers light blue button-down shirt, navy pants, and Allen Edmonds black dress shoes, said, "Let's have a glass of wine before we leave."

She answered, "Sounds good to me." With that, he poured two glasses and handed one to her. "A toast for luck and a very Happy Mother's Day to you," Clay held his glass out, and Jill touched her glass to his.

"Do you know how to get there?"

"Of course, silly, I have been there three or four times." What Clay didn't know was that she deliberately did not mention that blind date fiasco that Wendy tried to fix her up with a short while ago.

Smiling, Clay said, "Just checking. I didn't want us to get lost."

Ignoring his comment, Jill continued, "It's an excellent five-star restaurant, and very famous. It has earned numerous culinary awards. You'll like this. It is also known as the most romantic restaurant in the San Diego area."

"Now, Jill, do you think we need a romantic restaurant to get us in the mood?"

Once again, disregarding what he had implied, she said, "It has three amazing views, the ocean, cove, and sunset for dining. I told Wendy to request a table with an ocean view."

"That's fine. Whatever Momma wants," he said teasingly.

"It will take us an hour or a little less to get there," and jokingly, she smiled, saying, "Don't forget your credit card; you'll need it!"

"Got it in my wallet... gee, what if my card limit won't cover the check?"

She gave him a friendly smirk and said, "We don't want to be the first to arrive, so I'll drive you along the beach before we pull in."

On the drive over, Jill began to reveal that she was apprehensive about leaving the kids she loved so dearly. "I hope they will understand and not feel that I am abandoning them." Tears filled her eyes.

"Oh Clay, we must do whatever we can to ensure that they are not left with the impression that you are luring me away. They have been through a lot of anguish brought on by both the divorce and me moving out of the house."

"It had to have been a real shock when your boys, although they are nearly grown, suddenly discovered the one parent they could always depend on to fix their meals, do their laundry, and listen to their problems and help them work out reasonable solutions was leaving."

"Yes, and it also broke my heart, and now I am getting

ready to tell them that I am going to move across the country... Oh, Clay!"

Anxiously talking while she was driving, Clay noticed in addition to tears trickling down her cheeks, Jill had a stranglehold on the steering wheel, and her white knuckles were also a sign of nervousness.

"Jill, from everything I have heard about your ex, he's a good guy, and certainly not someone who would intentionally abuse his kids. You've got to calm down. Your kids are young adults, and I would be surprised if they didn't understand and support your decision. You know you have Wendy in your corner, and I would be shocked if she and your two boys haven't talked. You are likely worrying needlessly about something that is not a problem."

"Clay, I know, but this is such an important life-altering decision for all of us."

"Jill, don't worry; trust me. We'll all be fine."

"I wish I could... I've been working darn hard at it," she confessed.

Chapter 54

After a slow drive past the famous Torrey Pines Golf Club, and down La Jolla Shores, Jill drove past the luxurious La Jolla Beach & Tennis Club and turned into the valet parking area of the Marine Room.

Once inside the restaurant, the first noticeable thing was the magnificent ocean view. As they approached the reception desk, the *maître d* informed them that the rest of their party was already seated in the dining room with an ocean view.

He excitedly said, "You will be in for a real treat in forty-five minutes; that's the time of high tide." Once they neared the table, the *maître d* also wished Jill a Happy Mother's Day. Those at the table rose once Mom arrived, and each, including James, gave her a big hug. Since this was the first meeting between Tony and Joe, and Clay, Jill handled the introductions before being seated by the waiter. Wendy and James also warmly said hello again to Clay.

Once Jill was seated, her three children and James wished her a Happy Mother's Day, and one by one each again gave her a big hug. Once the drink orders arrived, things loosened up, and conversations flowed more freely. It was Mother's Day, and Jill's kids were hell-bent on making sure she had a fantastic day. No one, including Wendy, had the slightest inkling of the bombshell their Mom and Clay would deliver before they left the restaurant.

Tony and Joe had pre-planned their tribute by obviously taking words from either a greeting card or poem. The two had chosen to alternate by reading one verse to their Mom. Tony led off, and Joe followed. Mom was upbeat, smiling, and occasionally saying, "That's so sweet, thank you."

Everything was going great, that was until Tony asked both Wendy and Joe to also stand during his reading in honor of Mom. He commenced to read the ending verse, "We'll never outgrow our need for your smile, your hugs, and your warmhearted ways, we will always need you, always love you, and always be grateful for the wonderful woman you are... our mother."

That verse cut deep into Jill's heart. Suddenly she began having difficulty breathing and trying to catch her breath. Clay immediately sensed what was happening and tried to change the subject to something more pleasant. Too late! Jill broke out crying like the kids hadn't seen since the death of their dog, Mickey. She tried to speak, but the words stuck in her throat.

Confusion engulfed the table; how could such a heartwarming verse inflict such torment on their loving mother? James was overheard whispering to Wendy, "Something is wrong here."

Clay stepped in and attempted to intercede, but since Tony had already finished reading that tearjerking verse, the apparent stalling was rapidly reaching an abrupt end. It was now time for everyone to hear their plans for the future.

Clay mused to himself, "*Oh Lord, please give Jill and me the support we need to get through the remainder of this day.*"

Chapter 55

Suddenly, as if out of some ocean adventure movie, a huge wave struck the heavily fortified glass window startling those diners seated closest. Joe spoke up and said, "Neat, really neat. When we were being seated, the waiter told us this would happen; the high tide causes it. He also said we have a great table to view this reoccurring phenomenon."

Clay was thinking, "*This was a miracle if there ever was one. Perhaps God did hear me.*" Jill's focus had moved away from the hurt of leaving her kids. She had stopped her crying outburst and joined the others in talking about what just happened. Things returned to normal, at least long enough for everyone to order their meal and another drink.

As the meal portion of their celebration wound down, Clay thought to himself, "*One down and now comes the hardest part.*" Jill, now totally calm, tapped her knife against a glass. Part of her was wishing she and Clay hadn't come. As she looked into the joyful eyes of each of her three kids, Wendy, Tony, and Joe, pleasant memories of their childhoods flooded her mind.

"Besides those mundane things such as attending PTA meetings, volunteering for school field trips, and a batch of other demanding duties that goes along with good parenting," She smiled, *"I'll never forget the fun times of watching my kids grow up.*

"Sitting through hours of Wendy's field hockey practices and games, Tony's baseball games and watching him tinker with cars, and of all things having to keep Joe away from hanging out at the local Radio Shack. His insatiable desire for learning as much about electronics was almost mind-boggling."

She almost laughed out loud when thinking about, *"the time Tony came home with the dissembled parts of an entire car engine in the trunk of his sister's car, and Joe, for his fascination with a simple flashlight."*

Clay asked, "Jill, are you okay? From that smile on your face, you seemed to be having a pleasant daydream."

For a long moment, she stared into Clay's eyes and smiled before replying. "Yes, I was daydreaming. I was thinking about several fond memories I had with the kids when they were youngsters and teenagers.

"Oh, Clay, I love them soooo much! When I lived at the house, I always got a kick out of things my friends would say once they found out they were all in their middle to late teens. Comments like, 'Well, they don't demand much of your time now that they are nearly grown.' I would always reply, No, not really. As long as I'm up two hours before I leave for work and don't go to bed before eleven or twelve, it's not bad." Clay chuckled, recognizing Jill was starting to relax.

Suddenly she looked up, remembering to tap that glass again

to get attention. That she had now accomplished, and everyone was waiting to hear from her. She reached over and took Clay's hand in hers, gave him a loving smile as she looked directly into his hazel green eyes.

Wendy touched James on his arm and said, "Oh, boy! I know what Mom is getting ready to say."

A moment later, Jill commenced talking about how she and Clay first met and the growth of their relationship. She waded through some of the challenges facing them, and how their love for one another had developed.

Tony, with a glass of root beer in one hand, spoke up, "Mom, you couldn't have known Clay long. How do we know he is right for you?"

Jill didn't respond to that question but followed by saying, "I'm not here asking for anyone's approval. I'm here to tell each of you that I love you dearly, and since you are grown up, I now must make a life of my own... and that's why I am moving to New York in August to live with Clay."

Wendy spoke next, "Mom, you've got fantastic instincts about life in general. As the oldest, I am speaking for the three of us. Mom, we also love you dearly, and while I know little about Clay, James and I have watched him around you whenever we had a chance. We sincerely believe he loves you and will make you happy."

"Thanks, honey."

Wendy continued, "Mom, I don't want you to go to New York, but I do understand why it's important for you to go."

"Well, I think it's now my turn to speak," With a pause as if to gather his thoughts, Clay addressed Tony's question, "Tony, you are correct, your Mom and I haven't known each other long.

Will our relationship last? I hope so, but it would be impossible to give you my assurance that it will never falter. Therefore, you must listen closely to what I am going to say. First, Wendy said your Mom has... the term I believe she used was 'fantastic instincts'... this is one of the greatest survival tools any individual can have.

"Secondly, your Mom is an exceptionally talented artist. I have already met with the owner of one of New York's most prominent art galleries. He is an expert in corporate art. I showed him a few of her sketches and asked him to tell me what he thought. Bottom line, he was impressed enough that he agreed to help us connect with a major organization as soon as we can get back to Manhattan. We tentatively are going to meet with his contact in July. That means your Mom will fly to New York and spend three or four days there.

"I know she has the talent; she needs a break. And, I intend to see that she gets that well-deserved opportunity."

Jill was glowing with pride as Clay continued to speak, "Wendy, Tony, Joe, and you also James, I love your mother more than I have ever loved any woman. And yes, I have made more than my share of mistakes, and your Mom knows about them. I own a successful and growing business, and who knows what the future may hold. But, you can take it to the bank that I will give your Mom a great and secure lifestyle."

Driving back to the hotel, Clay asked Jill what she thought about the dinner meeting. She said, "Everything went much better than I expected. You won them over. Didn't you see them crying as they hugged me and wished me much success in 'The Big Apple.'"

Jill dropped Clay at the downtown rental car location where he had made reservations for the vehicle he would drop off in Los

Angeles. Once assured everything about the rental was in order, Jill told Clay she would meet him back at the Hilton. Less than fifteen minutes had elapsed since her arrival in the room until Clay was at the door.

"I hate to say this, but I told Guy I would be at the apartment by seven. We have several documents to go over, and that likely means we will be burning the midnight oil until the wee hours of the morning."

"Oh poor baby," Jill said, smiling as she touched him under the chin.

"Well, these hours we've been keeping aren't exactly invigorating to a guy as old as me."

With that teasingly remark, Jill laughing came back at him by saying, "I doubt that. You never seem to settle down."

"Kidding aside, how long do you think it will take me to drive up to L.A.?"

She hesitated and then replied, "It all depends on where in L.A. you are going? So, figure it will take you two to three hours; at most."

Clay gathered up his clothes, double-checked his room to ensure nothing was left behind, and the two went downstairs to checkout. They kissed and hugged in the parking lot. Jill went her way, and Clay, now driving his rental, headed up to Los Angeles.

♥ ♥

Chapter 56

S hortly after being processed for his rental car at the Los Angeles International Airport on Sunday afternoon, and while he had been to Los Angeles on several occasions, Guy Devine was unfamiliar with PMP's apartment complex and its location. Therefore, at the airport's exit, he asked the attendant for directions and carefully made a note: 'Down Century Blvd and take the ramp to I-405 North. Go several miles down, get onto 1-10 East. From there, take La Brea Avenue North exit. Follow to Hollywood Boulevard, turn left at that intersection. This will begin the residential area.'

"*Damn, I am sure glad I asked that attendant to give me detailed directions. I hope he is right. I can't imagine some New Yorker taking that amount of time to help me,*" Guy muttered to himself. "*Here I am, and I didn't get lost.*"

It was evident from the well-designed entrance, the picture-perfect landscaping, and overall exterior condition of the buildings and covered parking areas; Guy knew he was in at least a moderately affluent area.

Unlocking the door and walking in, *"Not bad,"* he thought. *"Two bedrooms, nice kitchen area, TV in each bedroom, and one in the living room."* Guy also noticed in the living room was a conference table and desk combination.

Two security lockboxes were sitting on the desk, and one folding table neatly stashed behind the sofa. As anticipated, the fridge was empty, as were the pantry cabinets. *"Next up a little shopping at that strip mall, I passed a couple of miles back."*

After the trip to the grocery store and a stop at Kentucky Fried Chicken, Guy had purchased the essentials needed to make his and Clayton's evening reasonably comfortable. Clayton wasn't expected until later, so Guy didn't mind the wait. He had enough to keep busy. As a precaution, Smythers had telephoned before Guy left New York and gave him the two lockbox combinations. He opened both boxes and started to peruse their contents.

Clayton arrived shortly after eight, and upon seeing the carryout boxes neatly stacked on the counter, he told Guy that he had a hamburger, fries, and a Coke on his way up. Guy then opened the box of fried chicken and sides. It contained coleslaw, baked beans, mashed potatoes, gravy, and biscuits.

"Sure you won't have something," Guy said, smiling as he waved a chicken leg under Clayton's nose.

"You damn well knew I couldn't resist. Pass me one of those plates. I'll help myself; any wine?"

"Nothing but Cokes, sorry."

After eating and unpacking, Clayton and Guy discussed the contents of the files. Guy, who rarely made predictions, said, "After looking at PMP's internal controls manual and going through several payment records contained within those," pointing to a box of file folders, "This case should be a 'piece of cake' for us to solve."

"I hope you are right," replied Clayton. The two men spent several hours studying the documents at their disposal.

Finally, at 2:00 a.m., Clayton said, "Let's get to bed. We have a meeting with Smythers in seven hours. Besides, I want to call Earl Williams at his home before he leaves for work."

Guy reminded him, "You know there's a three-hour difference in time between here and the East Coast. You need to make that call at 4:00 a.m. or shortly after."

♥ ♥

Chapter 57

As the 1981 black Lincoln Town Car pulled up to PMP Movie Studio gate, the guard approached the driver's side of the vehicle; Guy Devine lowered the window. "You have business here?"

"Yes," said Devine. "Mr. Smythers is expecting us; Clayton Clarkson and Guy Devine."

"I'll check," said the guard wearing a PMP security patch on the shoulder of his neatly fitting khaki uniform.

"How's that tailor job for class? Shit, I never see a rental cop in the City that looks that professional," said Guy in a whisper.

"You're expected. When I open the gate, pull to the curb on the right; an escort is on his way to take you to Mr. Smythers' office."

In less than two minutes, another neatly dressed guard pulled up in a converted electric golf cart.

Without saying a word, the driver motioned Guy to follow. In slightly less than the length of a football field, the cart guard came to a stop and pointed the Lincoln into an open space marked, *'Reserved Visitors Only.'* Finally speaking, the guard said, "Follow me. I'll take you to Mr. Smythers' secretary."

They did as instructed.

The party walked up three exterior stair steps, through a heavily fortified glass door, and into an elegant wood-paneled room that served as the waiting area.

"Once Mr. Smythers is available, she... her name is Margarita— yes, like the drink—will come to get you. Please have a seat. Water or soft drink?"

"No, thanks," Clayton responded. The guard turned, leaving through the same front door they had entered.

Looking around, several photos and award plaques adorned each of the four walls. Every picture was of Edgar Smythers in the company of a well-known actor or actress: John Wayne, Elizabeth Taylor, Rock Hudson, and several others. Smythers was also pictured in smiling poses with both U.S. Presidents Reagan and Carter.

"Gentlemen, I apologize for the delay. My name is Margarita. I am Mr. Smythers' secretary."

Clayton spoke up, "No problem. We found the memorabilia most interesting."

"Mr. Smythers is now ready to see you." Down the hall, they went and turned left as Margarita escorted the two men through an ornate wooden double door into the inner sanctum of one of the wealthiest mini-major motion picture studios in Hollywood.

"Good seeing you, gentlemen again. However, this time, welcome to the West Coast. I hope you found everything in the apartment satisfactory?"

"Yes, everything is fine. We spent several hours last evening and into the morning examining those files and documents we had requested," Clayton answered.

"A man who gets down to business," Smythers said. "I like that. Well, gentlemen, Earl Williams called me at home this morning. He briefed me on your call to him at 4:00 a.m. our time. You guys already appear hard at work, and I appreciate it.

Earl and I discussed your recommended plan; we both agree. Earl said he also told you that the subsidiary's financials are processed and kept on file within our Accounting Department. This should make it easy for you to check and confirm data without raising suspicions. Earl has sent his local audit supervisor who handles our account, to assist you. He was told you are from the IRS and are here to do a spot review of the subsidiary."

Clayton responded, "Great, now it's time to go to work. Mr. Smythers, one other thing."

"Yes, Clayton?"

"You should know that we will not communicate any of our suspicions or conjectures to anyone, including you and Mr. Williams until our findings are confirmed. You are our client, and we will make only you aware of our findings and provide you with our final report. It shall be your decision as to what you choose to share with Earl Williams, law enforcement, or others."

"Thank you, Clayton. I understand and appreciate your position," Edgar Smythers said as they walked to the waiting room. After having a few words with Margarita, he said, "Please be seated. Margarita has gone to get Dick Swartz. He is the auditor Earl Williams sent this morning. Dick is a fine young man and knows he is to supply you with any files or information that you request. He also has been given the authority to allow you to remove any files from our premises. However, we ask that you sign for anything you take off premises."

Both Clayton and Guy shook hands with Mr. Smythers and sat down to wait for Dick Swartz.

♥ ♥

Chapter 58

Based upon their analyses of the documents left at the apartment, Clayton and Guy identified three areas; check authorization signatures, vendor controls, and bank reconciliations as focal points of their investigation. Based on their preliminary research, their principal period would revolve around the past six months.

After meeting with Dick Swartz and the Accounting Department supervisor, Swartz took Clayton and Guy to a vacant office that would serve as their temporary office. He gave Clayton the door key.

Guy pulled out his focus list, jotted down one more request: the personnel folders of the subsidiary's executives. Handing Swartz his list, Guy stressed the need to gather all accounting activities for the past six months. If Swartz had any questions about why the IRS would have an interest in reviewing such documents, especially personnel files, he didn't ask. Swartz left the office, and, in less than half an hour, he returned with the personnel folders of twelve executives.

Before the end of the day, Swartz returned and said that six months of accounting data was taking longer than expected, but the supervisor assured him these files would be ready before 10 a.m. tomorrow. As promised, Guy's list was completed and on his desk at 9:30 a.m. This portion of the investigation was now fully operational, and it didn't cease at PMP's quitting time.

Several document folders were placed in two cardboard boxes, inventoried, signed for, and taken back to the apartment. The scrutiny work continued with only a brief break when their food delivery arrived. Working well into the night, Guy smiled and said, "Now this is what I call burning the midnight oil. I feel good... no great."

Clayton, while placing a file on the table, responded, "So do I. We now know the identity of the embezzler. Tomorrow we shall confirm."

Clayton and Guy were in their temporary office when Dick Swartz stuck his head in the door. "Good morning, gentlemen."

Looking up, both Guy and Clayton returned the greeting, "Good morning, Dick."

"I need to confirm that those folders you took last evening are back."

"No problem; I'll help you," replied Guy.

Once Swartz left the office, Clayton and Guy spent a significant part of the day double-checking and confirming their findings, making copies of critical documents, and labeling those of an evidentiary nature.

As quitting time approached, Clayton called Dick Swartz and asked him to come to the office and verify the removal of more records. However, this time, the document count was in greater detail. Individual documents, folders, and supplemental files were inventoried, dated, and verified and signed by both Guy Devine and Dick Swartz, and then placed in a box for removal.

After Swartz left the office, Clayton looked at his watch, picked up the in-house phone and dialed Mr. Smythers' extension.

"Good afternoon, Mr. Smythers' office."

"Margarita, this is Clayton Clarkson, is he there?"

"Sorry Mr. Clarkson, he had a meeting off-site and will not return until tomorrow morning."

"Is there a time available so Guy Devine and I could meet with him. It's important."

"Please hold, I'll check. He's unavailable most of the day. However, he is always in his office no later than 7:30. Could you meet with him that early?"

"That's fine. We will be here by 7:45. Please notify the gate guard and the person at the main entrance we will be coming in."

"Mr. Clarkson, be assured I will take care of you. See you tomorrow morning. I am always in before eight."

Clayton and Guy spent the evening organizing their notes to coincide with the evidentiary documents. Not having access to a typewriter, Clayton prepared a handwritten Executive Summary for their early morning meeting with Mr. Smythers.

♥ ♥

Chapter 59

The meeting got underway promptly at 7:45 a.m., and it was evident that Edgar Smythers was anxious to hear what Clarkson had to say. After their greetings and no offer of coffee, Clayton asked, "Mr. Smythers, is it okay if we ask you a few questions and take some notes?"

"I have no problem with you asking questions. But as I have told you before, this entire matter must remain completely confidential. If word leaked out, your investigation could impact the Office of the President of the United States.

Guy Devine, with a pen in hand, had already removed his note pad from his briefcase as Smythers was speaking. Upon hearing Smythers insistence that what is said between the three while in this office must be kept in secret, Guy discreetly returned the pad to his briefcase. After three or four unobtrusive questions regarding the lack of control over the subsidiary's executive staff, Clayton got down to business.

"Well, Sir, we have identified your embezzler. However, we

have both good and bad news."

"The good news first, please. For some reason, I feel that what's coming is going to be heartbreaking."

"The good news is that we found absolutely nothing that gives even the slightest indication that the Presidential candidate is involved."

"Well, that's a relief. But how can you be sure?"

"We'll get to that later. The bad news is that your embezzler is Stephanie Cheminski, the Vice President of Talent Relations. Do you know her?"

"Yes, but not well. I know she is a long-term executive who always works long hours and does a bang-up job."

Clayton said, "Makes sense she would be a hardworking and star producer so as not to create suspicion. She has been employed by your organization for ten years. And we were able to trace her fraudulent activities back at least four years. Our documentary evidence shows that she has used her corporate credit card to make personal purchases for years. She has fabricated expense reports and business statements, doctored or created fake receipts to make them appear work-related, and also turned in fake receipts for reimbursement for personal funds she allegedly used for work expenses.

Smythers looking shocked at what he was hearing, buried his face in his hands, and said, "Oh my God!"

"There's more," Clayton continued, "She created a fake company which she used to submit bogus invoices for style and makeup services provided to actors. But the services were never delivered, and those payments went into a bank account she had established under another name at a local bank.

We were able to identify 237 fraudulent invoices that resulted in your Accounts Payable Department paying out approximately $870,000. In addition to all of this, PMP paid out another $67,000 in nonbusiness car services for herself, family, and friends over the past three years. Bottom line, your executive embezzler has likely cost PMP over one million dollars through her fraud and embezzlement schemes."

"I am shocked that such things could be taking place under our very noses, and no one became suspicious... where in the hell were our auditors?"

Before responding, Clayton thought, "*It's amazing at the number of companies that think they are protected from these crimes because they have auditors.*"

He replied, "As we tell client after client, auditors do not normally check for internal fraud. I bet that if you look at the scope of your formal agreement, you'll find it states that fact."

"You are probably correct. I remember Earl Williams telling me something like that when he recommended you. He said Clarkson was good at finding embezzlers, but I am amazed that the two of you were able to identify all that you did in less than a week."

"Mr. Smythers, now back to our opinion about the Presidential candidate; we found nothing regarding any criminal activities anywhere within PMP; I suspect you may already know he is a wife cheater who likes to chase pretty women, and that's probably why he frequently shows up here. We also had a law enforcement contact check out three of Stephanie Cheminski's bank accounts, including the fraudulent one, to see if there was any movement of funds to him or his campaign. Nothing was found."

"I guess I should be thankful for that." "True, but mark my word, before his campaign picks up any real momentum, some hotshot reporter or tipster will blow the lid off his womanizing escapades. He is blatantly careless."

"Well, the next step regarding what actions we take is up to our Board of Directors. But my recommendation will be that we prosecute Stephanie Cheminski. However, be assured she will be fired before you reach the 405 freeway. If we need you further, we will be in touch. Well done, gentlemen."

Two days later, a national story broke connecting Arthur McDermott—a popular candidate for the position of President of the United States—in an illicit romance with Stephanie Cheminski, a recently arrested embezzlement suspect.

The media reported, "Cheminski was found dead in bed by her husband. No foul play is suspected; pills and a note were found at her bedside. The Los Angeles County Coroner, with respect to Ms. Cheminski's suicide, stated, 'Decedent was concerned that her arrest for embezzlement and her relationship with Arthur McDermott would have a detrimental impact on his struggling campaign.'"

♥ ♥

Chapter 60

Vivian, obviously happy to see Jill said, "Well friend, where have you been? I haven't seen or heard from you in ages. Phyllis told me that you were traveling and helping to train both staff and cosmeticians with our new computerized inventory management system at Mira-Mar, Yuma, and El Toro."

"For Heaven's sake, it sounds like you missed me."

"I did miss you, Jill. But now I must ask, how is your love life going with that New Yorker... Clay?"

"Oh, Vivian, I have so much to update you. Let's meet on the porch at lunchtime?"

"You're on. I'll see you at noon."

Both women arrived on the porch at nearly the same time.

Vivian, smiling, spoke first, "Well?"

"We are doing just great," Jill said, "I know you remember that rocky start. That's now history. Clay met my kids, and everything went well."

"Boy, introducing him to your kids, that's a huge step."

"That's only half the story, Next week I am flying to New York City for four days. And, in August, I am moving out there."

Shocked, Vivian said, "You're what?"

"You heard me. I am going to live with Clay in New York. So many good things have happened to me lately; my life has totally changed."

"What are you going to do there?"

"Get a job, of course. Clay has already been seeking out possibilities for me as an artist or working with him on what he calls a 'joint venture.'"

Vivian laughed at what was just said. "Are you getting married?"

"Well, not right away." The way Jill answered, it was as though she owed Vivian an apology for not giving her a firm wedding date.

"When?" Vivian asked.

"Not for a while. Clayton has some personal business to take care of before we tie the knot."

Vivian, concerned for Jill, said, "Honey, I know you came from a sheltered life back in the Midwest, and even here, you have not seen how rotten some guys can be. Oh, Jill, you don't know enough about this guy to leave the only place you have roots and go away to that hellhole, New York City. Sorry girl, I don't mean to upset you, but men only think with their dicks, not their heads."

"Vivian, I've got to get back to work."

"Me too, I hope I didn't upset you, sweetie. I just don't want you to get hurt."

Back in her department, Jill couldn't shake what Vivian had said. She knew her friend could be right. It took less than a year for Jill to become aware of the risks associated with dating; it can lead to falling in love; and falling in love can lead to heartbreak.

She had quickly discovered that most of the guys she had connected with only wanted to get physical. Once they felt the sting of rejection, they moved on in search of greener pastures. "*Not Clay, he is different,*" she told herself. Yet, in the back of her head, that haunting voice persisted, "*I'm just warning you, this guy is bad news, and an admitted liar. Don't be stupid.*"

With tears streaming down her cheeks, Jill abruptly walked off the sales floor and headed for the ladies' lounge. Inside a stall, she regained her composure and muttered to herself, "*Clay, I love you so much, please don't betray the love I have for you.*"

♥ ♥

Chapter 61

"Hello, beautiful!" Startled, Jill busy unpacking a carton behind her counter turned around, and there stood Clay and Guy.

"What are you doing here? I thought I wouldn't see you until Friday evening."

"We wrapped up before noon in L.A., so here we are. We are on our way to meet with Colonel Cooperswaite. Naturally, I had to stop and say 'Hello,' and let you know we are back at the Hilton."

"I take it you want me to meet you there?"

"You bet, room 415 or in the lounge?"

She said, "I'll be in the lounge at 6:45."

"Okay, see you there."

As the two men entered the Colonel's outer office, they were greeted with a friendly smile and welcomed aboard by Master Gunnery Sergeant, Ed Mulligan. He said, "Colonel is expecting you. I'll let him know you have arrived."

Shortly after that, along with their escort, the two civilians walked into the Colonel's conservatively-decorated office. Colonel Cooperswaite got up and walked around his desk to shake hands.

"So, you are here to finish the MCRD portion of your contract with the Corps?"

"Right, sir," Clayton answered.

Smiling, the Colonel said in his abrupt military voice, "Well, get to work. Gunny will get you set up in the vacant office you previously used. He will also take care of scheduling your meeting with Captain Marquez and his noncoms. I'll see if there is anyone else you need in your meetings."

Clayton and Guy had been in their makeshift office for less than fifteen minutes when the telephone rang. The two looked at each other, and neither picked up the phone. After five or six rings, their phone went dead.

Seconds later, a corporal stepped into the doorway and announced, "Mr. Clarkson... Colonel Cooperswaite is waiting on line one."

"Christ, we just got here. I hope we are not going to have to deal with some emergency."

"Clayton, I'm glad I could catch you before your meeting got underway."

"Good timing, Colonel. Captain Marquez has encountered a short delay."

"The reason for my call is that I just spoke with Martha, and she is insisting that I invite you and Guy Devine to dine with us this evening, say at 1930 hours. Naturally, you don't want to disappoint Martha, do you, Clayton?"

"No, sir. We cannot disappoint your lovely wife."

"Fine, 1930, it is. Oh, by the way, Clayton. If you would like to bring along Ms. Simpson, you are more than welcome."

Surprised by that invitation, Clayton slightly stuttered and said, "Thank you very much, Colonel. But how ..."

Cooperswaite interrupted, "How did I know? Clayton never underestimate a Marine, especially if he is in charge of a military base. My boy, not even a gnat can take a shit on this base without me finding out... understand? See you, Guy, and Jill at 1930 hours."

After hanging up the phone, Clayton looked at Guy and starting to speak, and Guy said, "I got it. I could overhear most of your conversation. Now, you need to get word to Jill about her command performance, so she can go home and change into a fresh outfit."

"Guy, I'll be back in fifteen minutes. If Captain Marquez arrives before I return... stall him."

♥ ♥

Chapter 62

Clayton caught Jill between customers and gave her an abbreviated version of what had taken place, and he made it back to the office before Marquez arrived. His only comment to Guy before flopping down in the corner chair was, "Message delivered."

Clayton, driving the rental Lincoln Town Car, pulled to the curb in front of Jill's apartment building. In less than two minutes, she appeared carrying a beautiful bouquet of long-stemmed roses. Guy jumped out of the passenger seat and held the door as Jill got in. He then got into the back seat.

"Wow, you look like a million bucks," Guy said, "I hope you don't make Martha Cooperswaite envious."

"The flowers... damn," said a smiling Clayton, "I never thought about bringing a gift. Good thinking."

Jill responded, "I figured you two wouldn't, so I stopped at the florist on my way home; beautiful, aren't they?"

"Yes," answered Clayton as he pulled away from the curb, "Now we're off to dine with the Colonel and his lovely wife, Martha."

Once inside the Colonel's charming home and greetings shared, Jill's roses were a big hit with Mrs. Cooperswaite as she commented, "Jill, I am certain you are the one responsible for selecting these long-stemmed beauties. Thank you so very much." She turned to her husband, "Honey, I'll get a vase for the flowers; you take the drink orders."

With the drinks served, the Colonel said, "As you can see, the *hors d'oeuvres* are on the serving table; please help yourselves." He then went into the dining room to help his wife as she prepared a salad dish for each place setting.

From the appearance of the dining room and place settings, it is evident that Martha Cooperswaite was an experienced entertainer. Once the entrees and small talk ended, the group returned to the living room for cognac, dessert, and espresso. The ambiance of the room had changed from its initial greeting area to one of comfort and relaxation, consisting of low-burning candles and easy listening instrumental music.

Once everyone was seated, Colonel Cooperswaite looked at Jill and said, "Jill, you two seem to be getting along pretty well. How did you and Clayton get to know one another?"

"It's just... I was with a friend when I met him in the lounge at the Hilton. *Not exactly a lie*"...

He smiled and replied, "Ah, Jill, that's not what I heard." She blushed and said, "Colonel, there's a saying around the base that you know everything, including something about a gnat... you know what I mean?"

"Sure do, Jill. So, spill the beans."

She quickly turned to Clayton and said, "Clay, do you tell

him or do I?"

Guy laughed and said, "Prepare yourselves, a hand grenade, with a pulled pin, is on its way."

Martha, looking confused, said, "Prepare ...Guy, what do you mean?"

"Okay, I'll take over from here," Clayton said, as he sat his nearly empty glass of cognac on the coffee table. He told the entire story about how they met and fell deeply in love. He also broke the news that he had asked Jill to move to New York and that she had accepted.

When he finished telling their story of love, Martha had tears in her eyes, and even the hard-nosed Colonel pulled a handkerchief from his pocket and said. "The pollen is bad this time of year, and it makes my eyes tear up."

Clayton thought to himself, *"Pollen here in Southern California... Yeah, right, Colonel."*

They all said their good byes with hugs and man-to-man handshakes. Moving towards the door, Colonel Cooperswaite reached out with each hand and took one of Jill's and Clayton's within his. He softly squeezed each and said, "Martha and I are so happy for you. However, you both must remember that I am the man responsible for bringing the two of you together."

Clayton replied, "Sir, you truly are, and we shall never forget it." Jill leaned forward, kissed the Colonel on the cheek. Stepping through the door, she turned and said, "Good night, and thank you both for a most wonderful evening."

Time flew as Clayton and Guy wrapped-up their projects at MCRD, El Toro, and Camp Pendleton. It would be another two weeks before Jill would see Clayton at New York's JFK Airport on a late Sunday evening.

Even though Jill was looking forward to spending those four days in Manhattan with Clayton, her inner voice was again actively punishing her, "*I'm warning you, this guy is bad news, and an admitted liar... Are you stupid!*"

♥ ♥

Chapter 63

O n her way to the airport, tears filled Jill's eyes as she lifted her slightly trembling hand and wiped away a tear from her cheek. No matter how hard she tried, she couldn't erase Vivian's words from her mind, '*Are you out of your mind? I can't believe you are thinking about moving way across the country to live with a man who caused you so much heartache.*'

Wendy's voice returned her to reality as she said, "Well, Mom, we are here."

As Jill turned and smiled, her final thought was, *"Vivian's correct,"*

Wendy, driving her Mom's 1978 Datsun, pulled to the curb in the passenger unloading zone at San Diego International Airport. Jill blotted tears from her eyes before stepping from the vehicle. By the time she reached the rear, Wendy had already removed her Mom's two pieces of luggage from the trunk.

On this inactive Sunday morning, a baggage handler quickly appeared, greeted the two women, checked Jill's destination information, and placed her bags on his cart, ready to proceed to the check-in counter; final destination, New York JFK Airport.

"Mom," Wendy said, "I can tell you are upset. Just remember you will only be away for four days. So treat this trip as a 'try it to see if you like it' type of visit. If you don't like what you see, or the way you are treated, just cancel your August trip back East."

The two women wrapped their arms around each other, tears flowed, and good byes were said. As a parting comment, Wendy quickly added, "Mom, Tony, and Joe, said to tell you to enjoy yourself. Always remember, whatever happens, we love you and will always be here for you." Jill smiled ruefully.

Just as quickly as that baggage handler had appeared, so did a police officer signaling that the vehicle must be moved from this 'No Standing Zone.' With that, one last kiss goodbye, as looks of sadness flashed across their faces. Jill turned and commenced to trail behind the luggage handler.

As she approached the ticket counter, Wendy's pep talk had proven successful. Jill's tears were gone, and her appearance and body language exuded confidence. The agent took charge, and once all required documents were approved, the two pieces of luggage were weighed, tagged, and placed onto the conveyor. With the printing of the boarding pass, the check-in was complete.

Jill headed for Gate 16 in Terminal 1. After a short wait, the attendant announced the first class section was ready for boarding. Inside of the cabin, the flight attendant directed Jill to seat 6-A. *"Oh God, I pray that he is the one...* Pardon me; I have the window seat," Jill said, showing a little awkwardness as she maneuvered past the chubby man seated on the aisle in 6-B.

A short while after she was seated and the remainder of passengers on board, the flight attendant's voice spread throughout the plane.

To Jill, it sounded like a recording… smooth and professional.

"Good morning, ladies and gentlemen. Welcome aboard Delta flight 40 bound for New York John F Kennedy Airport. We will be taking off shortly, so please ensure that your carry-on items are properly stowed either under the seat in front of you or in the compartment above. At this time, please securely fasten your seat belt. Thank you."

Chapter 64

" *Fasten your seat belt... boy that fits this crazy plan of mine.*" Tears welled again in Jill's eyes as she struggled to conceal her emotion by ignoring an attempt to strike up a conversation by the man seated alongside. To avoid any unwanted chats, Jill focused on whatever was taking place outside of the window. However, as hard as she tried, she could not escape Vivian's words of warning, including those ghostly images of what possibly lies ahead as they fought hard to take center stage. "*This is no time for tears and heartache,*" she scolded herself. "*He is the right one!*"

Comfortably seated, Jill, for some odd reason, rechecked her seat belt, knowing full well it was secure. Her heart now racing faster than it had during those hundreds of times, she had cranked up her jogging pace and turned it into a quarter-mile sprint within the confines of her neighborhood.

Jill tried—every way possible—to keep her mind from wandering back to negative thoughts. She focused on her positive relationships with her loving twenty-one-year-old engaged daughter,

Wendy, and her two sons, Tony and Joe, both now in college.

She knew what was happening; an insidious invasion of shameful guilt was tearing at her very heart and soul. *"Damn,"* she thought as that haunting Armageddon message began to replay in her mind and not missing a word, *"Here I am planning to leave my three nearly-grown kids, a nice home, and a good job in San Diego to go live in New York with Clay Clarkson, a man I hardly know... And what I already know about him would likely cause the most tenacious gambler in Vegas to tell me to avoid this guy like the plague and to stay put on the West Coast. Am I crazy?"*

Somewhat startled, Jill heard a flight attendant say to the gentleman in the adjoining seat, "Oh, I am sorry, your bag does not fit properly under the seat. I'll place it in the overhead bin."

Moments later, the Lockheed L-1011 lifted into the air. Jill Simpson was on her way to the "Big Apple." Still peering outside, but not visualizing whatever movements there was, she again allowed her mind to return to those haunting words... *Fasten your seat belt!*

♥ ♥

Chapter 65

Clayton had taken care to ensure that every moment of Jill's and his time would be both enjoyable and productive. He rented a room at the New York Hilton, as this would be the place where the most extensive retail conference in the City would take place in January. He wanted to make sure Jill was comfortable in her surroundings, and that she understood how easy it would be to gain access from anywhere within the hotel to the exhibit floor, and where Clarkson International would have their booth.

Jill often smiled to herself when thinking about how caring Clay was in looking after her. At times she would jokingly criticize him by saying, "Clay, I am not a little girl. I have survived on my own most of my life. Yes, even when I was married."

Jill had always tried to play by the rules, but had learned quickly, that like the unstable sea below the ascending airplane, life was not always fair. But she knew that if she persevered, one day her dream man would bring her the companionship and happiness she wanted so badly. She reassured herself, "*Clay is that man.*"

After a quick breakfast at the hotel, the two arrived at the Clarkson International office at a couple of minutes past eight.

"Tomorrow's a big day for us," Clayton said. "Jules Edwards did as he had promised. He got us an appointment with William Gordon, Sr., and now it's up to us to show, or better yet, prove to Mr. Gordon we can become a valuable vendor for AUSRM."

Guy arrived in the office at eight-thirty, and Marsha at a couple of minutes to nine. This was the first meeting between Jill and Marsha.

Later Marsha whispered to Guy, "She's really wonderful." "See, didn't I tell you so," Guy replied.

In addition to her regular duties, Marsha was learning the importance of product sales within an organization such as Clarkson International. She had often heard Clayton refer to product sales as 'bread and butter' income, but wasn't quite sure what he meant. Now getting a good look at the preparations involved, and hearing her associates' discussions revolving around the upcoming Gordon meeting at AUSRM, was a real eye-opener.

She knew the management consulting practice was the sole source of Clarkson's revenue. However, she had never thought about the peaks and valleys of income flow that can realistically occur when no physical product sales are available, although this was always a real concern for Clayton. He knew the firm had to develop an affordable and effective product that would help enhance the firm's reputation and provide a steady flow of income.

Marsha mulled to herself, "*So that's what Clayton means when he says, bread and butter money.*"

As the AUSRM planning sessions were winding down, Clayton knew he had found a winner in Jill. "*Now, we need to come up with something creative that will knock management's socks off."* Clayton recognized that Jill and her artistic talents were destined to play a critical role in landing the AUSRM account. He did not take this opportunity lightly.

He, Guy, and Jill tossed ideas around for hours. Jill also worked on sketches, Guy played devil's advocate, and Clayton focused on coming up with a variety of employee motivational strategies. He confidently said, "Tomorrow is zero hour. Today, once we finalize our approach, we'll do a dry run to help ensure our best presentation possible."

Marsha was asked to listen to the presentation and give her opinion. She responded with six words, "If this doesn't sell, nothing will."

At quitting time, both Guy and Marsha passed along their wishes for a successful meeting tomorrow. Clayton and Jill spent an additional hour reviewing final preparations. "Jill, we're as ready as we will ever be. Let's drop our materials at the hotel and go get something to eat."

♥ ♥

Chapter 66

"Well, today is our big day," Clayton said as he stepped from the curb, waving a cab to stop. "Let's take this cab down to lower Manhattan and show that Mr. William Gordon Sr. just how talented we are."

Jill, obviously nervous, smiled and mumbled, "Okay."

At ten-twenty, Mr. Gordon's secretary said, "Mr. Gordon will see you now."

"Ten minutes waiting beyond our appointment time is not bad," Clayton whispered. Once inside Mr. Gordon's office, the meeting was strictly business. No mention of Jules Edwards; for this, Clayton was grateful.

Mr. Gordon listened attentively to their presentation and examined three of the five sketches Jill had placed on the conference table. Suddenly, he laid down one design, turned and reached across his desk, picked up the telephone, and dialed what appeared to be a three-digit extension. "Come into my office, please: I need your opinion on something." He then hung up his phone.

Within a minute or so, a neatly dressed woman, likely in her mid thirties, walked in. Gordon introduced Clayton and Jill to Becky Tuchman, VP of Personnel and Administration. Gordon gave her an accurate and concise version of the purpose of the meeting and asked her to take a look at the materials and sketches displayed on the table.

Ms. Tuchman, while examining the contents, asked both Clayton and Jill a few questions revolving around their perceptions of how these materials could be used to help strengthen the culture of a retail organization and in motivating its employees to become more productive. She listened attentively and pausing for a few seconds said, "I like what you two have put together."

She turned and said, "Bill, this could be right down the alley for what we have been looking for."

"That's why I wanted your opinion." Gordon's next comment was an apparent negotiating ploy. He looked towards Ms. Tuchman and said, "Becky, I just hope they won't burst our bubble by giving us quotes well beyond what we can afford."

Clayton, looking very sincere, replied, "We are looking for a long-term relationship with AUSRM. Furthermore, we recognize that your organization serves as the supplier to hundreds, if not thousands of retailers, both large and small, and that you must also make a reasonable profit."

"Good, glad you have a realistic understanding of what is involved. What do you need from either Ms. Tuchman or me to get a proposal together?"

"Bill, I am already running late for a meeting. Charlotte can give them whatever they need from my department."

"Fine, I'll take it from here." Another thirty minutes was

spent gathering information for the proposal. Clayton explained that because of their busy schedules, and the complexities involved in locating a qualified printing service, the proposal might not arrive until mid August.

As they were leaving the office, both Clayton and Jill shook hands with Mr. Gordon. The ball was now in their court. As they walked towards the elevator bank, Clayton smiled and said, "Good meeting... no, it was a great meeting! Jill, you did a superb job with your portion of the presentation, and your sketches were phenomenal... no bull." For the first time in her business career, Jill Simpson felt that her input and talents were truly appreciated.

♥ ♥

Chapter 67

Clayton recognized that delaying the proposal another two months was risky; clients likely lose interest. He looked at Jill as they stood waiting for the down elevator and said, "There's an old proverb, 'strike while the iron is hot.' My gut tells me that if we wait too long, they've seen what we have to offer, and that puts us at risk to them giving the job to someone else."

"Do you think they would ..." The elevator arrived, and their conversation ceased until they stepped onto the sidewalk in front of the building.

"Do you think they would do such a thing?"

"Absolutely, it all gets down to timeliness and the almighty dollar."

"Then, we have a problem?"

"Yes, Jill, possibly so. Now the real challenge is that we live approximately 3,000 miles from each other. Not good working conditions, agree?"

"Yes, but Clay, I know that won't stop you."

"Won't stop us, Jill. We'll figure out a solution. But first, we need to come up with alternatives.

"By the way, I think it would be appropriate for us to thank Jules Edwards. After all, it was he who got us in to see William Gordon... Senior, that is. Taxi." The cab stopped suddenly in the middle of the street.

"Clay, we can't get in. We'll get hit by a passing car."

"Come on, Jill, you're in the big city now. People here ignore pedestrian laws. Give me your hand." He opened the rear passenger door, and Jill got in, sliding across the seat to make room for Clayton.

"Cabby, take us to Edwards' Art Gallery, corner of 72nd and York." Speaking in broken English, the cabbie said, "You got it. I saw your lady friend not want to step into the street... she a tourist?"

"That she is my man. She's from California, where they obey pedestrian laws or pay big fines."

As they departed the cab, Clayton pointed to the building on the corner, "As you can see from the large sign that is the world-famous Sotheby's Art and Auction house."

Walking into the gallery, Clayton noticed Jules was speaking with one of his staff. Looking up, Jules saw Clayton with the lady he assumed was his newly discovered West Coast artist.

"Clayton, I presume you are here to update me on your meeting with Bill Gordon this morning... But first, introduce me to this beautiful lady."

"Jill as you likely have guessed, meet Jules Edwards."

Taking Jill's hand, he smiled and said, "Jules, I want to introduce you to Jill Simpson. We both wanted to come by, and personally, thank you for setting up our meeting. It went fantastic."

"So I heard," Jules answered.

"You already heard?"

"Yes, Bill called me minutes after you departed. He wanted to thank me for the connection, saying this could work into a good business relationship. But he said he was surprised the submission of your proposal would take so long. I told him this delay was likely because of your busy schedules."

"Thanks, Jules."

"Oh yes, Jill, he was impressed with your artistic talent and curious as to your relationship with me. I told him that I had only seen three or four of your sketches, and the jury was out as to whether we shall pursue any formal relationship. I also told him that whatever decision the two of us made would not interfere with any work involving AUSRM."

"Jules, we are most appreciative of your help. How about going to lunch with us?"

"Okay, I'm game ...where?"

"I was planning to take Jill to the Tavern on the Green, how about having lunch there?"

"Perfect choice. Jill, as an artist and lover of nature, you'll appreciate the overall ambiance of this landmark restaurant. It's nestled in an idyllic Central Park setting, and unlike any other. If my memory serves me correctly, it was built sometime around 1870 and initially used as a barn for sheep that grazed in the park's meadows. This historic restaurant has served locals, presidents, royalty, actors, artists, and first-time visitors such as you, since the middle 1930s."

♥ ♥

Chapter 68

After lunch, Clayton said he needed to return to the office to take care of some work. "Jill and I are driving up to Dutchess County early tomorrow. Then on Thursday afternoon, she is flying back to San Diego. I want to make certain we can spend as much time together as possible and also take in a little sightseeing."

"Jules... may I call you Jules?"

"Of course, my dear."

"That was a wonderful history about Tavern on the Green. I truly appreciated you pointing out things that only an experienced artist could envision and appreciate."

Jules looking at Clayton, said, "Clayton, I am planning on attending an artists' wine social down in SOHO this evening. It's very exclusive, gorgeous, and highly restricted. However, as a member, I am allowed to bring two guests. There will be musical performances, comedy routines, good food and drinks, and a way to meet and socialize with new friends. Some of the City's best artists, gallery owners, and prominent art aesthetes will be there.

However, I should also mention that your former friend may also make an appearance."

Jill smiled and said, "You mean Taylor Lee?"

"Uh, yes. Have you met her?"

"No, but I figure it's only a matter of time until we cross paths. Oh, don't worry." With a slight laugh, she said, "I am too much of a lady to show my claws." Taking Clay by the hand, "Clay, this sounds like fun. Let's go. I'll behave myself; I promise!"

"Okay, Jules, we'll gladly go."

"Good, where are you staying?"

"The New York Hilton over on Times Square."

"Pick you up at seven; in front. Thanks for lunch, it was enjoyable. Wear casual clothes, nothing fancy, or you'll be out of place."

"It's such a beautiful day, let's walk," Clayton said, looking at Jill. "Then I'll leave you at Bloomingdales so you can do some shopping, and I'll show you an easy short cut over to Saks and, more shopping. You know where our office is, a couple of blocks over, on Park Avenue. I'll wait there for you."

Clayton hugged and kissed her once they arrived at the entrance to Bloomingdales, and he said, "Now go inside and shop till your heart's content. See you back at the office."

"Love you," she responded.

After spending a short time in Bloomingdales, looking at the latest fashions, but not purchasing a single item, Jill returned to the main floor and stopped by the Cosmetics Department to watch a couple of makeup artists in action, " *Interesting*," she thought. *"Enough looking around in here. Saks Fifth Avenue, here I come."*

Inside Saks, Jill decided to purchase a pair of shoes to wear to

Wendy's wedding. With the salesclerk's help, she sat down in a comfortable chair to try on one pair. Standing, while checking for comfort and looks, Jill took a few steps over to the mirror. When she returned to the chair, she noticed her purse was open and her wallet missing.

She screamed, "Pickpocket! Thief!"

Two women took off running down the escalator with a store clerk chasing. Within three or four minutes, the clerk returned with Jill's wallet. He explained that during the chase, he saw one woman hurl the billfold into a rack of dresses. He gave up the chase and recovered the wallet.

Jill checked its contents and said, "Only fifty or so dollars is missing. Thank God, my credit cards and identification are here." With this theft, Jill's first day of shopping in Manhattan came to an abrupt end.

Off the elevator and as she opened the office door, Clayton was standing at Marsha's desk with a piece of paper in his hand. He looked up, "Back already... where are your purchases?" She looked into his eyes and gave a steely reply, "A damn pickpocket stole my money in Saks."

Marsha blurted out, "No, shit! No fucking shit!" Clayton took Jill in his arms, hugged and kissed her, and said, "Welcome to the Big Apple, honey!"

Chapter 69

As promised, Jules picked up Jill and Clayton at seven sharp. The townhouse in SOHO was everything Jules had described. The evening was spent sampling fine wines, snacking on *hors d'oeuvres,* listening to live music, and a few 'open mike' comedy skits that had an odd resemblance to a couple of Karaoke evenings that Jill had attended in San Diego.

Through most of the evening, she sensed that Clay appeared a little nervous; he frequently glanced towards the front door. Without saying a word, she wondered, *"Is the anticipated appearance of Taylor Lee troubling him?"*

As the evening was winding down, Jules suggested it was time to leave. Jill turned to Clayton and said, "Ah, heck Clay, I didn't get to meet your ex-flame."

"Okay, don't rub it in." It was indeed an upbeat and fun evening. When Jules pulled in front of the hotel, both Jill and Clayton most graciously thanked him for such a wonderful evening.

In the room, a brief conversation revolved around who would

shower first. Clay was the winner since it took Jill much longer to get ready for bed. Clay, now waiting, lay on top of the bed's turned-down sheet. "How much longer," he called out.

She answered, "Only a couple or so minutes."

"Hurry, I am waiting for you to seduce me."

"Be patient, my love." With that teasing remark, Clay, wearing only a towel, slipped into the bathroom and swept her into his arms.

She said, "Oh, that's a romantic move if I ever saw one."

"It's the music," he replied.

"Listen, the radio is playing an instrumental by Kenny G. Let's dance, and with you in my arms, I guarantee I will not step on your toes."

She let out a snigger as she softly kissed the side of his neck and said, "You are so silly." He moved in rhythm to the music as he left the bathroom in the direction of the bed. Laying her down, he gently kissed her lips as he removed her towel and dropped it alongside the bed; his followed.

Clay's adult life, before Jill came along, was filled with mostly heartache and turmoil, and he knew she was the one gift in his life that mattered. She was the one companion and lover he would cherish forever.

Whispering words of his love for her, Clay kissed her softly on the lips and then moved his tongue slowly to each ear, down to her neck, and back up to her lips where he took soft and moist nibbles until they parted for his tongue. From her mouth, his tongue slowly moved downward and gently caressed the nipple of each breast, causing it to become hard. He pulled back, caught his breath, and leaning down, began to give her belly button a light, moist massage. He teasingly moved his tongue a little lower as he took more, just a little more. His every move was electric and seemed to make its way deep into her body... she was on fire. He felt her hands on his back, summoning him. "Don't stop!... Oh God, Clay."

With her back slightly arched and her body moving in an inviting rhythmic way, in one smooth motion, he was above her on all fours, his knees inside of her hips. In anticipation of his next move, she pulled his body closer and closer until she felt him go deep inside her.

While trembling beneath him, and with every breath, she felt his body's rhythm moving in harmony with hers. Slowly over and over with each thrust, she felt a gratifying sensation that went on and on until the last pleasurable aftershock had rippled through her, and she went limp.

As he had done the first time they made love, Clay lifted her head and looked into her eyes. He smiled and gave her a long and dreamy kiss that rose from his sole. He whispered, "I love you so very much! Please never forget that."

"And I love you every bit as much Clay," she said softly. They made love slowly a second time, and when finished, they fell asleep in each other's arms.

Chapter 70

After awakening on Wednesday morning, both were famished. They showered, dressed, and went downstairs for breakfast. While waiting to be seated, Clay filled Jill in about his 1820s country home named 'Evergreen.' He described it as settings on eighteen acres of land, adjoining an 850-acre government park.

He also told her that it's reasonably close to several historical sites, including Franklin D. Roosevelt's home, Vanderbilt's Mansion, Culinary Institute of America, the 1766 Beekman Arms hotel, a few antique centers, and three auction halls.

Over breakfast, the two continued their talk about Evergreen and the Mid-Hudson Valley. "How far from here," Jill asked.

"About ninety miles from Mid-town. A beautiful hour and a half drive up the scenic Taconic Parkway," Clay responded.

"Is your Evergreen livable?"

Laughing, Clay said, "Certainly it's fit for human habitation."

"No offense. You said it was built over a century and a half ago."

"Jill, Evergreen is now my permanent home. I only stay down

here when business demands it."

She came back with a snide remark, "Or when you were shacking up with Taylor Lee."

Uncertain of her exact meaning of that comment, he decided to follow up with "What's past is prologue... Jill, the day I met you was the most important day of my life. And, my dear, today is the first day of the rest of our lives."

"How sweet, and I can't believe you did such a marvelous job of getting out of that dig with that famous quote from Shakespeare's play, *The Tempest*."

Laughing, he responded, "Practice, my dear... Say, what would you say if I suggested we check out of the hotel this morning, and spend the night at Evergreen?"

"I'm game."

"Great," he said, "When we first go in, you'll find it a little cool and damp, but it heats up quickly."

She smiled and said, "Heats up... just like you. Kidding aside, it would be nice since it will become my new home in August."

"Great," Clay said, "I'll go check out. You go upstairs and start packing. It won't take me long at the desk."

As they left the City in Clay's 1979 Cadillac Seville, Jill asked Clay about his part-time driver, Arthur. "Arthur now has a full-time job out on the Island, and with me moving to Rhinebeck, it worked out best for both of us. He is available on occasions if needed, but only for around Manhattan."

Recognizing that Clay was somewhat of a captive audience for the next hour or so, Jill thought it an excellent time to move away from both small and business-related talk, and learn more about his personal life, of which she knew little. Jill, being especially curious about the daughter he had only mentioned a couple of times, asked, "Tell me about your daughter?"

Startled, Clay repeated, "My daughter?"

"Yes, I find it unusual you never talk about her. Do you have a bad relationship?'

"No, not at all. I love Lynn dearly, and I believe she loves me. I am sure you remember me giving you several details about her Mom, stepdad, and Lynn, during my heartbreaking confessional at the Hilton."

"Clay, you might view that talk as some forced confession, but I certainly didn't... your lies nearly destroyed our relationship."

"Jill, that day, I told you everything I thought was important for you to know. But there are a couple of other things I didn't mention. So, I shall explain: Lynn's Mom is a local judge in Virginia, although this has no bearing on my relationship with my daughter, except I certainly better not get pulled over for speeding. If I did, she would likely throw the book at me.

"And yes, I do have contempt for both Cindy and her husband. I believe they did everything they could to destroy the bond between Lynn and me. Oh yes, another thing, when she was in college, Lynn and I were talking on the phone, and she told me she was going to lose her dorm room over the summer because she did not have the money to pay for it. I sent her the money to ensure her room was reserved. A couple of years later, Lynn told me that her parents had found out about that payment, and her stepfather stopped talking to her. I never asked why. I figured if she wanted me to know the reason, she would have told me."

As Clay drove and talked, Jill noticed every once in a while, a tear would trickle down his cheek. She also saw he no longer would face her as he spoke, and the crackling of his voice revealed a nervousness Jill had not seen before.

"Not the time to talk about this," she thought. However, Clay continued with his tell-all.

"Naturally moving from Washington, D.C. to Boston, and later to New York, cut back on the personal time Lynn and I spent together, but we kept in regular contact by telephone and a few get-togethers at my Mom's house in Maryland. I strongly believe that my daughter and I will become even closer in the years to come."

Jill asked, "When did those two siblings find out that Lynn was not their full-blooded sister?"

"As far as I know, they still don't know. Lynn told me that when I would come to pick her up, Cindy always said to them that I was an old friend of Lynn's. So, please understand this is a personal matter that I'd rather not discuss.

"Jill, I bet you have one or two skeletons in your closet that you'd rather I not know about." Clay thought to himself, *"Damn right, Jill, I would be shocked if you didn't have secrets that you don't want to divulge... especially to me."*

♥ ♥

Chapter 71

As Clay passed the park, he slowed as Evergreen came into view. "Well, there she is," he commented. Jill could see the pale yellow, two-story house sitting on a knoll and surrounded by six huge maple trees. A medium-size pond with a waterfall was on the right lower portion of the front yard.

Clay explained, "The pond will be ideal for stocking with trout because it is fed with fresh spring running water... it never freezes during the winter, nor dries up in the summer."

"Clay, you never struck me as a fisherman."

"Well Jill, I am not. I just thought it would be a nice touch for any friends who like to fish."

"Good, I don't care for fish, and once I am here, you should know that I won't cook fish... that's a job for you and your buddies.

"The pond is beautiful, especially the way those white birch trees and wildflowers surround it. But, where is the water going once it goes over the falls?"

"You can't see it, but it is flowing underneath the lawn

and the road just ahead on the right. It continues through the adjoining neighbor's property and empties into a lake several hundred yards downstream."

First impressions mean a lot, and Jill was pleased with what she was seeing as the car turned right onto the small paved country road and continued up the hill approximately the length of a football field before making a right turn into the gravel driveway.

Situated directly in front of the car was an aging and somewhat dilapidated two-car garage, no automatic door openers, and in desperate need of a good paint job.

Once out of the car, Clay opened the wooden gate, and Jill stepped into the courtyard. Along this side of the house, stood another large maple tree capable of providing ample sunshade for the yard. As Clay opened the porch screen door, it became apparent the main entry to the home was here; on the kitchen side.

Now facing the locked door directly in front of her, Clay stepped in front and said, "Mind if I carry you across the threshold?"

"Oh, if you don't mind, I had rather wait until my permanent move out here in August."

"Of course, I understand," he said. He turned, unlocked, and held the door as she stepped inside to a reasonably well-decorated kitchen. Looking around, she formed a quick thought, *"This kitchen definitely has a woman's touch."* She looked at Clay and, with a slight pause, asked… "Taylor Lee?"

Without speaking, he nodded.

Walking from room to room, Jill began to realize this house was much larger than it appeared from the main road. It contained seven rooms, including four bedrooms, an office, a small library, a fair-sized vacant room, two and a half baths, front and kitchen porches, and an extensive cellar that included a separate pantry/wine room.

"I love it! It has a true feeling of warmth and friendless. If ghosts live here, they are the good guys."

"Why would you bring up ghosts," he asked.

"Well, since I was a little girl, I was always told that ghosts live in old houses. Besides, just last year, I read that book, *The Amityville Horror,* that took place on Long Island. It scared the bejeebers out of me."

Clay laughed and said, "No unfriendly ghosts here; only good ones."

Jill gave him a mischievous stare.

A third exterior door on the south side of the house led into the back yard with its rustic brick patio and an ancient stone fireplace. More large maples, a small, although neglected, apple orchard, and an even better view of the pond; it was much larger than it looked from the road. The back was amazingly level, with an open view of a nearby hillside and beyond.

Clay said, "I call this 'the south forty.' See that stone fence on the hill," he was pointing, "behind it is an 850-acre government park."

Back inside, Clay told Jill to notice the temperature. She replied, "It's much cooler in here than on the outside."

"That's because of the placement of those large maples," he proudly said. "They protect the house from the sun's heat. The first owner, some 160 years or so ago, planned and planted those trees for that very purpose. Also, it's worth mentioning the thickness of the outer walls. They are insulated with stone to help keep pipes from freezing in the winter, and in the summer, the walls serve as heat barriers. Upstairs, you'll see wide-plank flooring throughout, and in the attic, the roof is supported and braced with hardwood tree limbs that still have their bark intact. In the bedrooms, you'll find lower ceilings."

"Ah ha, that's something I understand. Being raised in Minnesota, my Daddy did the same. He told us kids, this was done to keep the heat in during cold periods."

Once Jill had the total picture of what she anticipated would soon become her new home, Clay looked at her with worry in his eyes. "Well, what's your impression?"

"Wow, I am not going to lie to you. It certainly will require a major mental adjustment for me. I have lived in modern homes for decades, and this is like stepping way, way back in time, well over one hundred and fifty years. But Clay, I am here because of my love for you... we'll make it work."

♥ ♥

Chapter 72

"I'm curious, how long have you owned this place and why did you buy it?"

"Good questions. Sometimes I wonder the very same," Clay answered. "I bought it about two years ago from a couple who were moving to California. A real estate friend told me about this property when we were talking about investments in real estate.

"He said he had a Manhattan couple who were very anxious to sell and would consider self-financing. My friend gave me the address, so I stopped by and looked at the vacant property, but made no effort to see inside. A couple of weeks later, he again called and said a real deal was to be had if I was interested. Taylor and I drove up so I could see inside.

"Overall, it looked tired and untended. I estimated it would need a great deal of work, especially in places you cannot see from the outside. I got back to my friend and told him I was hesitant.

"Two days later, he called again, saying the couple indicated they were now considering offers. I thought, here's my opportunity if I want a place where I can make a profit. I made a lowball offer of fifty-two thousand below their asking price and asked that they hold the mortgage. They agreed, and the rest is history."

Jill looked at him and asked another question, "What caused you to move up here?"

"Hmmm, two reasons actually: The high costs of living in the City keep getting higher, for example, I was paying eighty-five dollars a month to park my car at the apartment building, and it would be even higher elsewhere. Secondly, after Taylor and I split, I was traveling a great deal and knew that if I signed a monthly rental agreement, the costs would be ridiculous.

"So, I chose to stay in hotels. Believe it or not, the luxurious Plaza Hotel gave me my best deal. While they were most accommodating, living there was also expensive. Buying this house put me in the right spot. First, it was a good investment and reduced my cost of living significantly. Jill, perhaps best of all, that purchase relieved the mental pressure of apartment hunting, and having this house gave me the ability to break off from Taylor much more quickly. Okay, enough of your third-degree," he said defensively.

Jill looked at him for a moment and feeling slightly embarrassed by Clay's momentary testiness, smiled and said, "Let's go into town, have lunch and pick up a few items."

He added, "And then take a cruise around the surrounding area."

She, after giving him a peck on the lips, replied, "I'd like that."

On their way down Route 308, on the left, Clay noticed a large sign, '*N & T Printing*,' at the intersection of Old Schoolhouse Road. Without saying a word, he suddenly swung a quick left.

"Why did you make that turn," she asked.

"We need a printer, and surely one up here would be much

cheaper." Following the road one-half mile, Clay pulled in front of the print shop, and said, "But will he be able to deliver what we need?"

They spent close to an hour talking with the two owners, Nick and Tommy, and looking at some recently printed work. Jill explained what she had in mind and asked lots of questions as to what they would need from her.

The elder printer, after much discussion, asked, "Are you able to bring us camera ready print overlays for each of the posters?"

Without hesitation, she responded, "Yes, I am quite familiar with print overlays, especially where color is involved."

Clay, somewhat amazed, stepped aside. "Jill, I don't know a darn thing about this type of printing. It's out of my league."

"Clay, that's no problem. I'll take over and give them enough information so they can work up a cost projection, say for a run of one thousand full color, 24 x 30 inch, quantities for five different posters. Such a quote should give us a head start on the AUSRM proposal."

"Great thinking Jill, once I have their prices, I'll make a comparison to a couple of printers in Manhattan. That way, we'll know if their prices are similar or better."

As the conversation was winding down, Clay asked for three local references that he and Jill could contact. In giving their final pitch, the two printers proudly talked about the type of work they could deliver, their client list, and their length of time in business.

Back in the car, Jill and Clay talked about the excellent quality of work they examined, the two printers' knowledge about dealing with their needs, and that they even offered a couple bits of advice that made good sense.

Clay spoke up, "I'll bet they will come in much cheaper than the others."

She followed, "After looking at the quality of their printing jobs, I'll be surprised if we hear any negative feedback from their references. Also, remember, Nick, is to have their proposal to you by Tuesday."

In town, things went like clockwork; good lunch, N & T's references panned out as expected, and the tour around the charming communities was enjoyable. Jill, pointing to the small grocery store near the corner in the town of Red Hook, said, "Let's stop here and get some food and wine. I'm in the mood to fix dinner."

"No wine, I have plenty. Jill, are you sure you had rather cook than eat in one of Rhinebeck's nice restaurants?"

"I'm positive. You know what?... I could start liking your old Evergreen, and the artistic beauty of those small towns we passed. Besides, I have a few ideas of ways we can heighten the charm of our new home and its surroundings."

Clay smiled, "I like that, especially when you said... our new home."

♥ ♥

Chapter 73

Back at Evergreen, Clay said, "Let's have a five o'clock happy hour even though it's an hour early?"

Jill responded, "That's good with me."

"Okay, you go sit on the sofa," Clay said, "And I'll go down to the wine cellar and get us a nice bottle of red wine."

"Wine cellar, where?" asked Jill. "When you gave me my tour, I didn't see a wine cellar."

"Well, I probably should have introduced you to the wine cellar when I opened that pantry door, the small room in the basement... you only glanced in. That small room is a nearly perfect wine cellar. Its temperature constantly holds at fifty-seven degrees Fahrenheit. Great for storing both red and white wines."

While sitting on the sofa and waiting for him to come back, Jill studied the living room and its furnishings. Once Clay returned with two nice size glasses of red wine, she said, "I didn't notice before, but you don't have a TV in this room."

"Nor will you find a television anywhere in this house. I

would rather listen to music or read."

She picked up her glass from the coffee table, raised it, and said, "A toast to no TV." She clinked glasses saying, "Cheers."

After going through two bottles of wine and reliving the highlights of their meetings at AUSRM, and the newly discovered printer, Clay said, "Let's eat. How long will it take you to cook whatever it was you bought at that market?"

"Oh, less than five minutes."

"Come on, Jill... how long? Do we have enough time to drink another bottle?"

"I have a confession to make."

"Confession... what?"

"I decided it was too risky to cook on an unfamiliar stove. So, I bought some fried chicken, fresh steamed asparagus, homemade coleslaw, and freshly made Amoroso bread; the grocer said you'd die for that bread."

"Sounds good, now let's eat."

Later that evening, they became lost in time as they listened to soft music, finished off another bottle of wine, went upstairs, and made the type of love that pleased them both.

♥ ♥

Chapter 74

When Jill opened her eyes, Clay was not in bed. She turned towards the clock on the nightstand; 7:00 a.m. "*That smell*," she thought as she placed her feet on the floor. "*It's bacon frying.*" Grabbing her robe, she tip-toed down the steps and moved silently towards the kitchen.

There on the front burner of the stove was a pan half-filled with bacon strips. "*Frying bacon was the culprit for that inviting smell that had worked its way upstairs.*" Quietly peeping to get a full view of the kitchen, Jill first spotted a medium size plastic bowl with beaten eggs ready for scrambling, sitting on the counter. Next, looking frazzled and confused stood Clay near the kitchen window, wearing only his boxer shorts, looking desperate as he tried to read the baking directions taken from the piece of curled wrapper he had peeled from an opened tube of Pillsbury Grand biscuit dough.

The muffled sound of Jill's laughter caused Clay to turn around. "Good morning, chef," she said.

"Well, I just wanted to surprise you with breakfast in bed," he answered, "But I guess it didn't work... ever try to read directions on a piece of paper that keeps curling up?"

"Can't say I have. Here, let me help."

Clay moved aside and said, "I accept your offer. You take over scrambling the eggs, draining the grease from the bacon, and baking the biscuits. I'll wash the dishes, cups, pan, and whatever else. I'll also put them away... the coffee's ready. Do you want me to pour you a cup now or when we eat?"

"Waiting until we eat is fine," Jill replied, "I'll have everything ready and on the table shortly."

During breakfast, Clay did most of the talking, mainly chitchatting about his plans for the garage. Once finished, he took the dishes to the sink. The only leftovers were four baked biscuits. He wrapped and placed them in the refrigerator and commented, "For tonight."

Looking at his watch but not speaking, his sad expression and look in his eyes revealed he was likely calculating how much longer they had together before having to leave for JFK.

Jill, with a tremor in her voice, whispered, "Clay, I'm also sad. I'm sorry that I must go. I know our love for each other is real, and I promise to stop letting others, or even my foibles, question the genuineness of the love we share. She moved closer alongside him, reached out, and took his hand in hers, and with a gentle pull, she turned and headed upstairs to the bedroom.

After making love, as he had always done, Clay held her close, hugged, and kissed her tenderly, pledging his love for her. To him, these embracing moments were just as important as the physical intimacy they'd shared.

Chapter 75

After his shower, Clay got dressed, picked up Jill's mid-sized piece of luggage containing everything but the clothes she would be wearing, and her cosmetic bag. He went downstairs and placed the bag into the trunk of his car. When Jill came down carrying her small overnighter and purse, he met her at the foot of the steps and could see that her eyes were bloodshot, obviously from crying.

"Here, let me take the bag," he said, "the other one is in the car."

Jill said, "I checked upstairs; you don't need to go up."

Smiling Clay said, "Okay." He looked at her and asked, "You will be coming back in August... won't you?"

"Silly, you know I will." He took her in his arms and gave her a big hug.

With her overnight bag in hand, he opened and held the door as she stepped onto the kitchen porch. He turned, locked the door, and followed as she walked to the car. "It'll take us around two hours to get to JFK, give or take a little, by bypassing the City."

"That's too soon. Oh, Clay, I really hate to leave you." He opened the passenger door for her to get in, and as she moved forward, he kissed her on the lips.

She told herself, "*I'm not leaving Evergreen forever; I'll be back here in less than two months. Besides, he'll be in San Diego for our drive back within a month.*"

On the way to the airport, they talked about their plans, the AUSRM proposal, and the fun they'll have traveling across country in her three-year-old Datsun, with less than thirty thousand miles on the odometer. And laughing, she added, "And, no air-conditioning."

Once through check-in at JFK, they went to the gate to await Jill's Delta flight to San Diego. As first-class boarding got underway, Clay took her in his arms, kissed, and hugged her for a much longer time than usual. "I'll see you next month."

As she walked towards the passageway, Jill mouthed, "Next month." A moment later, she was gone.

He stood by the window, watching as the plane moved from its gate position and headed out to the waiting line on the tarmac. He remained by the window until the aircraft rolled out of sight. Clay then turned, made his way out of the terminal, and headed to short-term parking. On his way home, he stopped at a pizzeria just off the Taconic Parkway at Route 44 and purchased a medium size pepperoni pizza to go.

Once home, he opened a bottle of Chardonnay, poured a glass, and placed the bottle on the side table next to the living room sofa. He walked over to the radio and turned it to his favorite music station. He next picked up his glass and sat down. Holding his glass in the air, he whispered, "*Here's to you my beautiful love,*" with a slight pause, he continued, *"I'll be with you forever in one short month. Safe Trip to San Diego... Cheers!"*

After drinking two glasses, he walked into the kitchen, opened the pizza box, put two barely warm pieces on a plate, and placed the container in the refrigerator. Clayton returned to the sofa and his music. He sadly sensed an odd chilling of loneliness in the room... almost haunting. *"Jill's ghosts are already missing her as much as I am,"* he thought.

With the two pieces of pizza and the wine consumed, Clay went upstairs. In the center of the neatly made bed was a note. He picked it up, read it, and reread it. And with eyes blurred and tears running down both sides of his face, Clayton folded the note and carefully placed it in the drawer of the nightstand.

♥ ♥

Chapter 76

Jill's flight back home was without incident, although she wondered about Clay's feelings once he read the note she had left. Upon arrival in Baggage Claim, she was happy, but surprised, to see her son, Tony, waiting. "Hi Mom, bet you didn't expect to see me here."

"No, is Wendy, okay?"

"She's fine. She and James had to make a change in a meeting about their wedding... that's all I know. She called this morning and asked me to pick you up."

"There's one of my pieces. Look, the other is right behind."

"I'll get them both," Tony said. "Let's go. Joe is outside waiting if a cop hasn't chased him away."

"Joe's here also?"

"Right, we both wanted to welcome you home and tell you we missed you, Mom."

Once inside the car and leaving the airport, the boys were anxious to get the lowdown on New York City and Clay. The first question, Tony, asked, "Is your move still on?"

"Certainly, now Tony, you guys didn't expect me to dump Clay... did you?"

Joe responded, "Well, not really... we kinda like the guy. He seems to be in love with you and will treat you right."

"Mom, one other thing," Tony interjected, "We have talked with Wendy and James, and we all are in agreement that you should invite Clay to the wedding.

Jill appearing startled said, "This has never entered my mind. I took it for granted that he would likely be unwelcome. My divorce to your Dad was the first in my entire family's history. Ooh, not good, he would draw too much attention. That wedding should be one of your sister's happiest days of her life."

"We agree." Joe interjected, "Mom, we don't mean to invite him to the ceremony in the church. That's not the best time for his coming out... if you get my drift."

"Yes, Joe, I get your drift."

"Mom, we all prefer that you invite him to the house for the small reception. Yes, we know Dad will be there," Tony said, "Surely you don't think he would cause any trouble; do you?"

"No, of course not. If he tried to say anything, I let him know in an instant to shut his mouth."

"Mom, now you are showing you have *hutzpah*."

"Joey, what are you saying... where did you get that word?"

"Mom, it means you have the balls, pardon me, to stand up for what is right."

"Okay, Mr. Smarty, where did you get that word?"

"Mom, it's American slang for the Yiddish word, *chutzpah*."

"And, you know I am always telling you boys that I do not

like it when you use derogatory words."

Joey responded, "Believe me, Mom... we know!"

Tony leaned forward from his seat in the back, "Ah, come on, Mom, give him a break for using that New York word."

"What do you mean New York word... where did you get that?"

"From Clay, we've heard him say it. You don't like it when we say someone has the balls to stand up for what's right," Tony continued, "So you must admit *hutzpah* is a better word than saying you have the balls to speak what you believe."

"Okay, Mr. Smarty, your point is well taken."

"Thanks, with your admission, Joey and I rest our case."

Jill turned sideways so she could face both boys, almost laughing out loud, she responded, "'*Touché*... Clay, hmmm."

♥ ♥

♥ ♥

Chapter 77

New York City

"Good morning, my name is Charles Jacobs, here's my card. I am an associate partner of the law firm, *Goldblatt, Ingram, and Jarvis.* I spoke with Mr. Devine last evening, and he told me Mr. Clarkson would be in the office this morning. Since I was in the area, I decided to stop by and take a chance that ..."

The office door opened, and Clayton Clarkson stepped in. Marsha turned away from Mr. Jacobs and said, "Good Morning, boss."

Hearing that greeting, Jacobs abruptly stuck out his hand while introducing himself, said, "Our firm represents E.P. Stores Corporation, and Paul Silverberg suggested I speak with you about an important confidential matter."

Marsha interjected, "Sir, sir."

"That's okay, Marsha; I'll take it from here. Let's go into my office." What Jacobs didn't know was that Paul Silverberg alerted

Clayton several days ago to expect someone from *Goldblatt, Ingram, and Jarvis* to contact him about a civil lawsuit matter.

"What can we help you with Mr. Jacobs?"

"Please call me Charles."

"Okay, Charles, call me Clayton. Now with the formalities aside, how can Clarkson International assist your firm?"

"Not your organization; we need only you, Clayton. Your references are top drawer, and they confirm that you are a man who stands his ground in litigation matters."

"What do you want me to do?"

"We are interested in having you testify in civil court as our client's expert witness."

With that, Clayton opened his door and said, "Marsha, hold my calls."

"We have already investigated your background and spoke with four of your past employers, including the Federal Bureau of Investigation, the Metropolitan Police Department's Detective Division, and two of your past private employers."

"I guess you have learned a lot of positive things about me, or you wouldn't be here."

"Right, we try to be as thorough as possible. We also have spoken to our contacts in the U.S. Attorney's Office about your testifying skills; they gave you glowing marks. So, if you are agreeable ..." Charles reached into his briefcase and removed what he said was a nondisclosure agreement.

"I must have you sign this before we can continue to discuss the specifics and your fees."

Clayton replied, "I completely understand that form serves as a legally binding contract. I have no objections to signing it."

The form was quickly passed, signed, and returned to Charles. Approximately another hour was spent discussing the case specifics, and Clayton's initial opinions relating to the evidence that would be brought forth in the trial.

Once Charles was satisfied Clayton's testimony would not be adverse to his client's position, he said, "The trial is to take place in the coastal city of Oxnard, California. Our team of attorneys, including you, will be staying in a beach resort not far from the courthouse. Clayton, this matter involves a multimillion dollar lawsuit filed by the plaintiff, and we will be representing E.P. Stores, the defendant.

So, when scheduling your time, you should plan we will be there two full weeks. The first week will be devoted to trial prep, and the trial is to commence on Tuesday of week two. I have no idea when you will be called to testify. But most likely, you will take the stand on Thursday or Friday. You will be our most critical witness, so you must be prepared to withstand a bombardment of questions and attempts to ridicule and discredit you in a variety of ways to make you look bad... that's why we conducted an extensive background investigation to identify if you have any skeletons in your closet."

Without saying a word, Clayton listened carefully.

Charles continued, "The plaintiff will likely do a similar investigation, and since no adverse information should surface, they will attack the high rate of your hourly fee and try to sway the jury into thinking the defense paid you an absorbent amount to get you to lie when on the stand. We know the opposing attorneys. They play dirty and will be out for blood."

Clayton paused after hearing what he would be up against, said, "You guys remember that you must not let them paint me as the typical expert witness who takes case after case to make a few bucks. As my track record will show, I only have testified under the most ethical circumstances.

"Furthermore, I am confident I can hold my own when testifying in jury trials against the most experienced and dirtiest playing attorney. Charles, perhaps at this point, I should quote that old colloquialism, 'This ain't my first rodeo.'"

"Great," Charles responded, "I'll have my secretary proceed with the bookings."

As Mr. Jacobs was leaving his office, Clayton said, "Charles, I imagine you were surprised when I signed that nondisclosure without taking time to read it in detail."

"Yes, to be perfectly frank, I was astounded."

"Well, Charles, the reason for my signing that boilerplate form and accepting this project was that I was expecting someone from your office to approach me. You see, I also have my sources. Once tipped off, I also did a background on your firm's integrity, identified your client, and reviewed a few critical circumstances of the case.

"Charles, I am looking forward to working with you and your team out in California. By the way, would you have any idea of how long it takes to drive from Oxnard to San Diego?"

Charles answered, "Well, I may be able to give you a reasonable estimate. I have driven between L.A. and San Diego a few times.

"Great, any help will be appreciated."

"Hmmm, let me think. Oxnard is sixty miles from downtown L.A. and add... say another one hundred and twenty miles to San Diego. You are looking at around three to three and one-half hours, possibly less if you drive straight through. Might I ask why?"

"I have close friends there, and I was just thinking about a quick stopover."

Chapter 78

San Diego

"I'm back," said Jill, as she pulled her car alongside Vivian's in the parking lot. After getting out of their vehicles, Vivian replied, "Well, from that big smile on your face, I would say your trip must have gone well."

"Yes, Vivian, better than expected." "Tell me all about it..."

"Okay, but first, I need to tell you to stop poisoning my mind with those rude comments about Clay and how he is not to be trusted."

Vivian, shocked at seeing the look on her dear friend's face and hearing those blunt words surge from her mouth, stammered and said, "Honey, you must know that I would never intentionally do anything to upset you. I said those things because I didn't want you to get hurt. Please forgive me."

"For what it's worth," Jill said, "I know you were only trying to look out for me, but Viv, Clay is my future. Your bull crap must stop. I love him, and he loves me... so there!"

Vivian, crying and at a loss for words, remained tight-lipped. Jill continued, "This morning, I am going to give Phyllis my two weeks notice. I am moving to New York on the first of August. Here's another shocker for you: The kids want me to invite Clay to Wendy's wedding reception. Can you believe it, they like him that much."

"How'd you pull that one off?"

"I didn't. It was their idea. The boys broke the news to me yesterday when they picked me up at the airport."

Vivian, feeling like she was getting an overload of shocking news, was dumbfounded. She said, "Wow, unbelievable. This guy must have something going for him that I missed."

"He does," Jill replied, "He loves and appreciates my kids and me. Vivian, things like that you can't fake. And, oh yes, even Colonel Cooperswaite and his wife gave us their blessings."

"You've got to be kidding... he knows about your relationship with Clay?"

"Yes, and this will make you really jealous; we had dinner at their house before I left for New York."

Vivian frowned and said nothing.

Without saying another word, Jill thought, *"Vivian deserved those digs. She shouldn't have been so nosy and preachy. Gee, with that bucket load of sass I just released, I think I just showed that I do have a touch of Joey's... hutzpah."*

Vivian, somewhat bothered by the verbal abuse she had just received, finally spoke up, "Boy, I bet Phyllis will be shocked when you break the news to her."

"She may not be as surprised as you think," Jill said. "She and the Colonel are close, and he may have already told her what to expect."

"Really," was Vivian's only reply as the two ladies walked into the building.

Jill's stomach churned as she gave a gentle tap on the open door and, without hesitation, walked into the Cosmetic Manager's office. Phyllis, seated behind her desk, looked up, seeing Jill standing in front of her. From the sad expression on her face, Phyllis sensed what she was about to hear.

Jill, with a slight clearing of her throat, said, "Phyllis, I have something important to tell you, I ..." At that moment, Phyllis sat her coffee cup down, looked Jill in the eye, and said, "You are here to tell me that you are going to resign."

"Oh..." Breaking into a nervous smile, Jill said, "I mean, yes. How did you know?"

Jill, as did most of the cosmeticians, regarded Phyllis as one of the girls—no different than Vivian or the newest hire, Sandra. She'd been to Phyllis' home four or five times over the past couple years—to drop off a holiday gift, attend the small party celebrating Phyllis' recognition as Salesperson of the Year, and a couple of other times when their department dramatically exceeded its sales goal.

"Jill, you know how the Colonel is when it comes to keeping secrets. He told me the day after you left for New York, what I should expect. He also said that both he and Martha thought you and your newfound love would make a very well-matched couple. Jill, as much as I hate to lose a cosmetician as talented as you, I am thrilled that you have found your Mr. Right."

Phyllis stood up, leaned over her desk, and took and squeezed Jill's hand. "Whatever you choose to do, it'll work out fine. Jill, you are a winner, and winners always find a pot of gold at the end of their rainbow."

"Phyllis, please, I'm blushing."

Chapter 79

New York City

Big box was the name given to the civil litigation case that Clayton was to fly to Oxnard, California, to serve as an expert witness. Once his level of involvement was nailed down, Clay called Jill late Saturday evening and gave her an update. "Can you believe it? I am headed back to the West Coast on Sunday, July 5."

"The day after the holiday?"

"Right. Then on that Monday, I will start a special project for a new client."

"Who's your new client, and where will you be... near San Diego, I hope?"

"Not that close. The city is Oxnard, just north of Los Angeles."

"Yes, I know where Oxnard is. One of my friend's parents used to live there. I remember her saying it is a beautiful oceanfront area. Oh, who's your new client?"

"Can't say, it's all hush-hush at this moment. But perhaps I can tell you later."

"Clay, your work is so odd and mysterious. One minute you are advising a company on financial management; in MCRD, you are helping with physical design, controls, and security; a couple of weeks ago, you and Guy were solving an embezzlement crime, and now you are doing confidential work on another mysterious project. Your work is confusing. Will Guy be with you?"

"No, this time it's only me."

"How long are you planning to be there?"

"My commitment is for two weeks."

"Hold on a minute, and let me look at my calendar. Am I correct that you likely will be wrapping up whatever you are doing on Friday, July 17?"

"Bingo, why the sudden excitement in your voice?"

"Clay, you are not going to believe this!" Excitedly she continued, "Do you believe in good omens?"

"Good omens?"

Jill, even more excited… and nearly shouting into the phone, said, "Yes, that's what I said."

"Well, I am not sure if I do or not. My Italian translator was the superstitious type. I remember her telling me that if a black cat crossed her path, that was a bad omen."

"Believe me; this is not a bad omen. It's a good one… no, oh, Clay, it's a great one!" Jill sounding more confusing as the conversation continued.

Clay said, "Well, let me in on your good omen so that I can become as excited as you."

"Okay, I wasn't going to say anything to you because I did not want to put pressure on you."

"Jill, where are you going with this?"

"Well, remember I told you about Tony and Joe picking me up at the airport."

"Yes, how could I forget? You said they were happy that we had a good time together."

"Yes, but there's more. It appears Wendy, James, and the boys got together, and they want me to invite you to a small gathering for Wendy and James at my house after the wedding."

"You're kidding!"

"No, I am not. Since the night I got back, I have been debating in my mind whether I should tell you or not. But when you told me the date of July 17, I knew this was a good omen, and you should come. So, as I have heard, you say... the ball is in your court. Clay, both the kids and I want you to come, so how can you refuse your future family... please say yes."

"Yes, yes, it is. I'll be there come hell or high water."

♥ ♥

♥ ♥

Chapter 80

Oxnard, California—Friday, July 17, 1981

C layton Clarkson spent five and a half hours on the stand until
the case was adjourned for the day as the six o'clock hour
approached. The presiding judge ordered the court back in session
the next morning, Saturday, at nine o'clock sharp. At which time,
Clayton would be the first witness called to retake the stand and
continue with his testimony.

As soon as he returned to his hotel room, Clayton called the
apartment; the answering machine picked up. "It's Clay. I didn't
expect you to answer the phone. You both are probably knee-deep
in getting ready for tomorrow's big day, and that's why this call. I
am involved in a major civil litigation trial that is taking place in
Oxnard. Today I was called to testify, and I spent over five hours
on the stand. Unfortunately, I did not finish giving testimony, and
we all have to be back in court tomorrow morning. So, here's the
bad news. I may not be able to finish in time to drive down there

to attend the wedding reception. So, if I am not there, you will know what happened. Give Wendy and James my very best wishes in the event I fail to show. If I miss the reception, I'll go to the apartment, so leave the key in your hiding place. Also, Jill, if you are late getting in tonight, please don't call me after nine. I am exhausted and have a tough morning ahead, so I want to turn in early. See you sometime tomorrow evening. I love you. Bye."

Clayton had barely replaced the phone in its cradle when it rang. His first thought, "*Must be a ring back from my call to Jill.*" He picked it up in silence, not uttering a word.

"Clayton, can you hear me?" "*I recognize that voice,*" Clayton muttered to himself. "*Charles Jacobs.* "Sorry, Charles. I thought I was having a phone problem."

"Clayton, our team is going to meet in the conference room on the second floor... you know the one. We would like for you to join us."

"Sure, no problem. What time."

"How about meeting us there in say... fifteen minutes."

"I'll be there. Do I need to bring anything?"

"Only yourself. We'll have dinners, or I should say sandwiches delivered. What would you like to order?"

"Charles, I don't care; I am not a finicky eater."

"You better name it, or you'll end up with crap."

"Okay, a hamburger, medium, lettuce, tomato, pickle, and side orders of French fries and coleslaw."

"To drink?" "I'd like a Chardonnay wine miniature... how's that, my man?"

"Great idea. You just broke the ice for all three of us. Instead of your miniature, I'll order three bottles of Chardonnay from the bar. That should be enough for all four of us."

"Okay, see you shortly," Clayton hung up.

After their miniature happy hour and sandwiches, Charles gave a quick overview of today's trial activities, and praised Clayton for his testimony, especially with his calm, but firm answers when questioned by the plaintiff's lead attorney. "Clayton, if you think today was challenging, wait until tomorrow morning. You made their attorney look unprepared, so you can expect that he will come at you with guns blazing."

"I'm not worried... all I have to do is tell the truth."

Charles set his glass of wine on the table, looked Clayton in the eye, and said, "Tomorrow, they will play dirty. And, if they can't penetrate your testimony, they'll do whatever they can to destroy your reputation."

As I mentioned to you when we first met, I am quite capable of convincing a jury that I am not one of those expert witnesses who take on all types of cases just to make a few bucks?"

"You got it. Remember, they know as much about you as we do, and perhaps even more. Oh yes, be ready for them to bring out their heavy artillery and go after your hourly fees. You are making more per hour than their lead guy. So be prepared."

"Charles, If I didn't have the utmost confidence in our being able to win this civil proceedings I wouldn't be here. So, be assured I won't let you down."

"Clay, we have decided that if your testimony goes well... when we are called to cross-examine, I will tell the judge that we rest our case. So, if you hear those words, you will be free to leave the courtroom and head down to San Diego."

"Really!"

"Yes, but you must come through for us."

"Charles... don't worry; I will."

Clayton had a restless night. While he always wanted his clients to see his best side along with a comforting show of confidence, his insides were churning and being eaten alive by his anxiety. *"Settle down,"* he scolded himself as he exhaled, *"I know how to close my testimony with these shysters."*

Shortly after breakfast, Clayton brought his things downstairs and put them in the trunk of his rental car. He then went to the desk and was checking out when one of Charles' associate attorneys, Larry Goodwall, walked by, "Now that's real confidence. Checking out before you testify."

"Well, I cannot afford any delays. I have to be at a wedding in San Diego later this afternoon."

Once the group of four attorneys stepped into the courtroom, Clayton was surprised to see the room was already starting to fill up. Larry Goodwall, noticing the puzzled look on Clayton's face, said, "Saturday trials are rare around here. So, the locals come to see the excitement and listen to what New York lawyers have to say."

"Come on, Larry, they wouldn't know."

"I'm not kidding; word spreads in these small towns like wildfire."

At 10 a.m., with all the courtroom seats filled, a row of spectators was lining the walls. Ten minutes later, a guard walked through the door behind the bench and called the court to order. The presiding judge stepped in and sat down behind his elevated desk. Once the jurors were seated, Clayton Clarkson was recalled to the witness stand.

Charles Jacobs was correct. The plaintiff's attorney wasted no time in focusing his attack on Clarkson. For nearly two hours, he was bombarded with one question after another, and the majority of what was asked had nothing to do with the lawsuit. The focus was on his childhood, his Dad's work as a coal miner, and as attorney, Jacobs had forewarned his hourly fee. To Clayton, it was as if everything was being thrown at him. But nothing raddled his testimony or threw him off guard. *"Just stay focused and keep telling the truth,"* he thought.

Finally, the plaintiff completed his interrogation of the witness. The judge called for the defense.

Attorney Jacobs stood and announced, "We have no questions, your honor."

The judge then directed his attention to the witness and said, "Mr. Clarkson, you are excused, and you may now leave the building." Silently Clayton mused, *"Thank God! It will be tight, but I still may be able to make the church reception."*

Clay had misunderstood his verbal invite. Jill's invitation was not for him to attend the reception at the church. To the contrary, she wanted to introduce him to her closest friends and family at an informal get-together at Roy's house after the church reception. Jill and Wendy knew that if Clay showed up at the church banquet hall, he likely would be walking into a beehive of unsuspecting attendees, who had no idea of the shocking announcement on the horizon.

♥ ♥

Chapter 81

San Diego—Wedding Day

Jill and Wendy were up before seven; they hugged as Mom said, "Well, my dear daughter, this will be the biggest day in your life, apart from childbirth."

"Oh, Mom, I am so happy... James is my Mr. Perfect."

"Wendy, as you know, I always liked James and his family."

Wendy looked at her Mom and burst out laughing, "Do you remember those other guys I brought home to meet you and Dad?"

"Yes, I remember all three ...why?"

"You were so unwelcoming and cool to each of them. Mom, you were on the verge of being rude."

"That was my gut feeling kicking in. They were not for you, and I wanted to make sure they would be uncomfortable around me."

"Mom, that was mean."

"Maybe so, but it worked, didn't it?"

"Yes, but James was the exception. He seemed to get your

approval the very moment I brought him home."

"Wendy, you are only partially correct. He did meet my approval until I saw that license plate frame on the back of his Corvette that read: *'Do it in a Vette.'* That I didn't like, and you know why."

"Oh, Mom, that's only a silly guy thing. I couldn't believe it when you started lecturing me."

"Wendy, just wait until you have a daughter, and then you'll understand why I was upset. I'm going to make coffee; would you like a cup?"

"Okay, but first let me put my wedding dress in its carry bag and get my shoes and other things together. I don't want to forget anything."

"Wendy, we don't have to be at the church until ten; that's an hour before the wedding."

Wendy, a little agitated, said, "I still want to do everything now, Mom."

"Be my guest. I'm still going to have coffee." Jill poured herself a cup of coffee and sat down at the kitchen table. Alone and undisturbed, her mind began wondering, *"What's the matter with me? Why am I so afraid for Wendy and James? Just because my marriage to Roy ended in sadness doesn't mean theirs will."*

Silently berating herself, Jill took a swallow of coffee. *"Stop this crap, Jill. Think positive. Think about Clay, the man I am madly in love with, and about those wonderful things he has said, and of our future together in New York."*

Wendy appeared in the doorway and said, "Mom... Mom, you didn't hear a word that I said."

"What honey, sorry I must have been daydreaming."

"I said, you need to let Clay know that when he arrives at Dad's for our other get-together with family and a couple of friends that you two should be ready to explain why you are moving to New York. I can hear Dad now; 'Are you going to... cohabitate with him?'"

"You are probably right, but I've decided to tell the truth. I am going there to work as an employee for Clay's company. We already have at least one big organization seriously considering my artwork... And, that's the truth.

Furthermore, it's nobody's business if we will be living and sleeping together, so other than some off-color comment coming from your Dad, I would be surprised if anyone mentions such a thing. But, I'll leave a note for Clay on the coffee table in case he doesn't get here in time."

♥ ♥

Chapter 82

Before pulling out of the Superior Court's parking lot, Clayton again picked up his map to double-check directions to San Diego. After perusing the map, and checking his watch, he mused, *"Once out of Oxnard, the drive down to San Diego should be a piece of cake. I should be there by three-thirty."*

Unfortunately, less than forty miles outside of Oxnard, Clayton's smooth sailing drive abruptly came to a screeching halt a few miles past his merge from US 101 onto I-5 South in the Los Angeles area.

Within a half hour of encountering stop and go traffic, the speed continued to worsen. It deteriorated into, at best, a crawl with frequent stops. After several miles with his top speed reaching only five miles per hour, Clayton again looked at his watch. In a low, but pissed off tone, he mumbled, *"Damn it. Even if the backup broke this very moment, I couldn't make it on time if I drove one-hundred miles per hour... damn it, damn it."*

Unfortunately, Clayton's three-hour estimate turned into a

grueling four hours and forty-seven minutes before he turned off the car's engine in front of Jill's apartment building.

"Now all I'll need is for that damn key not to be in Jill's hiding place. Well, what luck; it's here. There's no rush now. I'll hang out until she returns."

He returned to the car, removed one piece of luggage and his briefcase from the trunk, and struggled up the two flights of steps to the apartment. Unlocking the door, and once inside, in plain view on the coffee table was a note from Jill. It contained explicit directions on how to get to Roy's house, for the family-and-friends get-together.

Clay felt himself getting utterly excited, the way he always did when he started thinking about Jill. A check of his watch brought a smile to his face as he mused, *"I love you, girl. You are always looking out for me."*

As he turned left onto Coldfield, Clay could see several cars parked on both sides of the street about halfway down the block. Looking at addresses, he saw Tony and two guys standing out front of the house drinking bottles of Corona beer.

An instantaneous thought flashed into his mind, *"Tony, if your Mom saw you drinking a cerveza and not root beer, you would be in a heap of trouble."*

Tony shouting, "Clay, pull in here," as he pointed to the driveway next door. One of the boys, after hearing Tony call Clay's name, quickly reached on the hood of a car, grabbed the Corona six-pack container, and discretely placed it out of Clay's vision. *"Ah, to be a teenager again!"* Clay thought, trying to remember how many times he and his buddies had done that very same thing.

While closing his car's door, he heard Tony yell, "Clay's here...

Mom, Clay's here."

Inside, Clay first went to Wendy and James and offered his congratulations, and apologized for missing the reception. Wendy spoke up, "We understand Clay. I heard the message you left on the answering machine."

Jill walked over, took his hand, and said, "Come on, I want to introduce the man…" Clay picked up immediately on how she was going to handle their relationship. "I will be working for in New York."

"Well, let's get on with the introductions," Clay said. Jill winked and smiled in a flirtatious way.

The conversations revolved mostly around New York City, Clay's business, Jill's duties, and her artistic opportunities. He mainly talked about Jill, the praise she had received from the prominent gallery owner, Jules Edwards, and her instrumental role in getting AUSRM to ask for a detailed proposal.

Later, Roy approached Clay and began casually pumping him by asking how he and Jill had met. Jill, talking with Janet, her longtime friend, and neighbor, was standing close enough to overhear Roy's inquisitive remarks, and intervened at the precise time he asked Clay where he was staying.

"No more talking shop Guys, it's getting late." Roy, with a puzzled look on his face at such an untimely interruption, thought, "*I'll bet my last dollar she is cohabitating with him.*"

Jill pulled Clay aside and said, "I can't wait to get out of here. Wendy and James left about a half hour ago, and Tony and Joe split with their buddies shortly after you arrived. Honey, the party is practically over."

"Okay, let's finish our drinks, and we'll say our good evenings," Clay responded.

Looking lovingly into Clay's eyes, she whispered, "I'll bet they also want us out of here so they can gossip about what the two of us are up to." That remark caused him to smile, and moments later, they were out the door.

Chapter 83

Back in the apartment, Clay said, "First things first. Let's break out that bottle of Champagne, I saw in the refrigerator." With the bottle opened and the bubbly poured into two glasses, Clay handed one to Jill and raised his high. "To Wendy's and James' happiness."

With glasses touching, Jill delivered a second, "To their wonderful honeymoon on Catalina Island. Clay, do you realize that when they return, we'll be on our way to New York?"

"Another toast, honey, pick up your glass. To the two of us," Clay said, "may we always love each other as much as we do at this moment."

"Cheers."

"I received a little help on that one," he said.

"I don't understand."

"Well, Joe told me that the wedding song Wendy and James chose for their reception was, *Just the Two of Us,* sung by Grover Washington Jr."

"I didn't pay any attention. I was too busy wondering where you were."

Clay tilted the bottle towards her and asked, "Ready for another?"

Laughing, she replied, "Why not." He poured, as she gave him a detail-by-detail description of how beautiful both the church ceremony and the reception were. She continued, "This evening's get-together should have given you a firsthand look at a few family members, my ex, and neighborhood friends. When you walked in, I was reminded of that old Hollywood movie, *Guess Who's Coming to Dinner.* If they only knew..."

"If there were any suspicions about the circumstances of our relationship," Clay commented, "nothing was said to me."

"Nor to me either," she replied.

"Even Roy was every bit the gentleman you said he would be when we met."

"Clay, Roy is a good and kind person. He just has some serious issues." She shifted the conversation away from Roy by saying, "Didn't the kids do great covering for us? They protected our secret. I think they like you."

"Jill, are you feeling okay? You seem a quieter than usual." She hedged, looking at him, "I'm fine, just tired, and a little sad. My little girl is now married."

Clay was sensitive to Jill's sadness. Her daughter was now married and leaving home. To complicate the situation even more, she was also leaving her two sons behind and moving across the country to start a new life with a man she had barely known for seven months. Clay thinking, "*What she is doing takes guts...real guts! God, please don't let me screw up this relationship.*"

Once in bed, Jill flicked off the light, her heart was pounding, and her stomach felt as if it was twisted in a knot.

Clay sensed what was going on. He reached over and tenderly pulled her up close and into his arms. He muttered, *"No time for hanky-panky. Hold her close, and if she chooses to cry, let her do so... just hold her close."*

Without a word spoken, Jill sensed his deep affection and love. She closed her eyes.

Jill and Clay spent their remaining daytime hours in San Diego preparing for her move East and working on the AUSRM proposal. Clay, for a minor fee, made arrangements with Jill's bank to receive twelve faxed pages from his New York office.

In total, the information contained in those pages, plus what Jill and Clay had prepared at the apartment, was enough to put together a final draft version of the proposal in longhand. This draft was returned to the Manhattan office via FedEx for final proofing by Marsha and Guy. After a couple of minor corrections, Marsha transformed what initially was a hodgepodge of handwritten information into a professional proposal for Guy to hand deliver to Mr. Gordon's office.

The majority of evenings Jill and Clay spent with Tony and Joe, either at the apartment or dining out. During the daylight hours, the boys were also busy, making sure their Mom's 1978 Datsun B-210, was ready to undertake the demanding 2,900 miles drive to New York that Clay had estimated would take seven or eight days.

Chapter 84

Friday, July 31, 1981

"Jill, wake up, it's time to hit the road." Turning over and looking at the clock, she said, "It's only 5:00 a.m., are you sure you want to leave this early?"

"I'm good," he said, "I have been wideawake for over an hour. I'm glad we showered and packed the car last night."

Getting out of the bed, Jill said, "I'll make a thermos of coffee for the trip. Just don't let me forget to drop the keys at the rental office."

Clay was out of town before the rush hour. By the time they were only a short distance from the village of Alpine, the steep mountain was starting to take its toll on the packed and likely overloaded Datsun; its engine's temperature gauge had climbed well into the 'hot' range.

"Here we've been on the road less than forty-five minutes," Clay said, "and the car is already overheating—not a good sign."

Jill replied, "Well, we cannot blame the air conditioner; it doesn't have one. That's why I brought this spray bottle to help keep us a little cool."

"I can't believe it," Clay said, "a car with no air conditioner."

"Cars in San Diego don't need AC. It would be a waste of money," she countered, "So, that's one less thing we can blame."

"Right you are... but remember, once I get past filling a tank and checking air pressure, I am helpless. But in a couple of miles, we'll reach the top, and the downgrade should help cool the engine."

Jill replied, "This car has always been so reliable, and Tony knows his stuff when it comes to making repairs. I don't think he would have told us he checked out and replaced anything that appeared to be a potential problem if he hadn't done so."

"Jill, this car is loaded, and that could be our problem. We are climbing such a steep grade. I just don't know."

Once beyond Alpine, the temperature gauge dropped slightly, but it remained in the hot zone. Clayton, while not voicing his concern, was worried about the car making it to the East Coast, especially with the outside temperatures in the desert states running 110 degrees and above. After nine hours on the road, they finally reached Phoenix, and the temperature gauge on a local bank was showing 115 degrees.

The gauge was as far over on hot as it could go. Clay, afraid if he stopped the car, it would likely not restart. Taking a chance, he ran a red light and kept going up the highway until he saw a nice-looking motel and pulled in. Rooms were available, and Dan, the desk clerk, said he had owned Datsuns for years, and they always run hot.

He gave the two a little comfort in telling them there was likely nothing wrong, other than it running hot. However, to be on the safe side, Dan recommended that Clay have his friend's nearby auto shop check the car tomorrow morning; once it has cooled. He said, "It's just up the street and within easy walking distance."

"Good suggestion," Jill said, "Give us your friend's name and the address of his shop, and we'll be first in line tomorrow morning, once you tell us what time he arrives."

Dan replied, "You'll find him there around 7:30. Knock on the door and use my name." Clay spoke up, "Let's go to our room, shower, change, and go find a nearby place to eat. Dan said, he'll give us his recommendations."

The next morning Jill wasn't in bed. He'd heard her crying during the night but said nothing. "*It's about leaving her kids*," Clay thought. She was sitting on the couch when he turned on the lamp. He could see that her eyes were blood-shot. "Good morning, he ventured.

"Good morning," she said in return, "Please don't ask me what's wrong. It's a momma and her brood kind of thing."

He got up from the bed, walked over and reached for her hand. "Hey ..." "I'm okay," she whispered.

"Are you sure? Why are you so sad?" She turned, reaching for the remote, and turned on the television. Jill was lying to both Clay and herself. Sure, she was missing her kids.

But what she didn't dare mention was that Vivian's haunting remarks about Clay were crushing her. "*He's a proven liar and heartbreaker. I'll bet most Las Vegas gamblers would tell you to steer clear of this loser. Oh, God, I am so scared. I may have made the biggest mistake of my life... what am I going to do?*"

Chapter 85

Jill didn't have a faucet personality... the type that is easily turned off and on at the slightest whim. However, this time, she let her transparency show, and Clay, from the very moment he saw that she was upset, commenced reacting to his gut feeling that something more important than her having difficulty over leaving the kids was wrong.

"Jill, what's wrong?"

Just as he spoke, the waitress walked up to their booth, and politely asked, "More coffee?"

Jill, not saying a word, slid her cup to the edge for a refill. Clay signaled, no more, by placing his hand over his cup. He looked up at Jill and smiled, "What about breakfast?"

She answered, in a half-hearted tone, "I'm not hungry."

"Jill, we returned to this diner because I thought you liked your food last night, and you even commented that it might be a decent place to have breakfast."

Raising his voice while looking her in the eye, he said, "What the hell is wrong with you!"

The tone of his voice caused her mind to flash back to that previous evening when they had met at the Hilton bar after she had pried into his business and ended up apologizing.

Her gaze fell on him as she thought, *"Now, he's pissed, and it's my fault because I'm treating him like crap."* She looked up and sighed, feeling her body slump slightly as tears began to well in her eyes. Jill knew she had unfairly pushed and was on the verge of starting an argument.

"Back off," her inner voice scolded. A gasp escaped from deep inside as she said, "Clay, I am so sorry for picking on you. I am so frightened about what I am doing. I hardly know you, and here I am moving across the country to be with you."

"Damn," he responded, frowning with chagrin, "I don't know what else I can do to prove how much I love you. We both know I lied when we first met, but only because I didn't want to take a chance on losing you. I have told you every secret that I was justified to keep to myself, and all I have done since we met is to try to overwhelm you with the love I thought you so desperately wanted. Jill, I am starting to believe that for some weird reason, you are having second thoughts about this move. And besides, it appears that you no longer trust me."

Now sobbing, she huffed, "Oh Clay, don't be silly."

Sharply, he said, "Look, we are less than seven hours from San Diego, so if you want to go back, just say the word!"

"Clay, please calm down. You misunderstood me."

"Did I? Look, we'll finish this talk later. It's already close to eight, and I need to get the car to that mechanic. You can stay at the motel, and I'll take the car with me."

"Okay," she answered, "I'll get our things together, but not checkout because I don't know how long the car will take."

"Good point, and Jill, I wasn't kidding about returning you to San Diego, so I expect your decision when I get back." She looked at him and acknowledged by shaking her head.

Dan was correct about overheating. His mechanic friend confirmed that Datsuns are notorious for having this problem, especially when stressed. But to be safe, he tested the radiator and gauge. "There's no problem. However, just one bit of advice, prepare yourself mentally for this car to continue overheating under stress conditions."

"How much do I owe you?" "Oh, there is no charge. Have a safe trip."

Clay was back at the motel within a half hour. Walking into their room, he caught Jill off guard.

But she quickly said, "Everything is ready."

Clay's comeback was swift. With a stern look on his face and in a straightforward voice, he said, "Well, which way are we going... on to New York or returning to San Diego?"

♥ ♥

Chapter 86

S he found his question and the look on his face devastating. "Do you really mean that," she cried out, "*He's not kidding. Oh, God, what am I doing?*"

He shot an angry glance at her as he bent over and picked up their two overnight bags. He walked out the door, and went to the desk, checked out, and headed to the car; she followed. Clay tossed the bags on top of the clothes in the nearly filled rear seat and was about to get into the driver's seat when she grabbed, hugged, and kissed him.

"New York, here we come," crying, she shouted, "Oh, Clay, I love you so very much... please forgive me."

He responded, "Jill, and I love you too. But I don't understand why I haven't earned your trust yet?" With that remark, he reached into the back seat and pulled out their two lucky mascots, Snoopy and Tweety. They had won these two small stuffed animals at a carnival on the outskirts of San Diego. Once she was seated on the passenger side, he placed the two mascots softly in her lap, smiled, and said, "Jill, I would move heaven and earth for you. Now let's go home."

♥ ♥

As they pulled into the driveway at Evergreen, Jill, with a startled look on her face, said, "What's this?" The dilapidated old garage was gone and, in its place stood a new, although unpainted, two-story, three and a-half car garage.

"That evening, after I returned from taking you to JFK, I contacted a local builder and made a deal with him. If he could complete this job by the first week in August, I would give him a ten percent bonus. All problems or issues were taken care of through Guy when I was unavailable."

"I can't believe you did this," she said.

"As you can see, the builder came through."

Laughing, she said, "He sure did. And there's even a cupola."

"Jill, we are in snow country, and since this is now our primary residence, I think you would agree Evergreen needed a new garage."

"No argument there, but why is it so big?"

"Well, we will also need a storage place for inventory once your AUSRM posters are printed. So, putting on a second floor during the construction phase is both ideal and cost-effective."

"Okay, that makes sense, but aren't you reacting too quickly? We don't even know if we'll get that contract."

"Jill, Jill, we'll talk about that later. Come on, Evergreen is calling."

Once the kitchen door was unlocked, Clay turned to face her. As the corners of his mouth formed into a smile, he asked, "Remember what you promised?"

"Of course I do." With her arms spread wide, she jumped into his arms and gave him a big kiss on the lips. "Okay big boy, carry me into our new home."

That evening, after consuming the remains of their Kentucky Fried Chicken bucket, Jill spoke up, "I'll carry our glasses of Chardonnay into the living room, and we'll sit on the sofa. You bring the bottle."

"Uh-oh, I feel a décor criticism coming on," Clay said as he took a seat on his nearly new sofa, "Should I run for cover?"

"Silly boy, sit down and listen. Remember, during my first visit, I told you that your modernized kitchen décor had the marks of your past girlfriend all over it. So does this room and its furniture. Don't get me wrong; I am not criticizing her modern taste. I suspect her apartment in the City is beautiful. However, her taste is too modern for this 160-year-old home."

"When it comes to antique furniture and knickknack shopping, we couldn't be living in a better place than the Hudson Valley," Clay said, "It's filled with antique shops and auction halls."

Jill, in an upbeat response, "Shopping around here sounds fun."

"Auctions are the best," Clay replied, "Saturday night, we'll go to a nice auction hall down in Millbrook."

"It's a date," she said. "Can you imagine, I now have to depend on you to be the chauffeur? Oh, by the way, earlier when I mentioned the proposal for Mr. Gordon, you said you would explain later. Clay now is later... enough. So, what do you have to tell me?"

"Good news. Ah, I mean... excellent news! Guy will be up here by noon tomorrow. He is bringing two legal documents for me to sign."

"Tell me, tell me."

"Our AUSRM proposal has been accepted. I need to sign the acceptance copy, and Guy will hand deliver it to Mr. Gordon and pick up our initial payment."

"So, what made you so sure we would land that contract that you went ahead and had the garage's second floor added?"

"Jill, you are going to learn a great deal about how businesses succeed. Personal contacts play a critical role. Jules Edwards is a closer friend to Gordon than I realized. The two talked about our work ethic, and they even did a background check on Clarkson International, and believe it or not, Gordon even talked with Charles Jacobs of that law firm, *Goldblatt, Ingram, and Jarvis* where I testified as an expert witness in Oxnard; we passed with flying colors."

"Oh Clay, tell me what our next step will be in getting started."

"Hold on, didn't you hear me say Guy was bringing up two legal documents to sign?"

"Yes, but I don't see how we could get better news than that contract."

"Well, that depends," Clay paused, looking at her and smiling.

"Come on, Clay, please don't tease."

"The second document is a court order requiring my signature. Once signed and filed, Lorre's and my divorce will become final sooner than expected. I spoke with my attorney in Maryland, and because this is an uncontested divorce, and since we have been separated for over two years, once the papers are processed, the divorce will become final."

Jill burst out crying, "Oh Clay, you are so right. That is great news. I am so happy!"

"That goes for me too, Jill. I am slowly putting my life back together. I love you very, very much!"

♥ ♥

Chapter 87

Evergreen— November 1981

Standing on the bridge, looking out over the partly frozen pond, Jill, feeling the cold wind whipping through her hair, thought, *"Winter is already setting in'"* as she admired the acreage's natural beauty: Mounds of accumulated snow glistened in the midday sun, giant maple trees, with their limbs lightly covered with sparkling ice crystals, having their shadows cast over the knoll leading to the park next door.

The majestic structure of Evergreen covered with a blanket of snow, and scent from the woodburning fireplace, brought back memories of her childhood days back in Saint Paul, Minnesota. *"This place has all the makings of a Currier & Ives winter scene... if I ever saw one."*

Clay opened the door, stepping outside, his eyes traveling across the old brick patio, the small apple orchard, and there standing on the little bridge that led to Proposal Point, stood Jill, waving both arms to make sure he saw her. He did, and shouted, "Hey you, what are you doing?"

With her breath wafting in the cold air, she yelled, "Enjoying the beauty of this picture-perfect place. Come on over."

Zipping his jacket up to the lower part of his neck, he cut across the front yard toward the side of the pond. Clay called out, "I'll meet you on the Point."

Standing together, Jill asked, "Why is this spot called Proposal Point... does it have something to do with those heart-shaped carvings on that old swing hanging on that tree?"

"I honestly don't know," Clay said, "but this place makes me feel like I am living way, way, back in time. Jill, the old lady, who lives up at the end of this road, told me that her parents attended two weddings on this very spot over one hundred years ago."

"Clay, perhaps we can make it number three," she said.

"No rush, Jill, everything is just fine the way we are."

She didn't like that comment, and thought, *"I bet you are thinking why bother getting married when you have all the benefits without having to commit... Clay, you are likely in for a big surprise a lot sooner than you think."*

"Why so quiet," he asked. Jill, digging her hands deeper into her jacket pockets, answered, "No reason. Let's go back to the house. You lead, I'll follow."

As she tagged behind, she mused, *"Clay, if you think I am just another piece of tail like your Taylor Lee, you are seriously wrong, my love. Know it or not, you are on the clock... and I am not talking about some friggin sport's clock."*

Chapter 88

"Jill, that was Guy on the phone. He was telling me that IBM started selling their new personal computers during the same week we were driving across the country. No wonder we didn't know anything about it."

Looking up from the poster overlay she was preparing for the local printer, Jill smiled, "You mean a desktop computer is now threatening to replace my trusty IBM Selectric III?"

"Could be. I told Guy that since Hudson Valley is IBM's home territory, we would check it out over in Kingston."

She responded, "What a godsend this could be." "You're right," Clayton said. "No more having to FedEx handwritten documents to the office for Marsha to transcribe."

"Clay, don't overlook the work we have to generate because of those big client reports; you write, and I type. And if I make one little mistake, you won't let me erase. I have to retype that page, and once the report is finished and bound..."

"I know," he said, "We have to drive about six miles to Smith's

Hardware so that they can send it out UPS."

"Well, Clay, even all that is better than having to go into Manhattan and doing the same thing. Just imagine what we could do with a computer?"

"Guy gave me some information and said we should check out model number 5150, a desktop, selling for $1,500 up to $3,000, depending on how well equipped."

Jill, excitedly responded, "Sold!"

"I'm also excited. And I know that Artie Ellison, a member at our golf club, is a salesman for IBM. We'll talk to him on Saturday."

Before meeting with Artie, the two read every magazine and article they could find about the new computers. Convinced they needed one, cost became the only issue. Before leaving the clubhouse that afternoon, Clay and Jill had cut a deal with Artie that included a word processing software program called *WordStar*. And, the deal was closed the moment Artie promised to teach both Jill and Clayton how to use their new floppy disk computer system.

"A step to automation, or should I say... the electronic age?"

"Okay, Clay, don't get too carried away."

"Jill, this investment should give us a payback in three months or less. Next, I am going to purchase one of those expensive, and I do mean expensive... $4,000 Motorola portable telephones that are to hit the market in a couple of years."

"In 1983, are you serious?"

"Not really, but I can dream, can't I? Besides, from what I've read, they will be the weight and size of a brick."

She said, "I can hear you now, Jill, let's take turns carrying the phone. Imagine the hassle of carrying that thing around Manhattan and other cities, through airports and on the subways."

"Jill, it's not going to happen. Just think someday in this electronics age, someone will invent a portable telephone that competes with the one that Dick Tracy wears on his wrist."

"Who?"

"Dick Tracy, the detective in the comic strips. Until then, I'll stick to strolling into those nice clean hotels and using their pay phones. Only in a dire emergency would I use one of those despicable phone booths on the street. But if the situation did arise, hopefully, I would not be forced into one anywhere near 42nd and Broadway... UGH!"

"Speaking of phones, Clay, do you remember when I made my first visit here, you telling me that your house telephone was on a party line and cautioned me about how to listen for our specific number of rings?"

"How could I forget... that was like living back in the Dark Ages. But that's now past. I talked a manager of the telephone company into issuing us a single line at a higher cost.

"The telephone company wasn't our only challenge. Something else I did. I went to the Post Office, met with the local postmaster, and got her to allow us to use the mailing address of 405 Prevention Way instead of Route 2, Box 405."

"Are you serious... Did you really do that?"

"You damn right I did! I learned a long time ago that if you want to be successful, you've got to come up with creative ideas and convince others you are worthy of earning their business. The telephone company recognized that by giving us a single line to handle business calls brought them more income; the post office was similar. I showed the postmaster our postage receipts and politely explained that I would not dare send and receive business correspondence at a rural route address or box number.

"I did the same with both FedEx and UPS. Next, the mail about your motivational posters shall carry the name 'Creative Concepts' and use the Prevention Way address. Jill, it's all about image and the money game. We'll make it work up here; I promise."

Chapter 89

New York City—February 1982

"Clayton, you just received a certified letter from Italy. Hold on a second, Marsha is on the other line, and I need to take an incoming call."

"Okay, Guy, take your time."

"I'm back. Do you want me to hold the letter until you come to the office, or do you want me to FedEx it up to you?"

"Who is it from?"

"The University of Milan."

"Please open it and read it to me."

Once Guy had finished reading the letter, Clayton called, "Jill, come in here if you can. We have good news."

"I haven't seen you this happy in days. What's so important?"

"The University of Milan wants me to come over next month and give a fee-paid one-day seminar. Better yet, this trip in addition to my speaker's fee, includes all expenses paid for two people."

"For two people," she asked.

"That's right, everything! Airline tickets, three nights hotel, and meal expenses for two."

"All for just a one-day seminar?"

"Right, Jill, everything! The only out of pocket expenses I will have would be any side trips not associated directly with the university. We'll be able to visit Venice, Florence, and Rome. And we'll fly back to the U.S. from Rome."

"I hope you are taking me... and not Guy."

"You heard me say 'we' didn't you? Guy doesn't stand a chance. So, are you game?"

"Are you kidding? Clay, tell Guy I'll call him back in ten or fifteen minutes to get all the particulars, and after you finalize our travel dates, I'll call Myrna and get the ball rolling."

"Sounds like a plan. But first, I'll get Marsha and go over my schedule with her. Once I know my availability, I'll place a call to the University and speak with the professor handling the seminar and finalize the date. Life is funny. I met and talked with that professor at a business luncheon in Milan last March. We talked about this possibility, and the two of us even worked up cost estimates. But since months had passed and I did not hear back, I figured it was a dead issue."

Clayton called the office and asked, "Marsha, what does my schedule look like next month?"

"For March, you are pretty tight. You are booked for two separate two-day seminars in Texas, traveling on Sunday. Seminars in Dallas on Monday and Tuesday, and on to San Antonio on Wednesday. The same in San Antonio on Thursday and Friday. Back home over the weekend and on Monday of the second week, the eighth, you and Guy are meeting with our gold refining client in Connecticut. On Thursday, the eleventh, you and Guy are in Atlanta for your monthly meeting with the auto parts client. The third week you are doing a two-day Internal Audit workshop in Chicago on the twenty-second and twenty-third.

"On that Thursday and Friday, both you and Jill are down all day for computer training... whatever that is, in Kingston. Also, for the last week in March, Guy has you and him penciled in at your house prepping for the Charlotte project. That project is to get underway on April 5th."

After listening to Marsha recite his schedule, Clayton responded, "I see what you mean... tight. Marsha, thanks. Please ask Guy when he returns to study my calendar to see if he sees any way I can work in five days in Italy."

"Will do. Talk later. Bye."

"Clayton, it's Guy," Jill said after she picked up the phone. "Hello Guy, I didn't expect to hear from you tonight... burning the midnight oil, huh?"

"Now Clayton, you know better. It's only a little past nine, and Barbara and I still have a couple more hours of television to watch."

Barbara has always remained a mystery to Clayton. For all the years he has known Guy, he has never met or spoken to her on the phone. When invited up, for one reason or another, she's always unable to come. "*Barbara, the puzzling mystery woman,*" Clay muttered, "*So if that's the way Guy wants it, then that's fine with me.*"

"Clay, I found a way to schedule the trip."

"Tell me, please?"

"It's possible in week two. We have that meeting with Charlie

Huff in Connecticut set for Monday, the eighth. On that Thursday, we are to be in Atlanta to meet with Bob Woods. I'll handle both of those meetings."

"That'll work great. That's why I pay you the big bucks, Guy." Laughing, Guy responded, "Yeah, right."

"Now I'll check to see if it will work for them. I'll reach out to the University tonight, once I figure out the time difference. It's in the morning there. Talk to you tomorrow." Clayton hung up the phone and started to calculate the appropriate time to place a person-to-person call to Professor Giovanni Cammarano at the University of Milan.

♥ ♥

Chapter 90

Milan, Italy—March 1982

Thanks to Guy's creative scheduling, Clayton and Jill arrived in Milan a full day ahead of the pre-planned workshop at the University of Milan. Once checked into their hotel, the two showered and changed clothes. Jill, while standing on the room's balcony and wearing a chic light blue jacket, white blouse, and navy slacks, caused Clay to take a quick second look.

To him, she was the real deal. "Wow! You look just like that girl I first laid eyes on at MCRD." His comment made her smile,

"Oh, stop it. You don't look so bad yourself." He gave her a big hug and carefully kissed her lips, avoiding any smearing of lipstick.

"I cannot believe it. Who would have thought a year ago that I'd be standing here with you, the love of my life?" Gazing across the narrow street at the magnificent Domo Cathedral, she continued, "My God, Clay, this trip already feels like magic, and we've only been in Italy for less than three hours."

"Jill, let's go down to the restaurant on the Mezzanine level and get a quick snack. Don't forget; we have an appointment to go sightseeing in forty-five minutes."

"No, I hadn't forgotten," she said, "but I am also hungry."

As they stepped off the elevator, Clayton looked inside the restaurant and said, "Good, no crowd in here, so we should be able to get seated quickly. If you don't mind, I'll order for the two of us."

Jill let out a small laugh, "Just like Sofia did on your first day here?"

He looked up, smiled, and said, "Come to think of it, you're right." When the waiter arrived, Clay greeted him as if he was an old friend. "Pietro, don't you recognize me? I spent four weeks here last spring."

"Sorry, sir. You look familiar, but I am having trouble."

"Okay, never mind, we are in somewhat of a rush. Please bring us two Italian salads with the chef's special dressing. On mine, please add an extra spoonful of the dressing."

"Sir, now I remember you! I have been here for fifteen years, and you are the only guest who asked for that extra spoonful. Sir, you always insisted on a glass of Chardonnay and refused to drink our most popular, Sauvignon Blanc."

Jill, hearing that verbal exchange, asked, "Clay, what was that all about?"

"Well, Jill, it's sinful throughout Italy to have a meal in front of you without a glass of excellent wine. I happened to prefer Chardonnay. Unfortunately, Pietro's favorite is Sauvignon Blanc."

"But Clay ..." The salads, now sitting in front of them for at least two minutes, Jill said, "I'm hungry. What are you doing?"

Clay didn't respond, but he sat quietly with his eyes closed, "praying? I don't think so." For a moment, he could picture Sofia waiting for his assessment of the salad. She'd said, *"You like?"* in slightly broken English.

"Yes, I like."

He set his fork down, "Well, what do you think?" he asked Jill, after taking another drink from his glass of Chardonnay.

Unknown to Clay, Pietro had served Jill a glass of Sauvignon Blanc. She took a sip, paused, and blotted the edge of her lips with her napkin before replacing it on her lap and said, "I think it's marvelous. Sofia did an excellent job tutoring her new culinary trainee."

Their lunch now finished, Clay said, "We better get upstairs. It's almost time for our guide to arrive, and I didn't leave a message with the desk that we would be down here.

Shortly after returning to the room, the telephone rang; Clay picked up on the second ring, "Okay, we'll be right down. Our guide is waiting in the lobby."

In the elevator, Jill took Clay's hand, squeezed it, looked up with a big smile on her face, and said, "Clay, Italy is filled with a treasure trove of art and you bringing me with you on this trip is an adventure I shall cherish forever."

The guide, Francesco, was reasonably fluent in English, but still, Jill and Clay had practiced several essential Italian words that should help them to get along. Clay had said, "A few I remembered from Sofia's teachings. She called them politeness phrases; greetings, thank you, telephone courtesies, do you speak English, restroom, directions, especially to the train station, and buying train tickets." Naturally, just like every well-informed tourist, they both carried Italian translation books.

Francesco, a licensed guide for twelve years, knew Milan like the back of his hand. He not only gave Jill and Clay a tour of famous sites, but also provided a few historical facts to make each viewing more enjoyable.

Once the sightseeing tour was over, Jill said, "It was terrific, and we saw so much in only five hours. Our visits to the Duomo Cathedral, Sforza Castle and museum with its Michelangelo pieces, the Santa Maria Convent, and inside, Leonardo da Vinci's mural *The Last Supper,* were priceless. The only disappointing thing was that they only allowed us to spend fifteen minutes admiring this unique treasure."

Clay added, "Jill, last year Sofia brought me to see *The Last Supper* and we had a private tour. I never realized how special it was that we were under no time constraints."

Back in the hotel room, Clay prepared for the seminar the next day while Jill had the front desk double-check their late afternoon train reservations to Venice. They had planned to check out of the hotel, have breakfast with Professor Cammarano, and afterward, a driver was to take them to the train station when the seminar ended at three.

"One thing for sure, you will not have to rush when the seminar is over. The departure time is 6:37 p.m."

Professor Cammarano then asked, "So if students want to spend a little time with you afterward, that shall be okay?"

"Absolutely, otherwise we would be waiting in that station longer than it would take the train to arrive in Venice... ninety, or so minutes."

The seminar got underway promptly at nine and ended at three. The Professor, also serving in the role of translator, opened up the session for questions, and while there were a few, the attending students were more interested in hearing about the ways and trends of businesses in the United States.

Afterward, as normal during Clayton's seminars, there are always three or four individuals who remain and enjoy casual conversations about a variety of things; this group was no different. At 3:45, Professor Cammarano interrupted and told the stay behinds, in Italian, "Our guests must now leave to catch the train."

As they were preparing to exit the auditorium, the Professor said, "Clayton, your seminar was very well received, and we appreciate you and your lovely wife spending extra time with us. Also, since I already have your luggage in my car, I shall drive you to the Centrale Railway Station and escort you to the train."

Jill responded, "Professor, that's so very nice of you." "Yes, Professor," Clayton said... "*Grazie Mille.*"

Jill looked at him, smiling, she flashed a thumbs-up

When on the train and settled, Jill praised both the quality of the seminar and Clayton's slower speech delivery, which made it easier for its interpretation into Italian. "I also noticed that you became nervous after seeing those students having wine with their lunches."

"I could have bet that fifty percent or more would sleep through my second half... but they didn't."

"Wasn't it surprising to hear Professor Cammarano tell us about how so many students are moving back home because they can no longer afford to live on their own. Housing shortages, rising rental costs, and poor wages are taking their toll."

"Yes, but don't forget he also stressed this wasn't just a student problem; this is happening throughout Italy."

"I wonder how long before the United States will encounter

similar problems?"

Clayton looked at her and said, "Not long, many are already complaining about those same issues."

"Clay, talking about those negative things makes me sad. Let's talk about fun stuff... like the Professor thinking, I am your wife."

"Okay, okay, you made your point."

Jill turned and while looking out the window, mused, *"The clock's still running. Please don't underestimate me, Clay,"* as the train sped past a small town and its station without stopping.

Clay immediately changed the subject to trains. "The trains are undoubtedly the best way to get around Italy."

She said, "I am impressed with this one's comfort and cleanliness."

Clay followed, "Including this train, and we will be riding on three different ones; Milan to Venice, Venice to Florence, and from there on to Rome. The good news is each leg takes only a couple of hours."

♥ ♥

Chapter 91

Venice, Italy

"I think we were wise to rely on a walking tour guide to see the sights of Venice," Clay remarked, "I didn't come here last year. We were too busy working elsewhere."

Jill, gesturing as they crossed one of the many bridges, said, "To me, the most impressive points we are seeing are the beautiful architecture and design of the churches, bridges, and canals. I find it unbelievable that Venice has at least 400 bridges and 150 canals... no wonder this place is called the Floating City. I also enjoyed our guide showing us how life is on the backstreets and a few of those stunning churches filled with Renaissance art."

"Well, Jill, was there anything you didn't like, Clay asked.

"To be frank, when we first arrived, I was not sure we made the right decision by skipping a gondola ride. Nearly every advertisement that I have seen about Venice almost always showed a gondolier cruising down one of the canals. So, naturally, I thought this was a must go on attraction."

Clay responded, "I also felt the same, but after asking a few couples who had already taken these rides, it was good to learn that both the knowledge and personality of the gondolier were most important. Otherwise, the level of enjoyment from the ride was nothing more than a coin toss. So, Jill, like you, I am also happy that we jointly decided to stay with our walking guide."

"Oh Clay, this city is amazing, and I shall never forget our stop at Piazza San Marco and its view of Saint Mark's Basilica. That square looks like it is always filled with lots of people and hundreds of pigeons."

"Yes," he said, "but anyone who dares to make the slightest gesture like they were going to toss a piece of bread or anything else, are putting themselves at risk of being bombarded with pigeon shit."

"Oh, now Clay, be nice. How could you focus on those pigeons with that magnificent church looming next door? Our guide told me that Saint Mark's, because of its opulent design, gold mosaics, and its status as the symbol of 11th Century Venetian wealth and power—is known as *Chiesa d'Oro* or for we English speaking tourists, the 'Church of Gold.' And, Clay, I shall never forget that beautiful Gothic structure, the Doge's Palace, that's also at Saint Mark's Square. Remember the guide telling us that it was completed in the 15th Century, although portions had to be rebuilt after a fire in 1574."

"Jill, you certainly have been listening to our guide much more closely than anyone else, or you are recording everything he says."

She looked at Clay, gave him a big smile, and answered, "Both!"

"Uh-oh Jill, I almost forgot about the time. We need to go to the hotel, pick up our luggage, and get a ride to the train station. Boy, Myrna has us on a tight schedule."

"Well, what did you expect? You told her this had to be a whirlwind trip. I love it, and we are getting to see the highlights... Florence, here we come."

♥ ♥

Chapter 92

Florence, Italy

"Clay, I just finished reading the first several pages of our Florence guidebook. Now, this is my kind of city. It is home to so many pieces of Renaissance art and architecture, and as with Milan, it also has a Duomo Cathedral. However, this church is most famous for its terracotta-tiled dome by the great artist, Filippo Brunelleschi. And, Clay, the magnificent bell tower was painted by Italy's first master artist, Giotto di Bondone. I should also mention that Giotto is also revered as the father of European painters. Oh, so much to see and learn."

"Jill, I spent an enjoyable three-day Easter weekend here last year, and I know you will love Florence."

"Oh, Clay, I'm so excited," she said.

With their luggage in hand, Clay said, "Before we do anything, we must find our way from this train station to the hotel where Myrna made our reservations."

"Do you know how to ask for directions," she asked.

"Not really, it's getting late, so we better take a cab."

"Here comes one... I'll wave."

"Jill waving doesn't work in Florence. I remember it took me over an hour before I figured out that you can only hail a cab by either using a telephone to call for one or by going to a taxi stand. I remember one being here at the train station."

"Over there," Jill pointed.

Once in their room, Jill looked out the window and saw the imposing sight of one of Florence's most breathtaking attractions, especially at night... the Duomo. "Unbelievable, this view is fantastic."

"As I said, you are going to love this city. Now, let's go find a place to eat."

After asking, the hotel receptionist gave them directions to an English-speaking restaurant in the next block. At the restaurant, Clay said, "Easy communications, menus in English, good food and wine, and they accept American Express... what more can we ask?" "Have you eaten here before," she asked.

"I don't remember. Unfortunately, when alone, I focused on looking in windows for restaurant menus in English."

"Poor boy," Jill said as she patted him on the leg.

"Well, before we venture out in the morning, we need to decide if we need a tour guide or whether we can do it on our own. Keep in mind that during my visit here last year, I think that I saw practically every tourist attraction imaginable. But not with the passion you showed on the train by just turning the pages in that guidebook."

"Clay, earlier you said something about all the most interesting sights being within easy walking distance of the hotel. So, if you are agreeable, I say let's do the tour ourselves... after all, we have a guidebook and you — a winning team, if there ever was one."

Back in the room and while getting ready for bed, Jill noticed his eyes focusing on her. "What are you thinking," she asked.

"I'm thinking about you."

"What?"

"How much I love you and that I am a... lucky dog."

"Clay, I have heard you affectionately say that 'lucky dog' phrase several times before; why?"

"Well, much of my adult life has been in turmoil And, just like a dog that finds a devoted owner, I only want two things in life: I want you and I want us."

He held her close for a while, and then they made love into the night. When she awoke, Clay was not in bed. However, Jill was put at ease when she noticed a glimmer of light under the bathroom door. After lying there for several minutes and not hearing a sound, she hopped out of bed and opened the door. Startled, Clay dropped a guidebook as he looked up from his potty seat. "Clay, what are you doing?"

"I thought I could save us some time by putting together our day's itinerary."

"So, what are our plans?"

"I've jotted down a few places you might enjoy... here's the list."

"Once we are dressed and packed, let's go for breakfast and decide there."

"Okay, I should also mention that everything here is within walking distance."

Once breakfast was over, and their walking tour list decided, Clay said, "The most distant attraction shall be first... Boboli Gardens."

"What magnificent gardens," she said, "It's remarkable how they are divided into different sections: the main lawn with a fountain and obelisk, another of worldly trees, plants and flowers, and several large ponds complete with amazing water features."

Clay, busy reading the literature, added, "The gardens were created in the 16th Century and cover eleven-plus acres. This area also serves as an oasis, and visitors are encouraged to stroll down the twisted lanes and to take refuge from the heat in the shade of trees. The centerpiece is Vasari's Grottos. It's an artificial cave decorated with stalactites, stalagmites, sponges, shells, and rocks."

"Incredible, Clay, look at that view."

"Jill, listen to this. The garden lacks a natural water source. So, a conduit was built from the nearby river to bring water into the elaborate irrigation system."

"Clay, this brochure I picked up at the hotel talks about Piazzale Michelangelo being near this garden. It also claims this piazzale offers the best view of Florence and the Cathedral, and that several artists will always be there selling their stuff. So, let's see what they have to offer."

"Well, since we are already so close," Clay said, "let's also take in the Palazzo Pitti.... are you game?"

"Sure, I am. I brought my walking shoes."

"Let's go inside."

Clay, reading from his book, said, "This 1400s structure is another fine example of Renaissance architecture. Jill, this palace was once home to Italian royalty. Today, it is the largest museum complex in Florence."

"According to my brochure," Jill said, "inside, we'll find a myriad of different galleries; all richly decorated, but this palace also contains a host of Renaissance artwork."

"I just knew you would find this museum to your liking," he added, "The Jupiter room, for example, contains some amazing fresco paintings on plaster, and also the famous *Veiled Lady* by Raphael. Other well-known artists featured here include Titian, Rubens, Caravaggio, and Veronese."

"Clay, if I weren't able to see you referring to that book, I would swear you were a naturally born Italian guide who only speaks American."

"Very funny... only American!"

"There's a bench, let's take a break."

"Okay with me," he replied, "This book is excellent, and it makes the grade as our nonverbal guide."

"Jill, look here," as Clay pointed to the map, "This is the Galleria dell' Accademia. It's where I found the original Michelangelo *David* sculpture."

"And we also have to visit the Uffizi Gallery," she said.

"Okay, Jill, what's there?"

"Botticelli's *Birth of Venus* and da Vinci's *Annunciation*."

"Well, here we are," Clay said, "So let me get out my handy guide and start reading, Jill, aside from the David sculpture, this museum houses several other sculptures and works of Michelangelo, plus several different and interesting halls separate it. Here you can find a wealth of historical art, and also a great deal of history about 14th and 15th Century Florence. See, Jill, all I need to do is read and stay on the path. Finally, here we are at the Museum of Musical Instruments. According to the book, this building contains a myriad of old and unique musical inventions."

"Clay, let's just breeze through here if you don't mind."

"Good, I'm with you. No interest in musical instruments."

"Jill, those galleries that you were so excited about visiting took us an hour and a half. So, were they worth it?"

She replied, "I have only one word to describe what I saw... 'Magnifico.'"

"Glad you enjoyed them. Now it's lunchtime. So, let's stop for a sandwich and drink. Are you okay with that?"

"Yes, I'm hungry," she replied, "but let's find a fast-food type eatery where we can sit. A stop will also give our feet a break... Clay, aren't you tired?"

"Yes, but we are on a mission, and we can't rest too long. According to this book's map, there ahead is the Uffizi Palace and Gallery. It's considered one of the most famous Italian museums in the world."

"Look at this place," she said, "The building is a marvel to behold. Check out those ornate columns and marble statues in the courtyard."

"According to this guide," Clay said, "Inside, we'll find Renaissance Art by Botticelli, Da Vinci, Titian, and Raphael."

Jill responded, "Oh my!"

"Next up, the Florence Cathedral, better known as 'the Duomo,' the jewel of the City," Clay continued referring to his book...

"The exterior and front facade of the Cathedral are monumental—covered in white marble and red, pink and green polychrome designs; the color and style are breathtaking. Furthermore, an immense dome sits at the rear of the Cathedral and reachable by climbing a series of steps."

Both standing and looking at that staircase, Clay said, "Jill, are you game in taking on those stairs?"

"I'm okay if you are, big boy."

"Not me," he said, "let's go inside."

Jill mused to herself, *"I just knew he wouldn't go up those stairs. If he'd said okay, I would have likely peed in my panties."*

Once inside, the interior of the Cathedral was quite bare in contrast to the exterior. "Clay, I'm ready to stop."

"Okay, I'm also nearly exhausted. However, since we are here, let's do a pass-through of the Baptistery of St. John. According to this guide, it is one of the City's oldest buildings. The exterior features the beautiful 'Florentine' design similar to both the Duomo and Giotto's *Campanile*."

"Clay, look at those three sets of bronze doors... notice how they depict various religious scenes and human virtues. And here inside," Jill continues reading from a pamphlet, "just feast your eyes on that stunning golden Byzantine-style fresco that covers the ceiling and upper walls and depicts the last judgment and other stories from the Bible and Genesis."

"Finished, finito, or whatever... " Clay said, "let's go back to the hotel, get our luggage, and have them call a taxi to take us to the train station. Trains are frequent. Therefore, we shouldn't have to wait long before we catch one to Rome."

♥ ♥

Chapter 93

Rome, Italy

"Today should be a breeze compared to our whirlwind tours of Milan, Venice, and Florence," Clay said, "We have all day to sightsee and will not fly home until tomorrow morning."

"Clay, the first thing I want to do is find a nice restaurant and order a breakfast of scrambled eggs, bacon, a croissant, a small glass of their 'red' orange juice, and one or two cups of Espresso; with a bit of warm milk and capped with milk foam."

"Say, didn't you have that waiter in Milan write it down so you could remember how to order your coffee?"

"I did, and I have his directions in my purse... here it is, *'Un caffè per favore.'* I think I'll try ordering my coffee the Italian way when we first sit down."

Clay smiling said, "Good luck!"

After finishing breakfast, Clay picked up his book, *'Handy Guide to Rome,'* and pulled a folded piece of paper from his shirt pocket. On it, he had scribbled: Vatican, Sistine Chapel, St. Peter's Basilica, Coliseum, Trevi Fountain.

"Five places," she said. "I thought you said we are going to take it easy today."

"We are. Three are together, and the Coliseum and Trevi Fountain are within short walking distances of the other. Jill, according to this guide, it is thirty minutes at most between the Vatican and Trevi Fountain."

"Well, okay. I am still tired, but glad to know we are in the home stretch."

"Never fear, my dear. The hotel receptionist said we could catch a 'Hop on and Hop off' bus in front of the hotel and ride it to the Vatican and other places."

"Clay, according to the guidebook, the museums within Vatican City, should be more interesting than I initially thought. And, more than I expected."

"Jill, I didn't realize there were so many. When Sophia brought me here, it was near closing, and we spent very little time in the museums."

Jill commented, "Martina, our guide, is a jewel and she has plenty of knowledge."

"Well, she should, Clay responded. "She has been giving tours for, I think she said, ten or twelve years."

"Clay, that's good. She also told me that we have a choice of taking a two-hour tour of the highlights or spend about six hours seeing an endless number of things... want to guess which one I chose?"

"I know the one I hope you picked; the two-hour quickie."

"Correct, and Martina said she would limit it to what she called her must-see places of interest. She named off a litany of things. The ones I remember were Raphael's *Transfiguration;* da Vinci's *St. Jerome* and without a doubt, the breathtaking, Michelangelo's Sistine Chapel ceiling. Martina also said no photography is allowed in the Sistine Chapel and talking is also prohibited. But once we leave, we can ask questions."

"Jill, as you know, I've been here before. Therefore, I'll follow your lead as to what we see."

"I am more interested in Michelangelo's art," she replied, "so, once we have seen his works, I am okay if you had rather leave. I take it our next stop is the Coliseum and will Martina be escorting us?"

"'Yes' to the Coliseum question, and 'No' for Martina going. She will remain here."

"Clay, I want to forewarn you about me and the Coliseum. I know that it may be one of Italy's largest tourist attractions, but now that we are getting ready to go inside, I don't want to stay long."

"May I ask why?"

"To me, it was a sadistic and inhuman slaughterhouse."

"Okay, I understand. We'll take a brief look at the seating area, which held 50,000 to 80,000 spectators. We can see most everything from there without going on a behind-the-scenes tour."

"Promise?"

"I promise, okay?"

Standing in an upper aisle, Jill, reading from the guidebook, said, "Listen to this: 'The Roman emperor Trajan, who was in office between 98 and 117, was declared by the Senate as Rome's best ruler. According to this guidebook, he is remembered as a successful soldier-emperor, and his philanthropic work earned him second place among the five best emperors who presided over an era of peace and prosperity.'

"Clay, this article credits 'one of Trajan's most notable acts was his hosting of a three-month gladiatorial festival in the great Coliseum in Rome. This event, although the precise dates are unknown, combined chariot racing, beast fights, and close-quarters gladiatorial bloodshed.' Oh God, Clay, listen to this, and I am quoting: 'This gory spectacle left 11,000 dead, mostly slaves and criminals, not to mention thousands of ferocious beasts killed alongside them.'

"Oh, God! I can't even imagine that 'fifty, let alone five million spectators, would attend such a horrific event.'"

Jill looked up from the Coliseum guidebook and said, "Do you think this stuff is accurate?"

He answered, "I don't know. Centuries-old happenings make for good legends and storytelling."

"Wait, there's more, 'Such events were occasionally on a huge scale; Trajan is said to have celebrated his victories in Dacia in 107 with contests involving 11,000 animals and 10,000 gladiators over 123 days. During lunch intervals, executions *ad bestias* would be staged.

"Those condemned to death would be sent into the arena, naked and unarmed, to face the beasts of death, usually lions or other big cats, which would tear them to pieces. Other performances would also take place by acrobats and magicians, during the intervals.' Unbelievably horrible! Look down there, Clay. I cannot even imagine the numbers of humans and animals slaughtered in that arena over the centuries. Let's get out of this place... before I get sick!"

Chapter 94

Rome, Italy—Trevi Fountain

"Jill, standing here today, I am reminded of two things. First, it was eleven months ago when I stood at this fountain with Sophia. One evening after work, we came here because Sophia said she was able to see in my eyes and hear in my voice that I was in love with you. She told me about the legend of Trevi Fountain. 'If you throw a coin with your right hand, over your left shoulder, and with your back to the fountain, your wish shall be granted, and you and your love will return to Rome within one year.' When she mentioned that coin toss myth, I said, "The 1954 movie, *Three Coins in the Fountain*." She answered, "Yes, that was filmed here at the Trevi Fountain.

"Jill, keep in mind that Sofia was a true believer in the supernatural and prophecies. I, a nonbeliever and thinking such legends are nonsense... just like those ghosts at Evergreen. I began to waver and thought, *I have nothing to lose, and it would satisfy her.'* So, I followed Sophia's instructions to the T. She cautioned me; I must never tell anyone what my wish was until after it came true. If I revealed *The Wish,* it would never materialize."

"Clayton, what are you saying?"

"The wish I made that evening was that the two of us would return to here, Trevi Fountain. Remember, the legend says it will come true within one year from the day the wish was made."

"You're telling me that your wish came true?"

"Yes, and with one month to spare!"

"Clay, I don't believe it. Are you are just telling me that tale because we are standing here?"

"No way! Jill, I swear what I have said is the truth."

"Okay," she said, "I believe you."

"Jill, do you believe in logic?"

"Of course I do."

"Okay then, look at our history: My life was a total mess, and it made a remarkable change once I flew across the country and found you."

"That could have been nothing more than a fluke," she said.

"Okay, explain this, how can you forget your attraction to me... even though we had never spoken?"

"Hmmm, yes, that was unusual."

"Jill, I'm just getting started. Here's another, explain this one: You met me for a drink after I dropped the worst pickup line ever on you, remember? 'You have the most beautiful blue eyes I have ever seen.'

"Even now, I can't believe that I didn't just ignore you. I had never done such a thing in my life."

"See Jill; our relationship was meant to happen. Now, what

about all of those times you were going to dump me, yet you didn't."

"I still have no idea why I gave in, particularly with Vivian trying to put the kibosh on you every time I turned around."

"Do you need more evidence?"

"There's more?" she asked.

"Well, we cannot ignore the weird ways that I kept landing those jobs in California; San Diego, Oxnard, San Francisco, Los Angeles, and Hollywood. Look at our connections with art and our working compatibility, and the chance you took in moving to New York. Call it synchronicity, or call it coincidence, whatever you like, Jill, but I am unwavering in my belief that we are meant to be together, and this togetherness is our destiny."

"But Clay ..."

"Jill, hold on. I am on a roll, so let me keep going. Look at this trip; it came out of the clear blue. Sure, I had a brief conversation with Professor Cammarano months ago about my seminars and fees. But how can either of us think that an Italian university could afford to fly the two of us to Milan for a one-day workshop... now that was beyond coincidence... agree?"

Standing there, dumbfounded, Jill wondered, *"Just coincidences, or could these phenomena be real?"*

"Jill, did you hear me?"

"Yes, Clay, you have always said that fate brought and keeps us together."

"Jill, we are a match made in Heaven, if there ever was one. So, take a coin out of your purse, and I want each of us to follow Sofia's prophecy."

"What's wrong with me using one of your coins?"

"Nothing that I know of... I don't want to take a chance, like avoiding a black cat from crossing your path."

"Aha, I think your Trevi wish has made you a believer."

"You could say that. Okay, Jill, it's your turn. With your back to the fountain, using your right hand toss the coin over your left shoulder, and make a wish."

"How was that?"

"Good toss, just remember, you must never tell anyone your wish until it comes true."

"It's now your turn, Clay."

"Okay, I am now an old pro, so here goes." Clay flipped his coin high ensuring that it turned end-over-end several times before splashing into the fountain water. Turning and looking at the ripples, he muttered to himself, *"Wish made."*

Jill kissed him on the lips and said, "Clay, when we walked up to the fountain, you told me you were reminded of two things. The wish was one. So, what was second?"

"Well, after we got into all of that talk about whether those unusual happenings were the result of amazing coincidences or unexplained phenomena, I got sidetracked. Sorry!"

"I'd like to hear what you have to say."

"Well, my second remembrance has to do with the words that an unknown poet wrote some time ago." Clay took her hands as he looked deeply into her eyes, "Jill, with you standing by my side, I feel compelled to recite my version of that poem:

Dear Jill, I'm not perfect, I'm me.
I've made bad decisions and wrong choices, but I'm me.
I've said the wrong things; I've told the right things because I'm me.
I don't like everything I've done, but I did them because I'm me.

I've loved the wrong people and trusted the wrong people, and I'm still me.

If I had the chance to start again, I wouldn't change a thing. Why? Because I'm me.

There are good things about me; you have looked past my imperfections and can see what's right. You have forgiven me many times for being the stubborn me.

You've helped make me the best I can be. Today, I stand with you at the Trevi Fountain and say, I love you with all my heart... because I am me."

♥ ♥

♥ ♥

Chapter 95

"Oh Clay," Jill said with tears in her eyes, "This has been such a wonderful journey, even though you preferred to call it a whirlwind trip."

Clay looked at his watch, "It's approaching five o'clock. Let's go back to the room, and uhh... rest," Clay, with a big smile on his face, uttered the following words, "then we can go out and find one of those touristy restaurants and have an early meal."

"You can't fool me any longer, you sex hound. I know what your... 'uhh' means."

Back in the room, he swept her up into his arms.

She gave out a long sigh and whispered, "I love being in your arms." She gave him a long passionate kiss as he picked her up and held her tightly as he gently placed her on the bed.

He closed the curtain and turned off the bedside lamp. With only the bathroom light glimmering through the partially open door, he removed his shirt, pants, and undershorts, tossing each towards the corner chair, not caring where they landed. She had never shied away when he had undressed her before; this late afternoon would be no exception.

His mouth drifted from her lips as his tongue took over, teasing and stimulating the passionate parts of her body. Her heart pounded with desire as she embraced each sensual moment. Everything inside of him was on fire, hungrier, giving her no chance to catch her breath. He whispered, "Give yourself to me."

They made love for over two hours, and when finished, she affectionately laid her head on his shoulder, and while holding her in his arms, he kissed her on the top of her head. His tender embrace was always comforting. It let her know that their cuddling was just as important as the physical intimacy they'd shared. Snuggling deep into his arms, she closed her eyes, *"Here I am in the arms of the man I love so dearly."* She turned on her side, trying to cuddle even closer. *"Oh, how I wish he could hold me like this for the rest of our lives."*

After returning from their eight o'clock dinner... early by Italian standards, they stopped by the hotel reception desk to ensure everything was in order for their morning ride to the airport. The clerk opened his shuttle log and said, "Yes, Mr. and Mrs. Clarkson, I have your itinerary here. Your flight to New York Kennedy airport leaves at 12:50 p.m. from Leonardo da Vinci International. Therefore, you must take the ten o'clock shuttle. I will assign you two reserved seats, although I do not expect the shuttle to be full at that time of the morning."

"Thank you very much. I'll take care of the bill in the morning," Clay responded.

In return, the desk clerk said, "Have an enjoyable flight back to America, Mr. and Mrs. Clarkson."

Jill muttered to herself, *"Oh, those damn words, Mr. and Mrs. Clarkson. Why do they have to be so... counterfeit?"*

Chapter 96

Rhinebeck, New York—Summer, 1983

Jill Simpson, now co-developer of series of successful North American employee motivational programs, had reached a defining moment in her life. She and her boss, Clayton Clarkson, have lived together for two years, and Jill, a divorced forty-two-year-old, after seeing no wedding plans in sight, was overwhelmed with her unresolved situation.

Clay's attitude is just the opposite. Anytime the subject of marriage came up, he sidesteped the issue. One of his favorite excuses was: "I read an article in one of those airline magazines about a nationwide survey showing that 59 percent of those 18 to 44 individuals surveyed now live with a partner they aren't married to, compared to 50 percent who took the plunge. Jill, cohabitation is on the rise. It's now the 'in thing to do.'"

Whenever Jill challenged what she believed was nothing more than a bull crap excuse, Clay was unable to produce any evidence of this article's existence. Furthermore, not a mention of this study was identifiable by using his latest toy, the new IBM desktop computer.

She asked, "Why are you trying to talk us out of getting married, Clay?"

"Now calm down, I'm not trying to get out of marrying you," he said, "Jill, you know good and damn well that I love and adore you more than words can say."

To some extent, Clay was getting cold feet and stalling. He'd spent the last three years thinking about the bad choices he'd made. His track record was poor. He'd had two former wives and a live-in girlfriend before Jill came along. If he'd learned nothing else, he'd taught himself to be cautious and not jump in headfirst until he knew how deep the water.

Jill, setting her sketch aside, looked up at him and started to speak, but paused as she let her mind revolve around the thought that Clay had little to gain by taking a walk down the aisle. *"We're traveling and working together twenty-four-seven, having sex almost every night, and living a lifestyle that most couples would die for... so, why should he run the risk?"*

Her beliefs as to why Clay didn't want to get married were unsupported assumptions. *"I need a plan. But first, I need to speak with Guy. If anyone knows what's on Clay's mind, it would be Guy."*

She picked up the phone and dialed the office. After a brief and polite chitchat with Marsha, Jill asked, "Is Guy in?"

"Sorry, Jill, he's on a sales call."

"Would you please look at his appointment calendar and tell me what time he will be in the office on Monday?"

"Okay, hold on a sec... I need to answer the other line."

"No rush, go ahead."

"I'm back. You said Monday?"

"That's right."

"He's down to be here by nine-thirty to meet with Clayton. Wait a minute. He also has penciled-in, 'Jill re: AUSRM, 1:00 or 2:00 p.m., and a question mark.'"

"Thanks, Marsha. Have a good day."

Clay's noncommittal attitude to at least getting engaged was eating at her heart. Several times, when he had ample opportunity to give her a rational explanation for his reluctance, he always kissed it off by saying something trivial.

She mused, *"Damn it, I am sick of hearing those disgusting comments he had the nerve to say, like his latest one when I hinted about us making it wedding number three at Proposal Point: 'No rush, Jill, everything is just fine the way we are... No, things are not just fine, Clay! This is a serious moral issue for me. My love, you should know that I am not the shacking up kind of woman, and I am not about to mope around like a scolded dog with its tail between its legs."*

♥ ♥

Chapter 97

Clay, sitting at his new computer, turned his chair to face Jill and reminded her of this evening's 5:00 to 7:00 p.m. preview at Windsor's Auction Hall.

She replied, "I thought you would prefer to go early tomorrow... say a half hour before the auction starts. Remember, this is the second Friday of the month, and we usually go over to the Club, play nine holes, and stay for dinner."

"You're right, but I ran into Ellie Windsor at the bank this morning, and she excitedly told me they had just taken in one of the best antique pieces their auction had received in years. I told her we would stop by this evening, and if we had any interest, we would be sure to attend the auction."

"The best piece they have auctioned in years? Wow, that's some statement," Jill said, "especially since we have bought six or eight very nice collectibles from them."

"Yes," Clay said, "didn't those two 1860s rosewood chairs from Lincoln's White House come from Windsors?"

"Come to think of it they did," she responded, "and so did my walnut roll top desk.

"Clay, what is her exciting find?"

"She wouldn't tell me. All she said was that I was going to be excited... really excited!"

"What about me?"

"She never mentioned you. Besides, I had told both Ellie and Bill to look out for any pieces that would make a great addition to Evergreen. So, I doubt if she even associated my request with you."

"Makes sense," she replied, "So, when do you want to leave?"

"Sometime after five. But not before we get to savor the taste of my mail order wine from that Napa Valley winery."

"I still can't believe you paid seventy-eight dollars, plus shipping, for two bottles of wine that you know nothing about."

"Jill, it's an exceptional wine for a special occasion."

"Okay, Clay, what's the occasion?"

"Oh, I don't know. I just said that to get you off my back... wait, I have a good reason."

"Okay, smarty, tell me."

He smiled and simply said, "That's what I work for."

"Well, I can't argue with that," she jokingly said, sticking her tongue out. "But I feel you are up to something sneaky. So, spill the beans, buster."

He replied, "Oh, Jill, don't be silly. I'll be back in a couple of minutes." As Clay walked back into their makeshift office, he said, "Jill, here, I poured each of us a glass of Shafer Winery's award-winning California Chardonnay. It's five o'clock and time for us to relax a bit before we head over to Windsors."

"So, this is your special occasion," she asked.

"Not really, this glass is more like a peace offering. Jill, lately, the cool ways you are reacting to almost everything I say and do is unnerving, and I don't know why."

Unbeknown to Clay, Jill was disgusted more with herself than Clay. She was wondering why. *"Something's wrong,"* she thought. Since their return from that whirlwind trip to Italy, Jill has felt like she was a deer caught in Clay's headlights, or could it be the other way around? She thought, *"Lately, I have been nagging about everything Clay does... most of it unfair. I can hear him now. 'Jill, could it be that living up here in the boonies is making you homesick for the kids and San Diego?' No, I love this place. God... Clay, I cannot believe you don't have a clue about what's bothering me. Damn it, I've hinted to you in every way possible that I want us to get married, or at least formally engaged. You're not stupid, and I'm getting afraid you are going to dump me just like you did the others."*

♥ ♥

Chapter 98

After pulling the car into an open space on the grass-covered parking area at Windsors, the two paused briefly to say hello to a couple they had casually talked with at two or three other auctions. Clay said, "Anything in there that makes tomorrow night worth attending?"

Jim responded, "Nothing for us, so I doubt if we will show up." His wife abruptly interrupted, "Jim, don't say that. You know I like to go, even if we don't bid."

With that comment, her husband shrugged his shoulders and showed a frown on his face.

Jill smiled, "Well, I guess we'll see you tomorrow evening."

Inside, while eyeballing the sales display area, Ellie spotted Clay and pulled him to the side and away from Jill. "Clay, remember you once told Bill and me in secrecy to be on the lookout and let you know if a super-nice diamond ring comes along?"

"Sure, how could I forget?"

"Well, it's here," Ellie whispered.

"I didn't see anything special listed in your ad in Wednesday's paper."

"That's because it just arrived last night. We haven't even put it out on display yet."

With what appeared to be a covert signal between Bill and Ellie, Bill walked over to Jill and struck up a conversation as Clay and Ellie continued to chat quietly. Jill didn't fall for this slipshod diversionary tactic, she walked over to Clay and asked, "What's going on?"

"That antique piece I told you about, well follow Ellie, and we'll get our very own private preview." Ellie walked into the rear office; the two followed. Bill remained on the floor to assist others and answer questions. Ellie, opening the safe, took out a small blue velvet ring case removed a diamond ring, and carefully handed it to Jill. The accompanying diamond certification certificate from Narome Jewelers, a reputable local jeweler, was passed to Clay. This document contained four close-up photographs of the ring and its description: rare mine cut antique 0.75 ct certified diamond solitaire engagement ring in 14 kt. white gold.

Jill, a former part-time jewelry vendor, was surprised at the distinctive features of the ring. "Clay, there's nothing more beautiful than a one of a kind old mine-cut diamond." She held out the ring for him to see. "Look at how it sparkles, even under this poor lighting. That's because diamond cutters back in the late 1800s and early 1900s cared less about saving weight, and more about the sparkle of the diamond."

Ellie removed a magnifying loupe from the desk drawer and handed it to Jill. Carefully examining the ring, she said, "Obviously, this diamond is hand-cut. Its shape is different from one cut by a machine. It also has different proportions, a smaller table, and larger culet. Hand-cut gems like this one are scarce."

Looking up, she directed her next remark at Ellie, "I understand most antique diamonds are kept within families and passed from one generation to the next as heirlooms. Ellie, where did you get this ring?"

"Sorry, Jill, but Bill and I cannot identify the owner; let's just call him Mr. X. I can tell you that he bought that engagement ring for his loving wife back in 1910, and they were married three months later in October. She passed away this spring, and there are no heirs. Mr. X told us that he is hoping this exceptional ring will go to a genuinely loving couple.

"He also said, 'Money was not the motivating reason for selling. If it was,' he said, 'I would have sold it to a fine jeweler.'"

"What a touching story, Ellie. The ring is beautiful." Looking at Clay, she said, "Don't you think so?"

"Yes, it is beautiful. Now try it on."

"I can't believe this. It fits perfectly."

Still smiling, Clay reached out and affectionately pinched her chin, "It's meant to be. It's what I call fate... Remember?"

"Jill, Bill, and I like both Clayton and you. Mr. X is a well-known local personality, and after his wife passed, we were discussing holding a possible jewelry auction. It was then we told him about Clayton and his secret search for a unique engagement ring to give to the lady he calls, 'The greatest love of my life.' Mr. X accepted our word about the two of you a while back. So, here's the deal... "

♥ ♥

♥ ♥

Chapter 99

"Jill, we three, including Clayton, expected this ring to reach the auction block two months ago. But we misjudged the length of Mr. X's difficult grieving period. It took him longer than even he expected before he was able to part with this highly sentimental ring. Even now, months later, it is still not easy, but he wants to see who purchases the ring. However, he has asked us to tell the buyer not to approach and speak with him... while he recognizes it will be an enjoyable experience for the buyer, it will be heartbreaking for him. Also, Bill has promised him we will not put the ring up for auction tomorrow night until we see him seated in the audience."

Looking at Clay, Jill asked, "You knew about this?"

Nodding his head and smiling, "And I was well aware that I was likely upsetting you when I kept ignoring your obvious hints about getting married."

"You certainly were right about that."

"I know Jill, but I was hell-bent on keeping this a secret." "Well,

I guess you can say, this was one secret you kept from me, that I wholeheartedly approve."

"Jill, I could have taken you down to Diamond Row in Manhattan, to other jewelers in Kingston and Poughkeepsie, and likely walked out of a store with a beautiful ring. But you deserve so much more. After hearing a brief version of this couple's seven-plus decades of their never-faltering love story, I knew this ring was a powerful sign of true love and good luck.

"To me, this ring represents another link in strengthening our love. As I told you at Trevi Fountain, it was fate that brought us together. This ring can seal the deal. Ellie, we will be here tomorrow night. Please reserve two front-row seats for us."

Saturday evening

At exactly four-thirty sharp, Jill and Clay walked through the auction hall's door, past the makeshift hotdog, drink, and pretzel counter that was being operated by one of Bill and Ellie's twin daughters. Clay stopped at the registration table to sign in and pick up his bidding number. His status as a frequent purchaser alleviated Clayton's need to produce a photo ID and verify his method of payment.

Jill, carrying a cloth shopping bag, continued into the auditorium like she was on a mission. Now well versed in ways to avoid having to sit next to a smoker, she had to find seats in the nonsmoking area. Moving towards two vacant positions, she suddenly remembered they had two reserved front-row seats also in the nonsmoking section, thanks to Ellie.

When Clay took his seat alongside Jill, he whispered, "The ring is now in the display case, and alongside it is the certification certificate.

"I told Bill that we hoped no New York City jewelry buyers would be in the audience. Bill said it was unlikely any New Yorkers would show up because the ring was not in the sale advertisements."

Jill responded, "I am more nervous now than I have ever been at an auction... we have no control over what others will bid."

"True, Jill, but we must have faith that this ring is destined for us. Hey, it even fits your finger perfectly. Oh, I almost forgot... Bill reminded me that the ring would not come up for auction until Mr. X arrives, and the earliest will be sometime after eight."

Clay reached into the bag and removed his old Wal-Mart twenty-seven-ounce thermos jug and two reusable plastic wine glasses. While handing one glass to Jill, he asked, "Ready for me to pour?"

Chuckling, she jokingly stretched her answer, "Wine... not, it's almost wine time." Clay poured two glasses of his special wine, and the two sat back for what likely was to become a long and worrisome evening.

♥ ♥

Chapter 100

Finally, at 8:45 p.m. Bill Windsor walked forward on the stage, made his announcement about the ring, and read a few highlights from the certification document. "Let's get moving on this beautiful ring... Give me a starting bid."

A man in the rear of the room shouted, "One hundred dollars!"

Bill, in a slightly respectful manner, said, "Come on, this official certification is worth that alone. What am I bid?"

Another voice, male, shouted $200, a female called out, $300. Jill looked at Clay,

"When are you going to bid?"

"I want to see how high those three and any other bidders are willing to go."

No sooner were the words out of his mouth when a fashionably dressed woman seated three rows behind Jill and Clay, but in the smoking section, called out, "$500" as she excitedly held up and waved her bidding number for all to see. The others ceased to bid.

"Well, we now have identified our competition."

Ellie, standing in front of the stage serving as one of the three spotters, looked at Clay and said, "Buy it, Clay!"

Bill said, "I have $500... who'll give me $1,500?" In an almost unnoticeable wave of his hand, Clay gave a one-half signal. Bill called into the microphone, $750; I have $750... Who'll make it $1,000?"

Clay leaned over, whispering to Jill, "Notice her pause, she's nervous and thinking. She'll do the $1,000, but that's it for her."

"$1,000," the lady shouted.

Clay, not wanting to give the lady any time to think about her next bid, immediately responded, "$1,250.

"We have $1,250. Who'll make it $1,500? The auditorium became silent. Jill whispered, "Even that noisy couple behind us aren't saying a word."

Bill increased the volume of his voice, "Going once... going twice... Sold to the gentlemen in the front row."

Once the excitement settled down, Clay whispered to Jill, "Pour us two glasses of our special Chardonnay. I'll be right back."

He stood and motioned for Ellie to meet him in the lobby. The two then vanished from the room. Ellie reemerged a few minutes later and stood to the side of the stage, waiting for Bill to complete the sale of the current piece on the block.

Bill, looked confused when Ellie stepped up and took the portable mike from his hand, laid it on the podium, and whispered something in his ear.

Bill picked up the mike and said, "Sorry, folks, we seem to have a small problem that requires my attention. I shall return in a minute."

This interruption made Jill nervous, but she could not leave her seat, especially since she was now holding two full glasses of

Clay's expensive wine.

"This must have something to do with Clay. First, he motions for Ellie to follow him outside, and then Ellie summons Bill right in the middle of the auction. Oh, God, what is going on? Oh, I hope Mr. X hasn't changed his mind and is now reluctant to sell the ring."

Within three minutes, Clay stepped back inside, Ellie right behind him, and Bill was bringing up the rear. *"What the heck is going on,* Jill thought as she noticed Clay was carrying the small blue velvet ring box in his left hand. *"They're smiling, so it can't be too much of a problem."*

Bill returned to the stage, as he picked up his mike, he motioned for both Ellie and Clayton to come onto the stage.

Now really confused, Jill wondered, *"I can't believe this."*

Bill, now speaking into his mike, said, "Well folks, Ellie and I have been auctioning here for over twenty years."

Ellie spoke up, "Twenty-two years, Bill."

Everybody laughed, including Jill.

"As you can imagine, we've had all kinds of things happen here, but this has to be one of the best."

Ellie spoke up, "Bill, just give the mike to Clay and let him explain."

"Okay, okay. I guess everyone now knows who's the boss in our house and business. Folks, Ellie, and I take great pleasure in introducing Clayton Clarkson. He is the guy who just bought the magnificent diamond ring that I auctioned a few minutes ago. Clayton is one of our newer neighbors who recently moved up from the City."

After the intro, Bill handed the mike to Clay.

Clay stepped off the stage, and as he walked toward Jill, he opened and removed the ring from its box. At that very moment, Jill sensed what was about to happen as he lowered himself to one knee.

Speaking into the mike, he said, "Jill Simpson, will you marry me?"

"Yes, yes, I will!"

With that response, Jill struggled to keep from dropping one of the nearly full plastic glasses. The man seated beside her reached out and took the two drinks. Clayton then placed the ring on her left hand, as the audience applauded. With the two wines back in their hands, Clay and Jill touched glasses, and each took a sip and kissed.

Bill, holding the mike, said, "Well folks, ain't love grand! The show is over. It's now back to the auction. What am I bid for this early 1800's highboy?"

♥ ♥

Chapter 101

"Jill... Jill, wake up."

Confused, she responded, "What? ...what's wrong?"

Clay answered, "You were having a nightmare, calling out... 'no, no,' and as I touched you, you mumbled something about Trevi Fountain."

Now awake, she paused, thinking, and still slightly groggy, she reached over, took his hand, and said, "I remember. It was so real and frightening, Clay."

"Okay, go back to sleep, and we'll talk after we get up. It's nearly three o'clock."

Jill, pretending to go back to sleep so as not to disturb Clay, couldn't shake that nightmarish thought. Laying there with her usual suspicious mind in overdrive, it bothered her, on what should be one of the best days of her life that she had such a weird nightmare. "*It was so real.*" Starting to doze, she thought, "*Is this some warning for me... so clear. Could last night's auction hall engagement have been some ploy staged by Clay? Whoever heard of a perfectly beautiful diamond engagement ring just showing up at an auction, especially one that exactly fits my finger? Then he admitted he was well aware of my hints for us to get married, and that sad story about some 'Mister X arriving on his white horse to save the gladiator who is about to lose his Lady... me. I don't care what he says about fate or his wish at Trevi Fountain coming true. Something must be wrong here."*

Clay was wide awake and sitting up in bed when Jill opened her eyes, "Well, did you sleep okay?"

"I guess so, but it took me a while to go back to sleep. I couldn't get that bad dream out of my mind. Clay, it was so real and terrifying."

"Want to talk about it? I remember you said something about the Trevi Fountain and mumbled a few other indistinguishable words."

"Clay, I'd rather not talk about it. What time do we have to leave for the City?"

"I told Guy I would be there by nine-thirty. So, we should leave here around seven-thirty to seven-forty-five."

♥ ♥

Chapter 102

"Good afternoon Marsha, I got a little delayed at AUSRM. I hope Guy hasn't waited too long."

"No, Jill, Guy, and the boss went on a last minute appointment after they finished with their meeting. He told me that Clayton was going to lunch with a friend, so he bought the two of you a salad. Guy said he picked out the choices; it's in the fridge."

"So, Guy's here?"

"Yes, he's waiting in the conference room."

"Eating his salad?"

"No, he said he'd wait for you so the two of you could kibitz before getting down to business. Here, let me help carry your salads and water."

"Great, and thanks."

As Jill and Marsha walked in, Guy looked up and, with a big ear to ear smile, stood up and said, "Congratulations!"

"I see Clay told you."

Marsha, nearly dropping one of the salad dressings saying,

"Congratulations... for what?"

Jill smiled and held out her left hand, now sporting a sparkling diamond ring. Marsha hugged and kissed her on the cheek and said, "Oh, Jill, I am so happy for both of you."

Guy followed with his hug and best wishes. "Thanks for the salad. I guess since we are celebrating my engagement, I should buy."

"Too late," Guy responded, "This is on Clayton."

When Marsha left the room, and while eating their salads, Jill briefed Guy on her meeting with AUSRM's Vice President of Personnel and Administration, Becky Tuchman. "She wanted to know if we could develop a series of motivational signs and messages in French."

"In French?"

"Yes, they have a Canadian company based in Ontario that is interested. However, everything we produce must be in both English and French. I told her that either you or I would get back to her."

"Jill, I just thought of something. Translating messages into Canadian French may not be a problem."

"What do you mean?"

"We have very close contacts at BYU."

"Oh, Yes," she responded, "Clay's two partners in the psychological testing company are professors at that university. Quick thinking, Guy."

Once the briefing was over, Jill said, "Guy, last week, I wanted to get your advice about Clay's and my relationship."

"Trouble in paradise?"

"Not now. But up until a couple of days ago, I would have bet he was stringing me along and had no plans for us to get married. But as you see, things changed dramatically on Saturday evening.

Did he tell you what happened at the auction hall?"

"Yes, he did. Jill, I have known Clayton for years, and we have traveled extensively together. I know him well enough to tell you that you are the love of his life!"

Guy continued, "Sure, he's played around, just like most men. And, he's made no bones about it. I wouldn't be surprised if you haven't heard him say, 'Sex makes the world go 'round.' Sure, Clay's romanced many women in his life. Please notice that I said 'romanced' and not loved. As you know, there's a huge difference."

"I know, Guy. But it's those wham-bam romances that frighten me the most."

"Jill, don't condemn him for his past transgressions. You must trust him until he betrays you. I sincerely believe Lorre was his only other love, and that's why he didn't give up on her until he realized she was on the verge of destroying both of them."

The longer Jill let Guy's words sink in, the more she knew he was right.

"Jill, are you prepared to start trusting him? I mean truly believing in him and trusting that he loves only you?"

With a quivering smile, she said, "I get it, Guy. However, at first, I was sure we didn't live in a fantasy world controlled by weird acts of fate and granting of wishes. But when it comes to our relationship, he always says we are a match made in Heaven. God, Guy, at first, I didn't want to admit it, but I now believe that the wish Clay made at Trevi Fountain really did come true."

Silently, she began thinking, "*We don't live in a world controlled by uncertainty. But, The Wish and all those bizarre twists of faith were too crazy. Thank God, I have finally found my true love! Therefore, happiness cannot be far behind.*"

Chapter 103

Friday, October 7, 1983

Shortly after lunch, Jill and Clay strolled up the steps of the City Clerk's Office for the town of Poughkeepsie, New York. Inside, they completed a marriage license application and paid the forty-dollar license fee. When the paperwork was approved, the clerk on duty explained that New York State law requires a twenty-four-hour waiting period before a wedding ceremony can legally take place. "Is there anything else?"

With that comment, Clay said to Jill, "While we are here, is it okay with you for us to make an appointment to get married?" Overhearing Clay's question, the clerk politely interrupted, "Monday is Columbus Day, and government offices will be closed."

"Thanks for reminding us," Jill said as she turned to Clay, "I know we have talked about this, but are you sure you don't want to invite anyone?"

"I'm sure. Most people up here think we are already married, so let's not feed them more juicy gossip."

The clerk placed a calendar on the counter and asked, "Which day and time would you prefer?"

Clay spoke first, "Jill, if you don't mind, I would like to pick the thirteenth... October 13, 1983."

Surprised, she responded, "The thirteenth? I know you have always said thirteen is your lucky number. But for a marriage?... ah, what the heck."

Leaning over, she gave him a little peck on the lips. "Clay, I love and trust you. I'm fine with Thursday, October 13th. I bet you were hoping the date would have been Friday, the thirteenth."

"How right you are, but Jill, I am not going to wait around until next year before that date appears on the calendar."

♥ ♥

Thursday, October 13, 1983 – Wedding Day

"Good Morning," Clay said, "We have a 10:00 appointment with Judge Iverson; Jill Simpson and Clayton Clarkson."

"Oh, yes, you're in our appointment book. I am Heloise, Judge Iverson's clerk. He will be with you shortly. Have a seat."

In less than five minutes, a guard appeared in the reception area, "Follow me, please. I will take you to the judge's chamber."

With the introductions aside, the judge asked, "Do you have two witnesses?"

Clay spoke up, "No, we do not, your honor." Judge Iverson

turned to the guard and said, "Get Heloise and tell her the two of you are going to serve as witnesses to this marriage."

When the ceremony was complete, Judge Iverson shook both Mr. and Mrs. Clarkson's hands and said, "Congratulations! I am so pleased to start this morning with such a happy event. "

♥ ♥

Chapter 104

Thirty-Five Years later. The Villages, Florida

O utside, the rain was softly falling. Clayton Clarkson stood alongside his lanai's window, listening to the pitter-patter, as he tossed his lucky baseball from hand to hand. His mind drifted from the present to the past, *"I can't believe how my life has changed for the better since I fell in love and married Jill. Four decades ago, I was on the verge of becoming a psycho. My personal life almost beyond repair, and through all of that turmoil, I was trying to survive in the business world... Whoa, enough! Damn it, not today."*

Clayton wanted to savor his happy memories of last Saturday. It had been their thirty-fifth wedding anniversary. As part of his gift to her on that extraordinary day, Clayton surprised Jill by planning an all-day visit to Epcot Center, Orlando... and what a beautiful day it had been. Fun rides, snacks at the food pavilions of various countries, a couple of imported beers, friendly chats with four or five other park visitors, and more rides.

Moments after departing their last ride, '*Soarin'*', Jill took Clay's hand and squeezing it, said, "When I heard the ride's attendant announce for everyone to fasten your seatbelt, I had a flashback. I remembered hearing those very words thirty-seven years ago. It was when my New York-bound airplane was leaving San Diego."

Jill continued, "In 1981, those three words, 'fasten your seat belts,' were worrisome. I wondered if what I had heard was a bad omen. But here we are more than three decades later, and our marriage continues with every bit of romance, respect, and fun that it was when we first met back in 1981."

Clayton had ignored Jill's 'declaration of guilt.' Instead, all he cared about was pleasing her. And, thinking back, he knew he had hit an ultimate *Grand Slam* home run when he surprised Jill by taking her to the Park's five-star French restaurant, *Chefs de France*.

Clayton, letting his mind recapture the events of that beautiful day, thought, "*Everything was fantastic; the food, service, and our perfect evening topped off with the restaurant's staff joining together and singing, 'Happy Anniversary' in French, as they brought to the table, a specially prepared anniversary dessert. The day couldn't have gone better! Even the weather was perfect.*"

Clayton, slightly startled, returned to reality when Jill's favorite song, *Born to Give My Love to You*, by Martina McBride, commenced playing on the stereo. Seconds later, he knew it was Jill's doing as she walked into the lanai. Clayton turned and greeted her with a warm smile and a tender hug. He teasingly said, "Fasten your seat belt."

Jill smiled, "Well, how could I have known this would be the smoothest ride of my life?" Looking into his eyes, she said, "Clay, I have a great idea. You have now written seven award-winning books.

He interjected, "Don't forget one was the first runner up for Book of the Year in 2017." Laughing, she replied, "I doubt if you would let me forget. Here's what I am thinking. Why don't you write a romantic love story inspired by our lives? I also have a great title."

"Okay," he said, "What's your title?"

She paused, looked him directly in the eye, and said, "*The Wish.*"

"Hmmm, Jill, I like it. I take it you are referring to my first wish at Trevi Fountain?"

"Yes, I was."

"Say, I had forgotten about those other two wishes we made there when we returned together, eleven months later. By the way, what was your wish? You never mentioned it, so I figured it didn't come true."

"Wrong, Clay, it did come true on October 13, 1983!"

"Our wedding," he asked. "Yes, it was one of the happiest days of my life."

"Jill, you're not going to believe this. My wish was almost identical. I wished that we would get married and live happily together for the rest of our lives."

Reaching out and taking her hand, he said, "Come on."

"Where are we going... Uh-oh, I know that look in your eye. Clay, you're getting too old for that stuff."

"Never, Jill, never."

♥ ♥

Epilogue

Life goes on:

Two years after Lorre moved in with Clay's Mom at Solomons Island, Maryland, she had resurrected her life and was now committed to being on the wagon. Alcohol was no easy demon for Lorre to defeat. However, a considerable portion of the credit must go to Mom, for without her consistent help, Lorre's battle against alcohol would have been lost.

Mom's rules of visitations were simple, but firm: You're welcome to visit, even hang out on the pier, do a little crabbing or fishing, but absolutely... no alcohol allowed in any form.

Lorre, with her sister deceased for more than three years, began to have a gentleman caller on occasions. And, then, he started to visit more frequently, up until the time that this teetotaller, widower husband of Lorre's sister, proposed marriage. The two got married, and Lorre moved back to his home in West Virginia. Mom missed Lorre, but she was both pleased and proud of the transformation in Lorre's life that had taken place.

Loyal friend and associate:

Guy Devine remained with Clayton through his company's formative years, up until the time a client offered Guy, a senior-level position in his multibillion dollar organization. While torn about leaving Clayton and unsure of what to do, Guy came to Clayton and asked his advice.

Clayton said, "You'd be a fool to turn down that offer, so take it. I wish you the very best, my dear friend."

Family:

Within six months of Guy leaving Clarkson International, Clayton made his step-son-in-law, James, a job offer, which he accepted. James, Wendy, and their one-year-old daughter relocated from California to New York. James spent nearly thirty years working closely with Clayton. Today, with both Clayton and Jill retired, James is the CEO and sole owner of Clayton Clarkson International, Inc. Wendy and James have a daughter and a son.

Lynn, Clayton's daughter, and her husband are both retired. They own a waterfront home in Smith Mountain Lake, Virginia, and a winter home in sunny Florida, one mile from her Dad and stepmom.

The relationship between Lynn, her Dad and stepmom, has materialized into one of real love and respect. Lynn has no children, but she does have two Schnauzer dogs

Jill's two sons, Anthony (Tony) and Joseph (Joey), both have one child each. Tony, keeping the Evergreen tradition alive, asked his wife to marry him at Proposal Point. And today, he and his wife live just outside of Rhinebeck, New York, and have one son. Tony is approaching thirty-two years with his employer, an international generator/high voltage corporation.

Joey, a true Californian, enjoys surfing, has a rock band, and performs gigs on weekends around the San Diego area. For the past sixteen years, he has worked for a prominent medical equipment corporation, and he currently holds a position in management. Joey is divorced, has a daughter and, like his stepdad, believes he finally has found the love of his life.

Made in the USA
Middletown, DE
13 September 2020